MASTERPIECES

OF

WESTERN LITERATURE

CONTEMPORARY ESSAYS IN INTERPRETATION

II

SHAKESPEARE TO ELIOT

Return this book on or before the last
date stamped below

Manufactured by WM. C. BROWN CO., INC., Dubuque, Iowa
Printed in U. S. A.

Preface

The essays collected in these volumes, taken as a whole, are meant to remind us that great literary works never cease to be contemporary. "A classic is a classic," Ezra Pound has written, "because of a certain eternal and irrepressible freshness." They speak to us as they have spoken to past generations, and perhaps they strengthen the hope not only that they will please coming generations too, but that there will be such generations. They are great despite the many years that separate us from them, despite the differences in the conditions of life, and even despite the translators. While they mean different things to different readers—as they should—there is no point denying that other readers can help us to a better understanding. First, of course, comes the reading of the work itself, second, another reading, and third, a third. One could go on and only be the wiser. But the following essays have been written and collected on the assumption that anything said about the masterpieces cannot possibly hurt them and might possibly help us. Or, at the very least, another precinct has been heard from, another measure has been taken, another prejudice has had its back rubbed— perchance the wrong way. Nothing astounds so much as the generosity of the great works: we are the gainers every time we explore them anew.

All kinds of things are tried out in the essays. Indeed, the editors have thought it a virtue that no one approach to the great works predominates in these two volumes. Some essays deal with the cultural background of the work, with the myths and legends the author refashioned; others examine a brief passage and pursue its ideas into larger meanings throughout the work; there are essays that analyze

v

language, or a character, or a scene, or the use of a certain convention; essays concerned with structure, or metaphor, or tone; Freudian essays and Jungian essays; and there may even be one in the tragical-comical-historical-pastoral mode. On the other hand, we have avoided general, all-embracing introductions (which are easily obtainable elsewhere) and very highly specialized studies in sources, influences, reputations, etc. The only requests to our contributors were to stay close to the work and to be partial. The variousness of the critical imagination is, we like to think, itself a tribute to the masterpieces.

As a glance at the Table of Contents will show, there is usually one essay on each of the masterworks chosen. In a few cases we have intentionally included pairs of essays on the same work or author (*The Odyssey, The Divine Comedy, Faust,* Wordsworth, *Crime and Punishment*) in order to provide a more dramatic contrast of approaches. The essays are arranged in a roughly chronological order according to the time of composition of the' work discussed. We have appended "Suggestions for Further Reading" to each essay, except where the footnotes are unusually full. The second of each paired essay has such a brief bibliography.

Of the 22 contributors, 15 are members of the Department of English at the University of Massachusetts; Hermann Weigand and Peter Heller are in the Department of German and John Brentlinger is in the Department of Philosophy. Further contributors are Angelo Bertocci (Boston University), Marilyn Gaull (formerly also of the English Department, University of Massachusetts, now of Temple University), Joseph Hilyard (Holyoke Junior College), and C. P. Segal (University of Pennsylvania). In addition to having published critical and scholarly studies in their special fields of interest, all contributors have had substantial experience in teaching the classics and western masterpieces. It is, as a matter of fact, from the conviction that teachers discover individual approaches to their favorite works that the idea of this anthology grew. But in a more practical way it owes its start to William G. O'Donnell and David Clark, the latter serving as its first editor. Howard Brogan has given the project his constant encouragement. On countless occasions Sidney Kaplan has readily and patiently shared his immense expertise. The design of the book is largely his, and so is the solution to some complicated editorial problems.

Gratitude is also due, and never more gladly given, to Leonard Baskin for permission to reproduce two of his works of art on the covers. The photographic reproductions were made by Russ Mariz,

University of Massachusetts photographer. *Cover of Volume I*: "Euripides," drawing by Leonard Baskin, reproduced by permission from Aristotle's *Poetics and Politics,* published for the members of The Limited Editions Club and The Heritage Club, copyright © 1964 by The George Macy Companies, Inc. *Cover of Volume II*: Medal by Leonard Baskin struck for The New York Public Library, reproduced by permission from The New York Public Library, Astor, Lenox and Tilden Foundations.

Permission has also kindly been given to reprint the following essays: "Sophocles' Praise of Man and the Conflicts of the *Antigone*" by C. P. Segal from *Arion*; "The Journey to Hell: Satan, the Shadow and the Self" by Charlotte K. Spivack from *The Centennial Review of Arts and Science*; "Love and Order in *King Lear*" by Marilyn Gaull and "Molière and *The Misanthrope*" by Seymour Rudin, both from *Educational Theatre Journal*; "Goethe's *Faust*" by Hermann J. Weigand from *The German Quarterly*.

We wish to thank the University of Massachusetts Office of Research Services for assistance in preparing the typescripts, and we hope that a general acknowledgement of many anonymous helping hands and helping heads will at least show an awareness of our indebtedness.

A. P.

Contents

David R. Clark

The
Tempest

~◆◉◉◉◆~

To an understanding of Shakespeare's *The Tempest* an examination of the role of Prospero is central. In presenting Miranda's father, the Duke of Milan, ruler of the isle, and an old magician, the play goes far beyond Prospero's literal roles to say a great deal about fatherhood, kingship and good government, and about man's control of the elements. It is a study of the nature of true freedom, moral freedom first—freedom within the individual—but afterwards freedom within the family and within society. Personal discipline and social responsibility are seen as the conditions of freedom. To the achievement of these aims the moral magic of Prospero's art, and of Shakespeare's art, are seen as aids.

Shakespeare finds one of his great themes in the "rage for order" in the family, in the state, and in the universe and in the correspondences among the three. As the good father wisely orders family affairs, so does the king the state, and God the universe. Prospero, as father, Duke and magician, has power in all three realms and represents a principle of order interpenetrating all three. He is "So rare a wond'red father and a wise" (iv, i, 123),[1] as Ferdinand says, carefully guiding and guarding his daughter's future; he is the model governor whether of the isle or of the dukedom; and he is a "god of power" (I, ii, 10) who through his magic controls the spirits of the elements and who raises and controls tempests.

Many things could be said of Prospero's fatherly dedication to the care and education of Miranda, but note particularly his willingness

---

[1]William Shakespeare, *The Tempest,* ed. Robert Langbaum (New York, 1964), the Signet Classic Shakespeare, gen. ed. Sylvan Barnet. All quotations are from this text.

1

to set her free. Lear was a sentimental father, yet one of childish rages. Prospero is hardly sentimental—at any rate Ferdinand would not think him so after finishing a day of log-carrying. Yet though Prospero is brusque, his anger is feigned. He does everything in care of Miranda even to plotting how Miranda shall leave him for another man. Lear cannot endure to hear Cordelia say that she will love her husband more than her father. Prospero is wise and makes plans for his daughter to disobey and leave him. He knows how to love her enough to set her free. This is, of course, the great lesson the older generation always has to learn.

Prospero, as Duke of Milan and ruler of the island, raises the large question of kingship, of good government, of order in the state. It would be hard to exaggerate the importance of this theme in almost any Shakespearian play. Here it strikes one that Shakespeare is making his point immediately—at the very opening of the play. "*A tempestuous noise of thunder and lightning* [is] *heard*" (I, 1). The ship is being blown hard, which is safe if it misses the island, but disastrous should it be forced too close to shore and into a reef. The first line of the play is given to the Master, that is, the captain of the ship, the person in command—and the first word is a command:

> *Master.* Boatswain!
> *Boatswain.* Here, master. What cheer?
> *Master.* Good, speak to th' mariners! Fall to't yarely, or we run
>   ourselves aground. Bestir, bestir! *Exit.* (I, i, 1-4)

This is the last word we hear from this mysterious master, though he appears at the end when the sailors recover from their sleep and rejoin the king and his party.

The Boatswain is ready to hand, responds quickly and cheerfully to his master's orders, and transmits them to the mariners: "Heigh, my hearts! Cheerly, cheerly, my hearts! Yare, yare! Take in the topsail! Tend to th' master's whistle! Blow till thou burst they wind, if room enough!" (I, i, 5-7) (—in other words, if there's room enough between them and the rocks so that the ship won't run aground. Blow us out to sea, free of the island.) Here we have an image of a just and harmonious government of the ship: the Master watching the situation and thinking up the commands, the Boatswain receiving the commands and seeing that they are carried out, the Mariners doing the work. There is no disagreement; everyone is trying to do his own job well.

Then enter Alonso, Sebastian, Antonio, Ferdinand, Gonzalo and Others.

Alonso. Good boatswain, have care. Where's the master? Play the men.

Boatswain. I pray now, keep below.

Antonio. Where is the master, bos'n?

Boatswain. Do you not hear him? You mar our labor. Keep your cabins; you do assist the storm.

Gonzalo. Nay, good, be patient.

Boatswain. When the sea is. Hence! What cares these roarers for the name of king? To cabin! Silence! Trouble us not!

Gonzalo. Good, yet remember whom thou hast aboard.

Boatswain. None that I more love than myself. You are a councilor; if you can command these elements to silence and work the peace of the present, we will not hand a rope more. Use your authority. If you cannot, give thanks you have lived so long, and make yourself ready in your cabin for the mischance of the hour, if it so hap. Cheerly, good hearts! Out of our way, I say. (I, i, 9-28)

The kind in a sense usurps a place not his own, attempts to do the captain's job. Here is an image of disorder, not only on board ship, but in the social world as well. For this king has conspired, we learn later, with Antonio, Prospero's brother, to displace Prospero, and Sebastian and Antonio will conspire to try to murder Alonso.

In fact this whole first scene is really the old ship of state metaphor in realistic guise, the metaphor that appears in Sophocles, where the Priest says to Oedipus:

> King, you yourself
> have seen our city reeling like a wreck
> already; it can scarcely lift its prow
> out of the depths, out of the bloody surf,[2]

or where Creon, in *Antigone*, says of the state, "She only brings us safe; her deck we pace,/Unfoundered 'mid the storm. . . ."[3] Plato, however, is the key allusion. One cannot read *The Tempest* and Plato together without noticing all sorts of connections. Particularly relevant

---

[2]Sophocles, "Oedipus the King," tr. David Grene, *An Anthology of Greek Drama*, ed. Charles Alexander Robinson, Jr. (New York, 1949), p. 53.

[3]Sophocles, "Antigone," tr. Robert Whitelaw, *An Anthology of Greek Drama*, p. 108.

to this first scene is Socrates' comparison, in Book IV of *The Republic*, between the true philosopher in his relation to the State and the true pilot in his relation to the ship. In a poorly commanded ship (like the Athenian democracy) the captain knows little more than the sailors about navigation, and they are eager to get the wheel away from him for the power's sake in spite of their ignorance of the stars. They recognize as their natural leader, not some man who has true knowledge of navigation, but some man who is clever at winning power and who, by taking their side, moves them to put the wheel in his hands. In spite of this mutiny, the man who has knowledge is, inescapably, the true pilot, even though he be scorned by the sailors. "He must and will be the steerer, whether other people like or not. . . ." He should not "humbly beg the sailors to be commanded by him—that is not the order of nature. . . ." In the same way, "He who wants to be governed" must go

> to him who is able to govern. The ruler who is good for anything ought not to beg his subjects to be ruled by him; although the present governors of mankind are of a different stamp; they may be justly compared to the mutinous sailors, and the true helmsman to those who are called by them good-for-nothings and star-gazers.[4]

The Boatswain makes the right choice to obey the ship's master and no one else and to care no more for the name of king in such a situation than do the roaring waves, whose destructive power the royal party is abetting by getting in the sailors' way. In a storm at sea the captain, not the king, must rule.

In Plato's ideal commonwealth, the philosopher-king would rule the ideal state with his wisdom, the guardians or warrior-class would carry out his commands with their power, and the artisans and laborers would serve all by supplying the means of existence. Such is a just and temperate state. The philosopher king rules not because he wants power but because all are agreed that he is the wisest in statesmanship. That is the way to run a ship and also a kingdom.

Notice that not only the ship image in *The Tempest* but also the three-part distribution of responsibility corresponds with Plato's thought. In Shakespeare's play we have the Master, the Boatswain and the Mariners. In Plato, as I have said, we have the philosopher-king, the

---

[4]Plato, *Apology, Crito, Phaedo, Symposium, Republic,* tr. B. Jowett, ed. Louise Ropes Loomis (New York, 1942), pp. 374-375. All references are to this edition.

guardians, and the artisans and laborers. Socrates invents a myth about three types of people—golden, silver, and iron or brass—fitted by nature for the three classes. Shakespeare would think, I imagine, of king, nobles, and commons. Later in the *Republic* a connection is made between these three classes in the state and the three-part division of the soul into Reason, Will and Appetite. Shakespeare's plays seem to assume Plato's doctrine in Book IV of the *Republic* that the individual has the same three principles in his own soul which are found in the state and is wise, temperate, courageous and just in the same ways that a state is. To Shakespeare the morally free man is one whose reason assures him that in God's service is perfect freedom and whose will and appetites are in spontaneous obedience to the reason. In *The Tempest* this three-part division is clearest in the masque. Juno, queen of the gods, patroness of Rome, may be taken to represent Reason. Iris, the rainbow, the messenger of the gods, who carries out Juno's commands as Ariel carries out Prospero's, may be regarded as Will or Spirit. Ceres, goddess of the earth and the harvest, represents the enlightened and obedient appetites. Venus and Cupid —lawless appetite—are not invited to this celebration.

A similar three-part significance attaches to Prospero, Ariel and Caliban, although the individual life of these characters overwhelms their allegorical significance. Caliban, "Thou earth, thou!" as Prospero calls him (I, ii, 314), certainly stands for the body, "Which any print of goodness wilt not take" (I, ii, 352), and which must constantly be kept in subjection. Caliban does at last learn obedience as the body may be taught useful habits. Ariel, diligently obedient, clings to Prospero's thought and carries it out as does the disciplined Will. The final freeing of this spirit is associated with Prospero's death. Prospero is himself man's Reason—without ceasing to be total man at the same time. He must struggle to make Will and Appetite, Ariel and Caliban, obey perforce, and finally—Will much more quickly than Appetite—to obey willingly. Temperance, the agreement among the three principles as to which should rule, is achieved with stern difficulty.

This, like many another allegorical pattern which has been discerned in *The Tempest*, will not fit every detail, but is nevertheless suggested in some of the other groupings of characters. Particularly, I think, Stephano, Trinculo, and Caliban are a comic reversal of the Prospero-Ariel-Caliban grouping. Stephano, like Prospero, has his magic book—his bottle—which seems to make all things possible. "Kiss the book" (II, ii, 135) he says to Trinculo and again to Caliban. "I will furnish it anon with new contents" (II, ii, 149). "The liquor is not earthly" (II, ii, 131) and it is the contents of this bottle-book "which will give language" (II, ii, 85) to Caliban as originally the wisdom of Prospero (or Miranda) taught him language (I, ii, 363). As Prospero later vows to drown his book "deeper than did ever plummet sound" (V, i, 56), so Stephano's bottle, in the previous scene, is lost "in the pool" (IV, i, 208) and Stephano resolves to face drowning again to restore this "infinite loss" (IV, i, 210): "I will fetch off my bottle, though I be o'er ears for my labor" (IV, i, 213-214).

As Stephano, who would be the king of the isle, seems a comic Prospero, so Trinculo his second in command, seems in some ways comparable to Ariel. He is slender, quick of movement and of wit. He has a healthy fear of Stephano, as Ariel does of Prospero. As a jester, he is in his small way an artist and an actor like Prospero's "tricksy spirit" (V, i, 226). At one point in the play Trinculo and Ariel are linked when Trinculo is chastised for something Ariel does—which is to shout "Thou liest" at Stephano and Caliban (III, ii, 48, 66, 79).

Caliban, the third in this grouping as of the other, here represents the ignoble slavishness of the appetites of an unjust soul, for—although he thinks he is winning his freedom—his servitude to Stephano is more abject and miserable than his orderly subjection to Prospero.

Trinculo is the very opposite of the disciplined Will. He is timorous and fearful and the specific virtue of the Will is courage. "I'll not serve him," says Caliban; "he is not valiant" (III, ii, 25). Trinculo, when he first appears, is afraid of the monster Caliban, of the thunder, and of what he thinks is Stephano's ghost. His fears make him comic throughout all the scenes in which he appears. He lacks decision and can effect nothing. When Stephano agrees to fall in with Caliban's plan to destroy Prospero, it is Trinculo who urges them to procrastinate. As Ariel pipes music, he cries, "The sound is going away; let's follow it, and after do our work" (III, ii, 154-155). And later it is he who is first distracted from the plot by the "glistering apparel" (IV, i, 193) which Ariel has hung on a line.

It needs no demonstrating that Stephano "drunkard" and "dull fool" (V, i, 297-298), is the very opposite of the sovereign Reason and wise Prospero. He would have been a sore king of the isle (V, i, 289).

These themes are strongly hinted at in the presentation of other characters. In both the original conspiracy against Prospero and in the conspiracy against Alonso, Antonio, whose true function is to obey commands, thinks up bad plans for his betters, for Alonso in the first instance and Sebastian in the second. And these slothfully take suggestion from him rather than think clearly for themselves. But to try to apply the three-part nature of man symbolism to the Alonso-Sebastian-Antonio group, or to the group which consists of Prospero and the lovers, will get us into unprofitable subtleties.

Shakespeare, like Plato, shows that in the just individual each principle—Reason, Will, and Appetite—does its own business. Shakespeare is also sympathetic, it appears, to Plato's idea that a just *state* is one in which each *class* does its own business. Now when Prospero was Master of the ship of state, Antonio was his Boatswain. Disorder reigns when he who knows only how to get the wheel into his hands displaces him who knows the changes of the stars: when Antonio, the crafty politician, replaces Prospero, the wise, liberally-educated statesman. We see Antonio and Sebastian later plotting against Alonso. We see Caliban plot with Stephano and Trinculo to overthrow Prospero.

However, Antonio, Caliban, Stephano and Trinculo, those who struggle for their freedom in this illegitimate fashion, win nothing but a more disciplined servitude. At the end of Act II Caliban drunkenly sings and shouts:

> No more dams I'll make for fish,
>   Nor fetch in firing
>   At requiring,
> Nor scrape trenchering, nor wash dish.
>   'Ban, 'Ban, Ca—Caliban
> Has a new master. Get a new man!

Freedom, high day! High day, freedom! Freedom, high day, freedom!
                                        (II,ii, 188-195)

Contrast this insubordination of a "howling monster" with his attitude at the end of the play. Caliban sees Prospero in a new light: "How fine my master is! I am afraid/He will chastise me" (V, i, 262-263). This combination of admiration and guilt-conscious fear is a new healthy attitude in Caliban. And when his chastisement turns out to be nothing but a bit of housework in Prospero's cell, Caliban shows not only relief but a healthy determination to do well as a servant:

> Ay, that I will; and I'll be wise hereafter,
> And seek for grace. What a thrice-double ass
> Was I to take this drunkard for a god
> And worship this dull fool! (V, i, 295-298)

Although his education is far from complete, Caliban can now distinguish the true master, the man fitted to rule. It is Caliban's fellow log-bearer Ferdinand, it is Miranda, it is Ariel, who win their freedom through obedience and diligent service. Ferdinand and Miranda serve not only Prospero but each other.

> *Ferdinand.* . . . .
> The very instant that I saw you, did
> My heart fly to your service; there resides,
> To make me slave to it; and for your sake
> Am I this patient log-man. (III, i, 64-67)

> *Miranda.* . . . .
> I am your wife, if you will marry me;
> If not, I'll die your maid. To be your fellow
> You may deny me; but I'll be your servant,
> Whether you will or no.

> *Ferdinand.* My mistress, dearest,
> And I thus humble ever.

> *Miranda.* My husband then?

> *Ferdin*and. Ay, with a heart as willing
> As bondage e'er of freedom. (III, i, 83-89)

Ariel has promised, "I will be correspondent to command/And do my spriting gently" (I, ii, 297-298). "Do so," answers Prospero; "And after two days/I will discharge thee" (I, ii, 298-299). Ariel works well for his freedom. "My industrious servant, Ariel!" Prospero calls him (IV, i, 33). "Was't well done?" Ariel asks eagerly of his work in restoring the ship and the mariners. "Bravely, my diligence," says Prospero. "Thou shalt be free" (V, i, 241).

The restored ship, which will take Prospero back to his dukedom, reminds us again of the ship-of-state metaphor implicit in the first scene, except that now, instead of disorder and shipwreck, we have "calm seas,/And sail so expeditious that shall catch/Your royal fleet far off" (V, i, 315-317). This is a great change from the tempest raging at the beginning of the play. The change is auspicious of order and harmony in family, state, and universe. These same correspondences are found operative in *King Lear* where the great storm scene on the heath dramatizes *dis*order in the family, the state, and, apparently, the universe. In fact, there are likenesses between the roles of Prospero and Lear as rulers (as well as fathers). Each made the mistake of renouncing power, of giving up his political responsibility—Lear resigning authority to Cornwall and Albany in order to "unburthened crawl toward death" (unburdened that is of all save his hundred knights and their expensive followers and equipment!)—Prospero resigning authority to his brother Antonio in order to pursue in private the study of the liberal arts. The storm figures largely in Prospero's history too: Recall the stormy sea which bore the bark in which he and Miranda were abandoned:

> There they hoist us,
> To cry to th' sea that roared to us; to sigh
> To th' winds, whose pity, sighing back again,
> Did us but loving wrong. (I, ii, 148-151)

The difference between Prospero and Lear, *The Tempest* and *King Lear*, is that in the tragedy we go beyond ethics and morality to face the terrible reality of death and loss, while in the comedy we see, years later, the man who has come through the storm, and we learn what it takes—what qualities—to weather the storms of this life. We also learn that it is essential occasionally to kick up a storm of your own!

There is the greatest contrast between Scenes i and ii of Act I in *The Tempest*. The storm and the sinking ship are presented with the most convincing realism. We are seeing events from the outside, from the aspect of physical appearance. Scene ii—Prospero standing majestically with wand aloft—shows us events from the inside, from the aspect of their cause and purpose. Instead of seeing our hero's old white head "bide the pelting of this pitiless storm," we see him standing, in his magician's robes, wand in hand, commanding it to cease. This storm is man-made. This play exists in the realm of what man can control—whether in himself or the external world. The tragedy—*King Lear*—exists in the total world—whose borders extend far beyond man's moral and practical achievements.

What makes Prospero at last a model ruler is also the secret of his power as a magician. His dedicated search for knowledge, while it loses him his dukedom to Antonio, is nevertheless part of the glory of that dukedom:

> Through all the signories it was the first,
> And Prospero the prime duke, being so reputed
> In dignity, and for the liberal arts
> Without a parallel. (I, ii, 71-74)

The dukedom is free under Prospero. Only under Antonio does it become subjected to Naples. Prospero was so good an administrator, through his learning, that he had the machinery of the state running in perfect order and could thus delegate his authority to another. That other, however, was willing to sacrifice the good of the state to his own hunger for power. Prospero should have foreseen that his brother would not resist this temptation. Nevertheless, his studies, though they lost him his dukedom, ultimately enable him not only to get it back and to regain its freedom, but also to arrange, through the marriage of Ferdinand and Miranda, that his descendants will be rulers of Naples as well. Moreover, the influence of his wisdom—what he has taught Miranda and indeed the royal characters Ferdinand and Alonso—will give both states good hope of wise government and prosperity in the years ahead.

Like the studies of Plato's philosopher king, which lift him out of the shadow world of becoming into the sunlight of the contemplation of pure being, Prospero's search at first separates him from his people.

> The government I cast upon my brother
> And to my state grew stranger, being transported
> And rapt in secret studies. (I, ii, 75-77)

Like Plato's philosopher king, Prospero, "neglecting worldly ends, [is] all dedicated/To closeness and the bettering of my mind. . ." (I, ii, 89-90). His "library/Was dukedom large enough" (I, ii, 109-110). Like the philosopher king he prizes the life of contemplation higher than the life of action, and Gonzalo furnishes him "From mine own library with volumes that/I prize above my dukedom" (I, ii, 167-168). It is therefore from a sense of duty that he finally drowns his book and returns to Milan, just as it is from a sense of duty that the philosopher returns to the world. They both act for the good of the whole rather than for their own pleasure.

It is not necessary to get extremely technical about the kind of magician Prospero was. His is, of course, white magic, in contrast to the back magic of the "foul witch Sycorax" (I, ii, 258). Theurgy, white magic, is described as "a kind of occult art distinguished by certain Neoplatonists, in which the operator *by means of self-purification and discipline,* sacred rites, and the knowledge of divine marks, or signatures, in nature is held to be capable of evoking or utilizing the aid of divine and beneficent spirits."[5] The italicized phrase is of im-

---

[5] *Webster's New International Dictionary of the English Language,* second edition, unabridged. Italics mine.

mense importance to an understanding of the interweaving of Prospero's literal role as magician with his moral role as man in pursuit of true freedom through self-discipline and self-knowledge. Plato's philosopher ascends, in his moral and intellectual training, from opinion of the world of becoming to knowledge of the world of being:

> A nature of wondrous beauty . . . beauty absolute, separate, simple, and everlasting, which without diminution and without increase, or any change, is imparted to the ever-growing and perishing beauties of all other things. . . . [It is by] beholding beauty with the eye of the mind [that] he will be enabled to bring forth, not images of beauty, but realities (for he has hold not of an image but of a reality), and bringing forth and nourishing true virtue to become the friend of God and immortal, if mortal man may. (Plato, "Symposium," pp. 202-203.)

In a similar manner, the Neoplatonic mage studied how, through moral and intellectual training, his soul might ascend by degrees through the elementary, celestial, and intellectual worlds "to the same very original world itself, the Maker of all things, and First Cause, from whence all things are, and proceed. . . ."[6] Prospero is such a mage; his spirits are spirits of the elements—earth, water, air, and fire—and it is through his intellectual and moral discipline that he controls the elements. Moreover, he recognizes the limitations of this elemental world which, like the masque which his spirits present to celebrate the betrothal of Ferdinand and Miranda, will melt

> into air, into thin air;
> And, like the baseless fabric of this vision,
> The cloud-capped towers, the gorgeous palaces,
> The solemn temples, the great globe itself,
> Yea, all which it inherit, shall dissolve,
> And, like this insubstantial pageant faded,
> Leave not a rack behind. (IV, i, 150-156)

Though our ephemeral world is beautiful, it is not Beauty itself, which is everlasting. To this high-minded vision Prospero's training in the magic art has enabled him to attain. It is a wisdom that goes with his control of the elements and his sovereignty over the human will. His power is gained through moral and spiritual self-conquest, and it is

---

[6]Cornelius Agrippa, *Occult Philosophy*, tr. J. F. (1651), I, i. Quoted by Frank Kermode, ed., *The Tempest* (Cambridge, Massachusetts, 1958), p. xl.

for purposes of moral and spiritual regeneration—not just the regain-
ing of political power—that he uses it. We would expect no less from
one who has learned the difference between reality and appearance.

The theory that Prospero the magician represents Shakespeare the
retiring playwright has had distinguished defenders and distinguished
attackers. It is really more important to note that there are many analo-
gies between Prospero's art of magic and the art of dramatic poetry
than to identify Prospero as Shakespeare. This play is a play about
plays. In the first scene, an extremely realistic and convincing one, a
ship sinks with all hands. Yet in Scene ii Prospero lays down his robe
and says to Miranda, the wide-eyed spectator of this catastrophe:

> Wipe thou thine eyes; have comfort.
> The direful spectacle of the wrack, which touched
> The very virtue of compassion in thee,
> I have with such provision in mine art
> So safely ordered that there is no soul—
> No, not so much perdition as an hair
> Betid to any creature in the vessel
> Which thou heard'st cry, which thou saw'st sink. (I, ii, 25-32)

The only place in our world where people drown and then come back
to tell about it and to do it again another day is the stage. These casta-
ways are not even wet. Gonzalo says later:

> But the rarity of it is . . . that our garments, being, as they were,
> drenched in the sea, hold, notwithstanding, their freshness and
> glosses, being rather new-dyed than stained with salt water. . . .
> Methinks our garments are now as fresh as when we put them
> on first in Afric, at the marriage of the King's fair daughter Clari-
> bel to the King of Tunis. (II, i, 61-74)

Only in the movies can the hero go through an avalanche or a stampede
and come out with his hat still on and his hair combed. And it is only
on the stage that shipwrecked men need not wring out their clothes
when they get ashore. It is only on the stage—for that matter, I suppose—that betrayed dukes are sure to get their dukedoms back, that
assassinations are blocked just in time, that the right boy always gets
the right girl and that he cherishes her as he should. Only the stage
has this kind of magic.

Another circumstance that suggests the stage is Shakespeare's ob-
servance of unity of time in this play: the action takes place in the

course of an afternoon, and the time is, for some reason, important enough to be called to our attention repeatedly. Shakespeare seems to want to impress upon us what time it is. He has Prospero pointedly ask Ariel "What is the time o' th' day?" (I, ii, 239). Falstaff, in *The First Part of King Henry the Fourth,* asks the Prince, "Now, Hal, what time of day is it, lad?" (I, ii, 1). But he does not get the information.[7] "What a devil hast thou to do with the time of the day?" (I, ii, 5-6) answers Hal, and goes on eloquently to make the point that time has no significance for idle Falstaff. In *The Tempest* the time does have significance. "Past the mid season," Ariel answers. "At least two glasses," Prospero confirms. "The time 'twixt six and now/Must by us both be spent most preciously" (I, ii, 239-241). I can think of no reason intrinsic to the plot why Prospero has to finish his work by six. Diligence and industry are thematically important—Prospero and Ariel must make every minute count. But why the specific hours 2 and 6? (Shakespeare did mean two o'clock by "two glasses," although the term is inaccurate.) The answer may lie in the time of performance. According to E. K. Chambers, "Performances were ordinarily by daylight; before the end of the sixteenth century the time for beginning had been fixed at 2 o'clock. . . . Plays . . . lasted at least two hours, sometimes half an hour or even an hour longer. . . ."[8] Chambers is speaking of the public theaters, such as the Globe, open to the sky. *The Tempest* may very well have been performed there, but its "natural home"[9] was a private theater, the Blackfriars, better suited to the performance of masques with elaborate stage decoration and music, which catered to an audience which could pay higher prices. At the Blackfriars, "performances . . . could begin rather later and go on rather longer than those out of doors, since they were not dependent on daylight."[10] The hours 2 to 6, then, probably give us the outside limits for the time of the beginning and ending of most performances of *The Tempest.*[11] And it is getting on toward six when Prospero finishes casting his spells, and decides to release his spell-bound victims. "How's the day?" he asks Ariel, who replies, "On the sixth hour, at which time, my lord,/You said our work should cease." "I did say so," recalls

[7]William Shakespeare, *The First Part of King Henry the Fourth,* ed. M. A. Shaaber (Baltimore, Maryland, 1957), gen. ed. Alfred Harbage.

[8]E. K. Chambers, *The Elizabethan Stage,* 4 vols. (Oxford, 1923), II, 543.

[9]Kermode, ed., *The Tempest,* p. 152.

[10]Chambers, II, 556.

[11]There was a performance of *The Tempest* on November 1, 1611, at the Banqueting House at Whitehall, for King James I. It may be that the six o'clock deadline for finishing alludes to the royal schedule. This is conjecture.

Prospero, "When first I raised the tempest" (V, i, 3-6). As a matter of fact, he said so when Shakespeare first raised *The Tempest,* that is, at the beginning of the performance (I, ii, 240-241), and one wonders if Prospero speaks as producer of a play as well as a magician. If some performances of *The Tempest* began at 2:30 and ended three hours later at 5:30, the time during which we are to imagine the action as taking place would approximate the actual hours of the performance. According to Alonso, the action of the play takes about three hours:

> If thou beest Prospero
> Give us particulars of thy preservation;
> How thou hast met us here, whom three hours since
> Were wracked upon this shore. . . . (V, i, 134-137)

When Prospero reveals Ferdinand playing chess with Miranda, Alonso, after welcoming his restored son, asks "What is this maid with whom thou wast at play?/Your eld'st acquaintance cannot be three hours" (V, i, 185-186).

It is possible that Shakespeare is so explicit about the time partly to show off to Ben Jonson and other dramatists that he could, if he wanted to, not only keep the action within the day's time required by some critics, but even within three hours time. (He doesn't usually do this. In *The Winter's Tale,* for instance, Shakespeare allows an interval of 16 years between the third and fourth acts!)

In any case, the time during which we are to imagine the action as taking place is very close to the time during which the audience would assemble, see the play, and disperse. Perhaps on some occasions it may have seemed simultaneous. This point seems to me one in favor of identifying Prospero's art in producing a tempest with Shakespeare's art in producing *The Tempest.*

Another point of interest is that all the characters are put in the position of spectators on various occasions. Prospero is always arousing wonder with a startling show. Miranda is principal spectator. The whole action is for her education as well as for the determining of her future. We have seen her as spectator of the shipwreck; later we enjoy her first sight of that rarity—a handsome young man. Leading her towards Ferdinand Prospero speaks a strangely rich line: "The fringèd curtains of thine eye advance/And say what thou seest yond" (I, ii, 409-410). And a rare sight he is to her and she to him. Later she is introduced to all the others—the King, Sebastian, Antonio, Gonzalo, etc. —and has her famous lines:

> O, wonder!
> How many goodly creatures are there here!
> How beauteous mankind is! O brave new world
> That has such people in't! (V, i, 181-184)

But there are better examples, including an actual masque in which spirits act out the roles of Juno, Iris, and Ceres at an entertainment in honor of the betrothal of Ferdinand and Miranda. As always the purpose of the show is educative: Ferdinand and Miranda are to learn the rules of chaste love.

No less effective is the show Ariel puts on for the king and his followers when he has a table of food miraculously disappear before them and Ariel, as a harpy, scold them for their crimes against Prospero. Here the theme of the moral effect of drama is at its strongest. Prospero compliments Ariel gaily on his acting. "Bravely the figure of this harpy has thou/Performed, my Ariel. . ." (III, iii, 83-84). He particularly liked the part where, by a stage trick, the food disappears. But Alonso, the audience, experiences the same strong reaction that the guilty king does in *Hamlet* to the play that represents a murder like the one he has committed. Gonzalo says to the king:

> I' th' name of something holy, sir, why stand you
> In this strange stare?
>
> *Alonso.* O, it is monstrous, monstrous!
> Methought the billows spoke and told me of it;
> The winds did sing it to me; and the thunder,
> That deep and dreadful organ pipe, pronounced
> The name of Prosper; it did bass my trespass.
> Therefore my son i' th' ooze is bedded; and
> I'll seek him deeper than e'er plummet sounded
> And with him there lie mudded. (III, iii, 94-102)

Alonso and the others remain under a spell until Prospero's act comes to an end. Prospero puts off his magician's robe and wears again the clothes of the Duke of Milan. As they come out of their spell they are like people extraordinarily attentive to a play who afterwards find it difficult to come back to reality:

> The charm dissolves apace;
> And as the morning steals upon the night,
> Melting the darkness, so their rising senses
> Begin to chase the ignorant fumes that mantle
> Their clearer reason. (V, i, 64-68)

Their understanding
Begins to swell, and the approaching tide
Will shortly fill the reasonable shore,
That now lies foul and muddy. (V, i, 79-82)

Dramatists Prospero and Ariel have put them through a purgatorial
suffering in which the result, for Alonso at least, has been "heart's
sorrow/And a clear life ensuing" (III, iii, 81-82). They have under-
gone the tragic catharsis and are restored to moral health.

It is a passage just before the charm is dissolved which has most
frequently been cited as evidence that Shakespeare is using Prospero
to give his own farewells to the theatre. The passage owes something
to one in Ovid where the sorceress Medea is also abjuring magic.
However, Shakespeare's choice of what of Ovid's to keep and what to
change is determined by his own interests. I accept the idea that one
of his interests here is to hint at his own career as a playwright. It
strikes my fancy anyway to be reminded of early romantic comedies
like A Midsummer Night's Dream when I read:

Ye elves of hills, brooks, standing lakes, and groves,
And ye that on the sands with printless foot
Do chase the ebbing Neptune, and do fly him
When he comes back; you demi-puppets that
By moonshine do the green sour ringlets make,
Whereof the ewe not bites; and you whose pastime
Is to make midnight mushrumps, that rejoice
To hear the solemn curfew. . . (V, i, 33-40);

of the tragedies such as Othello and King Lear where a symbolic storm
is important when I read:

. . . by whose aid
(Weak masters though ye be) I have bedimmed
The noontide sun, called forth the mutinous winds,
And 'twixt the green sea and the azured vault
Set roaring war; to the dread rattling thunder
Have I given fire and rifted Jove's stout oak—
With his own bolt . . . (V, i, 40-46);

of—I dare to say it—Macbeth when I read:

. . . the strong-based promontory
Have I made shake and by the spurs plucked up
The pine and cedar . . . (V, i, 46-48)

(You remember how Birnam wood comes to Dunsinane?); of *Julius Caesar* and *Hamlet* when I read:

> . . . graves at my command
> Have waked their sleepers, oped, and let 'em forth
> By my so potent art (V, i, 48-50);

and finally of the late romances, *A Winter's Tale* and *The Tempest*, when I read:

> But this rough magic
> I here abjure; and when I have required
> Some heavenly music (which even now I do)
> To work mine end upon their senses that
> This airy charm is for, I'll break my staff,
> Bury it certain fathoms in the earth,
> And deeper than did ever plummet sound
> I'll drown my book. (V, i, 50-57)

I'll retire to Stratford and never write another play until death takes me.

Prospero speaks an epilogue in which having freed the audience from the healthful spell of the play, he now asks them to free him by responding with applause. He steps down from being a magician-dramatist who is able to control our ideas and emotions by means of his play, to being plain man, dependent, as we all are, on the mercy of others. "As you from crimes would pardoned be,/Let your indulgence set me free" (Epilogue, 19-20). The spells that Shakespeare the dramatist cast are like those that Prospero the magician cast, and Shakespeare may be saying that they both had a moral purpose and that both must ultimately be renounced. All souls must ultimately be left free to make their own moral decisions. Art has a moral purpose. In Dante the graphic arts, music and poetry, figure largely in Purgatory, where the human will is perfected, but figure little in Paradise, after the individual soul, crowned and mitred over itself, is free. So in *The Tempest* the magic and aesthetic spells are broken when the characters and the audience, after a purgatorial cleansing, are restored to themselves.

All the characters are concerned with their freedom—from Ariel's first request for his freedom to the final words from the epilogue. We all want freedom, but what is it and how does one get it? Prospero's success in teaching and getting freedom is expressed in Gonzalo's speech:

Was Milan thrust from Milan that his issue
Should become kings of Naples? O, rejoice
Beyond a common joy, and set it down
With gold on lasting pillars. In one voyage
Did Claribel her husband find at Tunis,
And Ferdinand her brother found a wife
Where he himself was lost; Prospero his dukedom
In a poor isle; and all of us ourselves
When no man was his own. (V, i, 205-213)

It is of great importance for the moral meaning of the play that
Prospero gives up his magical power at last. He is in effect setting all
his erstwhile "subjects" free. The will must be free to choose. God
leaves it free to choose between evil and good and so must Prospero.
Prospero abjures his power as God abjures His that man may be free
to choose. In fact there is a sense in which Prospero—if not God, or a
"god of power" (I, ii, 10)—is a sort of Cato, a sort of guardian of a
purgatorial isle, and the whole play after the first realistic shipwreck
scene is a distant image of the state of the soul at and after death.
The shipwreck might be treated as an actual death and everything that
follows as a purgatorial after-life. "A brave vessel/(Who had no doubt
some noble creature in her)" (I, ii, 6-7) is shattered, as the body suffers dissolution.

Did Shakespeare have in mind some parallel with Christ—the stern
Christ of the second coming? Prospero has been defeated and restored
—resurrected; and he comes to rule Milan again. I am thinking of St.
Paul's first epistle to the Corinthians in connection with Prospero's
being able to say "At this hour/Lies at my mercy all mine enemies"
(IV, i, 262-263) and then being able to divest himself of his power
and present himself helpless to the higher power—the theater audience
—from which all his power comes:

Then cometh the end, when he shall have delivered up the kingdom to God, even the Father; when he shall have put down all
rule and all authority and power. For he must reign, till he
hath put all enemies under his feet. The last enemy that shall
be destroyed is death. For he hath put all things under his
feet. But when he saith all things are put under him, it is
manifest that he is excepted, which did put all things under him.
And when all things shall be subdued unto him, then shall the
Son also himself be subject unto him that put all things under
him, that God may be all in all. (I Corinthians 15: 24-28)

Look finally at the epilogue. Note particularly these words:

> Now I want
> Spirits to enforce, art to enchant;
> And my ending is despair
> Unless I be relieved by prayer,
> Which pierces so that it assaults
> Mercy itself and frees all faults,
> As you from crimes would pardoned be,
> Let your indulgence set me free. (Epilogue, 13-20)

Though some editors think this epilogue spurious, I do not, and I find this final abnegation and prayer of the humble Prospero as moving as anything in the play. Of course, on one level it is just a conventional compliment to the audience. But an allusion to *Ecclesiasticus*—"the prayer of the humble pierceth the clouds" (35:17)[12]—strengthens the biblical and religious overtones. I think the play leaves us at the point where man must abandon all his pretensions to practical and ethical achievement, and in the face of death, depend only on prayer.

Suggestions for Further Reading

Knight, G. Wilson. *The Crown of Life.* New York, 1947.

Murry, John Middleton. *Shakespeare.* New York, 1936.

Still, Colin. *Shakespeare's Mystery Play: A Study of "The Tempest."* London, 1921.

Tillyard, E. M. W. *Shakespeare's Last Plays.* London, 1938.

Traversi, Derek A. *Shakespeare: The Last Phase.* New York, 1955.

Wilson, J. Dover. *The Meaning of "The Tempest."* Newcastle-upon-Tyne, England, 1936.

---

[12]Authorized version, 1611. (See my "*Ecclesiasticus* and Prospero's Epilogue," *Shakespeare Quarterly*, XVII, 79-81.) Preceding versions of the Bible used "go through" instead of "pierces," so that if Shakespeare is thinking of this passage from *Ecclesiasticus* he is thinking of it in the 1611 version. If he had not seen the new version in manuscript while writing the play, presumably in the fall and winter of 1610-1611, he certainly had opportunity to know it well by the winter of 1612-1613 when *The Tempest* was produced at court in a version which is probably the basis of the First Folio text. The passage from *Ecclesiasticus* seems to have been a familiar one to Shakespeare. A famous passage in *The Merchant of Venice* echoes part of it: "Oh, how faire a thing is mercie in the time of anguish and trouble? It is like a cloude of raine, that cometh in the time of a drought" (35:19, Geneva version). The whole passage has to do with judgment and mercy, relevant enough to *The Tempest.*

Leon Barron

The Timid I and
the Uncouth Swain in "Lycidas"

❧⊙❦⊙❧

The baroque quality of Milton's mind and verse is perhaps nowhere more startlingly or effectively displayed than in "Lycidas," that amazing collection of heterogeneous elements by grief linked together. As in the structure of "The Nativity Ode" and in the texture of the later poems, we see here the casual integration of Christian scripture and pagan myth, of topical diatribe and ancient allusion, of modern occasion and, apparently, antique form. It is hardly surprising that Dr. Johnson's discussion of the poem is characterized by the same acerbity that eats its way through the analysis of the metaphysical poets. Regarded as decorations, these elements do seem fantastic, far-fetched, even, as Johnson implied, untruthful. But if we examine them as components in the total form, relate them to the psychological situation of the speaker, whose habits of mind, like Milton's, have been formed by traditional methods of symbolism, we see that instead of being extraneous they are indications of the speaker's progressively deeper awareness of the meanings of things, an awareness that enables him to move from initial timidity to the final courage of his affirmation.

This progression is similar to that of Dante's pilgrim in *The Divine Comedy*, who begins in timidity, forced by fear down to that depth where the sun is silent, and by means of grace is enabled slowly to rise, learning to understand his surroundings and goals. Having entered hell on Good Friday, he emerges, reborn, on Easter Sunday, reproducing the experience of Christ whose meaning was the grace which enabled him to do so. Reborn through the deepening of his understanding, Dante takes courage and is ready to become a literary crusader, to battle against evil by using the means at his disposal, the poetic talent which he had learned was death to hide. Originally lost in the dark wood, the bright light of God hidden from him, he had been unable to see the justice of things. His questions, though more elaborately theological, are like those of Milton's speaker, and have to do with cause and effect, with justice. His understanding of what he sees and hears in hell differs greatly from that of what he sees and hears later in the poem: he who had believed earlier that all the unbaptized were eternally doomed, discovers, once he has won through to the necessary stage of enlightenment, that even pagans can shine in God's light. The pilgrim at the end of the poem, having learned the mercy in divine justice, is thus very different from himself initially. He is not merely beside himself with ecstasy, he is above himself in understanding. He is a new man.

But in at least one respect, Milton's speaker is handled very differently from Dante's, for whereas we see the transformation of the pilgrim and hear him finally avow that his will is turning with God's, the speaker of "Lycidas," the "I" who mentions himself frequently during the earlier parts of the poem, suddenly disappears. "I com to pluck your Berries harsh and crude," he says initially, identifying himself to the laurels and myrtles; but such personal references vanish after line 154; and on line 186 we read, "Thus sang the uncouth Swain to th' Okes and rills." After line 185, in other words, the previous speeches are suddenly seen as utterances by someone else. The voice we hear in the conclusion is a new voice, and the conclusion itself becomes the indication of mortality transcended.

Since "Lycidas" is thus not merely a lyric but a dramatic monologue in which the speaker is changed from what he was, it is necessary, in attempting a more thorough interpretation of the experience of the poem, to see how this change is effected. Partially a therapeutic utterance, "Lycidas" is aesthetically important as the record of a struggle occurring within the psyche of the speaker and manifested by the images and patterns of his words. It is not sufficient to say that the poem shows the change, for being essentially dramatic the poem embodies the reasons for the change.

The largest and most obvious of the techniques used to fashion this drama is that of the pastoral elegy, a form which allowed both ancient authority and contemporary freedom. In its oldest form, so far as we know, this kind of poem was in itself a mourning and a celebration, for with the death of the subject of the poem, be he an Adonis or a human substitute, all nature dies, and its seasonal rebirth is evidenced as indication of the resurrection of the subject who is thus seen as a fertility god or, as in ancient tragedy, a substitute for him. *The Golden Bough,* of course, has many illustrations of this type of sacrificed God, and even in later uses of the form the ancient pattern of death and rebirth is still evident. In its broadest sense, the pastoral elegy is always the celebration of the meaningful death. Conventionally, such a poem begins with the lament for the subject and for nature, which, without the sustaining energy of the subject, has also expired. Following the lament for the season and the subject, the speaker tells of his familiarity with the dead man and records the lamentations of a series of mourners. At the conclusion of the poem, nature is seen to revive, the speaker interprets the revival as indication of the continued life of his friend. During the English Renaissance the lament for the state of nature was broadened to include a consideration of the world at large, political, social, and ethical, as it had been affected by the death.[1]

Roughly speaking, Milton's poem follows this pattern. It opens in the season of *The Wasteland*. The leaves still hanging on the myrtle are brown and brittle; the spring has not arrived:

> I com to pluck your Berries harsh and crude,
> And with forc'd fingers rude,
> Shatter your leaves before the mellowing year.

The speaker then relates his intimacy with Lycidas, the common early training, shows the loss in nature, listens to the laments of the Herald of the Sea, Hippotades, Camus, and St. Peter, details a return of natural beauty, and consoles the shepherds with the news that Lycidas "is not dead."

But there are significant deviations from the conventional pattern, the most obvious of which is that the speaker describing the return of nature says:

> For so to interpose a little ease,
> Let our thoughts dally with a false surmise.

The dismissal of the return of nature as a false surmise indicates that although the pagan forms and myths had great attraction for Milton, they were, as *Paradise Regained* makes dazzlingly clear, not enough. He had a higher standard against which he measured the ancient claims and often found them wanting.

---

[1]See Richard P. Adams, "The Archetypal Pattern of Death and Rebirth in Milton's *Lycidas*," *PMLA*, LXIV (March, 1949), 183-88.

In another context William Empson has explained the poet's frequent use of such forms and myths: "Milton intends no unorthodoxy, but feels the poetic or symbolical meaning of the stories to be more important than their truth. The effect is that he compares Christian and pagan views of life as equally solid and possible."[2] Support for Empson's belief is to be found in the analysis of standard symbolic practice given by Helen Flanders Dunbar in *Symbolism in Medieval Thought*.[3] Her discussion, which centers on Dante, emphasizes the use of "insight symbolism" as a common Christian device by which eternal truths were seen in temporal evidences, even in pagan myths. Thus to the faithful, the North Star is not only a symbol of navigation or a metaphor for high-mindedness, but an indication of the mercy of God who provides guidance and comfort for his subjects. Extended, the same practice explains why Dante could use Athena as symbol of Christ: she was born without sin and had as her purpose the bringing of wisdom to man. That such methods of symbolism were not uncommon in Milton's time and were in fact the object of study by such early humanists as Pico della Mirandola and the cabalists, and were even used in many of the paintings of the age is the thesis of Edgar Wind's *Pagan Mysteries in the Renaissance* (London, 1958). Milton, it seems to me, has used the pastoral form here, with its attendant references to pagan myth, to show the speaker's increasing ability to penetrate to the truth behind appearances, the strengthening of his own faith which finally allows him to consider the early death of his friend not an indication of injustice but rather of divine mercy and comfort for man. To one who understands, things are not what they seem.

The achievement of this understanding is painful, in itself a kind of agony; and its record is to be found in "Lycidas." In the first verse stanza, the speaker exposes himself as pagan. His fear is caused by his dependence upon external things; he cannot sing because the time is not right; fate rather than free will rules his universe. Ordinarily he would not dare to disturb the season, to act in his peculiar manner, i.e. poetically, but the untimely death of the peerless Lycidas has shocked him into an attempt at action. Justice demands that this builder of "lofty rhyme" be himself remembered in a song. A melodious tear must somehow combat the desiccation of the "parching wind."

---

[2]*Some Versions of Pastoral* (London, 1935), p. 180.
[3]*Symbolism in Medieval Thought and its Culmination in the "Divine Comedy"* (New Haven, 1929).

Although the speaker seems bound by fate, the very materials of binding will finally be seen as promises of liberation. In a time of parching wind (in retrospect, spiritual dryness), Lycidas has drowned. The question of the meaning of this death by water will form the central vehicle of the composition; Milton emphasizes its importance by having all the figures of the poem identified in turn with water. The Muses, for instance, will be "Sisters of the sacred well"; Cambridge will be the river Cam; St. Peter, "The pilot of the *Galilean* lake"; and Christ himself, He "that walked the waves." Secondly, the theme of justice is introduced. The speaker has not as yet begun to ask about the justice of his friend's early death, but he does feel that good actions should be rewarded, and in the world:

> He must not flote upon his watry bear
> Unwept, and welter to the parching wind,
> Without the meed of som melodious tear.

It is the desire for justice that forces him, despite his feeling of the season's hostility, to compose something that will be ever-green, an undying reminder of the life of his friend.

A third consideration here is the reference to poetry itself. The speaker desires a poetic laurel in order to perpetuate the fame of another poet. Allusions to rhyme, song, singing, and the organs of the transmission and reception of song, the voice and the ear, will combine with the references to water in contributing to the structure of the poem. In this early section, all we know is that poetry is the commemoration of a good life; in this case, fit reward for one who was himself a dedicated poet. (That the speaker has not yet recognized the spiritual implications of "lofty rhyme" is underscored in the second verse paragraph where we are told that he hopes that his own poem may be the means of his being remembered after death.) He is, then, singing for fame, a pagan type of immortality:

> So may som gentle Muse
> With lucky words favour my destin'd Urn,
> And as he passes turn,
> And bid fair peace be to my sable shroud.

At this point in the poem, then, fame after death is a kind of justice, and it is the purpose of art to perpetuate this fame.

After recalling the joy of their common education, their learning the ways of nature and of song, and their early history as favorites of Satyrs, Fauns, and old Damaetas, the speaker turns to mourn "the heavy change, now thou are gon." But here he does not insist that nature is dead, the claim of ancient elegists. He does say that

> Thee Shepherd, thee the Woods, and desert Caves,
> With wilde Thyme and the gadding Vine o'regrown,
> And all their echoes mourn,

and he goes on to indicate that nature will *seem* dead because the poet has expired:

> The Willows, and the Hazel Copses green,
> Shall now no more be seen,
> Fanning their joyous Leaves to thy soft layes.
> As killing as the Canker to the Rose,
> Or taint-worm to the weanling Herds that graze,
> Or frost to Flowers, that their gay wardrop wear,
> When first the White-thorn blows;
> Such, *Lycidas*, thy loss to Shepherds ear.

In other words, Lycidas' death will kill the joy of the speaker just as natural growth and bloom are killed by insect, diseases, or frost.

With nature then as something he no longer can enjoy, that no longer gives consolation, the speaker turns to attack it as if angered by a breach of faith:

> Where were ye Nymphs when the remorseless deep
> Clos'd o're the head of your lov'd *Lycidas?*

They were not where they should have been, celebrating ritual and art, "Where your old *Bards*, the famous *Druids* ly." But here he stops, as if checking himself before committing folly, before asking nature more than it can grant:

> Ay me, I fondly dream!
> Had ye bin there—for what could that have don?
> What could the Muse her self that *Orpheus* bore,
> The Muse her self, for her inchanting son
> Whom universal nature did lament,
> When by the rout that made the hideous roar,

> His goary visage down the stream was sent,
> Down the swift *Hebrus* to the *Lesbian* shore.

The reference to the death of Orpheus, a central passage in the poem, is just on several scores. Actually Orpheus' death was not by water. He was dismembered by the bacchantes, and his head, thrown into the Hebrus, was carried to Lesbos where it was discovered and given burial. Under the protection granted by this sacred presence, the island became a spawning ground for poets.[4] Milton, however, to establish a connection between Lycidas and the legendary divine singer, avoids calling attention to the actual cause of Orpheus' death. Instead he refers to the floating "visage," and then, with purposeful synecdoche, prepares for the association of the two poets by speaking of the drowning of Lycidas' head. For the remainder of the poem, only the head or visage of the shepherd will be mentioned, for Lycidas and Orpheus are fused. As the victim of a sacrificial death, Orpheus is an insight symbol for Lycidas, the poet-priest, although as yet the speaker lacks sufficient understanding to see that the truth behind such a death is Christ himself, the archetype who, being of the eternal present, existed long before the mythical poet. All the speaker can say at this point is that not even divine ancestry can assure justice for the good. He does not as yet understand the nature of the Orphic resurrection or, by symbolic transference, the promise of Christ. He has come sufficiently far to see ancient signs of consolation, but he is not ready to decipher them.

In this state of mind the speaker questions the value of dedicated effort when even the best, Orpheus and Lycidas, are fatally cut down. There evidently is no justice, no reward; Fame, the pagan equivalent of immortality, remains his obsessive concern:

> *Fame* is the spur that the clear spirit doth raise
> (That last infirmity of Noble mind)
> To scorn delights, and live laborious dayes;
> But the fair Guerdon when we hope to find,
> And think to burst out into sudden blaze,
> Comes the blind *Fury* with th'abhorred shears
> And slits the thin-spun life.

As balm to his anguish comes the voice of Phoebus, an unexceptional symbol for Christ the light-bringer, explaining the limitations of a worldly, hence pagan, definition of fame:

---

[4]See Caroline W. Mayerson, "The Orpheus Image in *Lycidas*," *PMLA*, LXIV (March, 1949), 187-207.

> *Fame* is no plant that grows on mortal soil
> Nor in the glistering foil
> Set off to th'world, nor in broad rumour lies,
> But lives and spreds aloft by those pure eyes,
> And perfet witnes of all-judging *Jove*;
> As he pronounces lastly on each deed,
> Of so much fame in Heav'n expect thy meed.

Although this statement is transparently Christian, Milton is content, for this phase of the speaker's development, to rely on the force of insight symbolism. He does not talk of Christ or God the Father, for his mourner, not yet ready for open declaration of faith, has arrived only at the point at which he can believe that there must be a difference between earthly and heavenly fame, between matter and spirit; but he has not yet won through to the understanding that makes contemplation of such a distinction possible.

The justice behind the young shepherd's death thus is still undiscovered, and it is to this problem that the speaker now addresses himself, listening to the parade of mourners who pass by in their conventional manner. First to arrive is the Herald of the Sea, who questions the natural elements about the cause of the shepherd's death. Nature, however, is limited in its understanding, and can only talk of fate. "What hard mishap hath doom'd this gentle swain?" the Herald asks and sage Hippotades brings the unenlightened answer:

> It was that fatall and perfidious Bark
> Built in th'eclipse, and rigg'd with curses dark,
> That sunk so low that sacred head of thine.

Next to appear in this procession is Camus or, if we translate the water symbolism, Cambridge University, mourning the loss of a favorite student. Unlike nature, Cambridge does not blame fate; a symbol of reason, it looks for an agent:

> Next *Camus*, reverend Sire, went footing slow,
> His *Mantle* hairy, and his Bonnet sedge,
> Inwrought with figures dim, and on the edge
> Like to that sanguine flower inscrib'd with woe.
> Ah! Who hath reft (quoth he) my dearest pledge?

Reason is well intentioned, but like the speaker himself at this point, it is slow to see the meaning of what it possesses. The "sanguine flower inscrib'd with woe" is the hyacinth, another insight symbol for death and rebirth, since Apollo had given this form of immortality to the favorite he had accidently killed. But the symbol is not understood; the figures are dim.

The final voice in this procession of mourners is St. Peter, announced as "The Pilot of the Galilean lake." Scriptural rather than mythological, he represents a further stage in the speaker's approach to the consolations of faith as he delivers his attack on the unworthy poet-priests who are interested only in material success:

> What recks it them? What need they? They are sped;
> And when they list, their lean and flashy songs
> Grate on their scrannel Pipes of wretched straw,

and concludes with a reminder of divine justice:

> But that two-handed engine at the door,
> Stands ready to smite once, and smite no more.

Having moved through the teachings of nature, reason, and scripture, in his desire to learn about justice and its rewards for one who seeks true fame, the speaker rather guiltily returns to the elegiac convention, for at this point nature conventionally revives. But he is now too far removed from the pagan point of view to put his faith in the natural, the material. After calling upon the "vernal flowers" "To strew the Laureat Herse where *Lycid* lies," he shows that he must part ways with the pagan convention:

> For so to interpose a little ease
> Let our frail thoughts dally with false surmise.

Dismissing the consolations of nature as unreal, he turns, in the same verse paragraph, to imagining the probable voyage of the corpse. Seeing it passing the lighthouse shrine of St. Michael, he prays for the first time in the poem:

> Look homeward Angel now, and melt with ruth,
> And, O ye Dolphins, waft the haples youth.

The reference to the Dolphins, anciently credited with being the saviors of the shipwrecked, especially of poets, is once more an example of insight symbolism. Once this appeal to grace has been made, the speaker *in propria persona* disappears from the poem, for having risen to the point at which he can believe in the efficacy of prayer, he is reborn. He can see the truth of the resurrection even behind the Dolphin myth.

Starting then in the pagan convention, Milton has his speaker refuse pre-Christian answers. He adopts the medieval pattern of finding truth by ascending through nature to reason, from reason to Scripture, and, finally, from Scripture to grace. Behind the stories of death and rebirth is Christ himself who had transformed the waves, changing them into a supporting rather than destroying element. Even the sun, here described as *head*, partakes of this miracle of rebirth, an analogue for continued life beyond the claims of matter:

> So sinks the day-star in the Ocean bed,
> And yet anon repairs his drooping head,
> And tricks his beams, and with new spangled Ore,
> Flames in the forehead of the morning sky:
> So *Lycidas* sunk low, but mounted high,
> Through the dear might of him that walk'd the waves.

Lycidas not only has gained eternal life; he is now at the very center of lasting song:

> With *Nectar* pure his oozy Locks he laves,
> And hears the unexpressive nuptiall Song,
> In the blest Kingdoms meek of joy and love.
> There entertain him all the Saints above,
> In solemn troops, and sweet Societies
> That sing, and singing in their glory move,
> And wipe the tears for ever from his eyes.

This, however, is only part of the reward, for like Orpheus on Lesbos, Lycidas has become

> the Genius of the shore,
> In thy large recompense, and shalt be good
> To all that wander in that perilous flood.

He has assumed the pattern of Christ, an inspirer and protector of life. He has received spiritual justice.

The concluding paragraph shows us the speaker surrounded by a nature very different from that which he recognized at the beginning of the poem. In seeing the birth behind the apparent death, he has been reborn in knowledge and now can refer to his previous self in the third person: "Thus sang the uncouth swain to th'Okes and rills." Recognizing his earlier ignorance, he has lost his timidity and can now sing his song "with eager thought." Because his new faith has transformed his surroundings, he is ready to act, no longer a scarecrow indicating the path of fatalistically parching winds: "Tomorrow to fresh Woods, and Pastures new." In baroque fashion, the drama of "Lycidas" has traced his progress as a late Renaissance soul moving from near despair to affirmation.

Stanley Koehler

Style and Meaning
in <u>Paradise Lost</u>

୶๏ฦ๏๛

Two sorts of difficulty confront the reader of *Paradise Lost* in the twentieth century. On the one hand are problems of meaning for which Milton cannot be held accountable. They persist in the poem largely because Milton had Renaissance ideas, thinking as a man of the seventeenth century rather than as one of our own contemporaries in matters of politics and art, sex and religion, the distance between Milton and ourselves being increased, admittedly, by the strong personal bias with which he treated such ideas. On the other hand there are peculiarities of style for which Milton can be held entirely responsible, which he seems even to have gone out of his way to introduce. Unless certain elements of the Miltonic manner can be seen as functional rather than merely eccentric, our understanding of the poem and our sympathy with the poet may both be in danger. Since these stylistic problems are the first to strike one, we may deal with some questions of style and usage before proceeding to matters of substance.

I

Paradise Lost is the famous example in English of a manner that is now wholly out of fashion. In fact, it is hard to imagine a time less well suited than our own day to enjoying the virtues and indulging the limitations of Milton's style—the grand style—at its most Miltonic. In the three centuries since 1667, when *Paradise Lost* was published, we have gone over to the other end of the spectrum, back to that other seventeenth century ideal of a style which emphasizes normal idiom, even at the expense of the rhythm, as in Donne. To this we have added certain more modern ideas that make equally against the grand style:

31

Wordsworth's theory, for example, that the ideal language for poetry is the "real language of men," his judgment "that there neither is, nor can be, any *essential* difference between the language of prose and that of metrical composition." We have a high regard for "sincerity" as almost the ultimate virtue in poetry, and it may be for this reason that we listen for the accents of a living voice behind the artificial rhythms of the line, finding particular assurance in the regional tones of Robert Frost or the "American idiom" of William Carlos Williams. To our ears, a poet who reflects neither an individual personality nor a region will sound somewhat isolated, unreal, even insincere. And one who magnifies the element of artifice, however skillfully, however deliberately, will find the virtues of such a style counted as defects.

Wordsworth made no such error as far as Milton is concerned. He did not confuse the resources of the grand style with the mechanical tricks and more limited effects of Milton's successors. Nor was he so in love with his own simplicity that the grandeur of Milton's line was wasted on him: "Thou hadst a voice whose sound was like the sea. . . ." It is different for us. If we accept the grand style at all, it will probably be as an interesting but remote landmark in the history of English prosody. We may honor Wordsworth's tribute to that style, but we still do not have his sympathy for it. Wordsworth, of course, judges Milton as belonging to a different order of men, whose very dedication cuts them off from other men. Milton was in a sense a Nazarite, like his own Samson, set apart for some high purpose in life, and his style was fitted to that special purpose. One other thing should be noticed about Wordsworth's sonnet to Milton: the fact that it ends after all with a tribute to Milton's humility, not to his pride:

> . . . . And yet thy heart
> The lowliest duties on herself did lay.

Milton's style is at times very much in key with such humility; it can be, in fact, as simple as it is sublime. A recent critic dismisses the "organ voice," "sea sound" notion completely, finding in Milton's cadences the effect of a spellbound silence rather than of overpowering sonority. However this may be, it is at least clear that monosyllabic simplicity and native diction are part of Milton's range, whether Dalila speaks, or Samson, or Milton himself:

I was a fool, too rash, and quite mistaken
In what I thought would have succeeded best.

No, no, of my condition take no care;
It fits not; thou and I long since are twain.

I wak'd, she fled, and day brought back my night.

This is admittedly not the usual effect, and perhaps we should go on to meet the critics of the grand style on their own ground.

The most formidable of these, Samuel Johnson, conceded, with mixed feelings, that Milton's natural port was a giant's loftiness. Before that high and noble mind, he confessed, "criticism sinks in admiration." Yet, for all his admiration, Johnson had some reservations, and Addision had still others. "I must confess," Addison wrote, "that I think his Stile, tho' admirable in general, is in some Places too much stiffened and obscured by the frequent Use of those Methods, which *Aristotle* has prescribed for the raising of it." He wished, in other words, "to give his Verse the greater Sound, and throw it out of Prose." Contemporary critics like T. S. Eliot, whose taste in poetry prefers the sound of speech or prose accompanied by the least distortion of language, find Milton's remoteness from ordinary speech at once a mark of his greatness, and an example to be shunned. In the most extreme instances, anti-Miltonists have compared Milton's verse to "a curtain of felt" or the great wall of China.

Unfortunately for our present purposes, the defense of the grand style, or Milton's version of it, cannot be based on specific passages alone, however extensively quoted. To see its value one must experience the movement and meaning of large units of verse through which the thought and rhythm run without hindrance of rime or punctuation at the line ends; for *Paradise Lost* is exactly what Milton called it at the beginning, an "advent'rous Song,"

That with no middle flight intends to soar
Above th' *Aonian* Mount, while it pursues
Things unattempted yet in Prose or Rhyme.

The language of prose may be fit for the visions of prose; but the grand style was, in Milton's estimation, better suited to the poet's visions of Hell, of Heaven, and of Earthly Paradise, with their unexperienced terrors, unimaginable glories, and lost delights. It takes verse of unusual energy to describe the incredible events of these regions—the journey through Chaos, the Creation, the battle in Heavn—and to carry us over the intervening distances. Nor can one see how a vision heightened like Adam's to cover the world at one sweep, and witness all the events of history in the last two books, can be contained in the limits of common speech. Perhaps we are no longer capable of bearing up under the heroic subject, or the tragic view of life; but Milton was committed to both, by tradition and by training. His style was no concoction but an instrument to these ends. If it seems to deal too much in rhetoric and stock responses, to be busy manipulating reader reaction and conducting rituals, let the reader consult C. S. Lewis' defense of this style in *A Preface to Paradise Lost;* or let him yield himself to the verse. He may just possibly be carried away by it, like Milton in one of his early elegies: "*Iam mihi mens liquidi raptatur in ardua coeli.*" Barely in his twenties, but already aware that the exalted subject could elevate both mind and style, Milton found himself seeking "some graver subject,"

> . . . . where the deep transported mind may soar
> Above the wheeling poles, and at Heav'ns door
> Look in . . . .

It was at this point, it should be noted, that he appealed to Language, this time his own, to yield him the grand style:

> . . . . search thy coffers round,
> Before thou clothe my fancy in fit sound.

There is still much pertinence, of course, to Johnson's complaint of that style, as Milton developed it, as being "harsh and barbarous," "A Babylonish dialect." To more and more of his readers it may have overtones of Babel, on whose builders God sent

> . . . . a various Spirit, to rase
> Quite out their Native Language,

as Milton puts it in Book XII. Yet even Johnson concedes its virtue as an instrument "of so much instruction and so much pleasure that . . . we find grace in its deformity." The present remarks are aimed at making Milton's language seem less eccentric than purposeful. We may look briefly at some of Milton's stylistic devices, not only to warn the reader of what difficulties he may expect in the way of style and idiom, but even more important, to suggest the virtues of these devices, and the uses to which they may be put.

Three elements of Milton's style are of particular importance in producing the highly mannered idiom of *Paradise Lost*. These are ellipsis, or the omission of words necessary to the syntax; inversion, or the changing of normal word order; and pleonasm, or the use of more words than are needed for the sense. Related to these, and to a large measure responsible for them all, is the all-pervading Latinizing tendency of Milton's classically trained mind, which not only colors his idiom, but dictates the choice of words; words which he then proceeds to use in their original Latin rather than contemporary English sense.

The device of ellipsis is habitual to Milton. "Lives there who loves his pain?" is typical Miltonic shorthand for the question, "Is there anyone that lives who loves his pain?" If one looks closely at the speech with which Satan begins his temptation of Eve (Book IX, 11. 538-548), he will be aware not only of genuine ellipsis—"all things (which are) thine by gift," for example—but of a general condensation of meaning to which the succession of participles and absolute constructions add their bit:

> Displeas'd that I approach thee thus, and gaze
> Insatiate, I thus single, nor have fear'd
> Thy awful brow, more awful thus retir'd.

One is tempted to think that the compression of such talk serves the dramatic purpose, contributing, along with the sleights of logic, to Eve's bewilderment. But Eve turns out to be even more elliptical:

> How cam'st thou speakable of mute?

It is Milton, not Eve talking. Stretched over the length of an epic, such closeness of expression can be overwhelming.

The second trick of Milton's style, already in evidence, is his way of inverting normal English word order, as when God says to Adam, "Whom thou sought'st I am. . . ."

> *This Paradise I give thee*, count it thine
> To Till and keep, and *of the Fruit to eat.*

Though it may not be to modern taste, the studied quality of such inversion lends authority to the speeches of God, and is part of the epic tone, as when the Son pauses at the edge of Chaos to still its confusion at the moment of the Creation:

> Silence, ye troubl'd waves, and thou Deep, peace.

The word order of the first command is inverted in the second; the result is a line in which the restless elements are bracketed by the concepts of stillness and quiet. Although this is not the place to examine it in detail, the line is really the last word in artful simplicity. Compare it with the routine inversion that follows it, to see the difference between the creative and the routine use of ellipsis: "Said then th'Omnific Word, your discord end." At his best, however, Milton verges on incantation. Needless to say, one does not achieve his sort of magic with the accents of common speech, and it is not surprising that Milton invokes his Muse in the same style, beginning Book I with one of his most sustained inversions:

> Of Man's First Disobedience, and the Fruit
> Of that Forbidden Tree, whose mortal taste
> Brought Death into the World, and all our woe,
> With loss of Eden. . . .

The sixth line gets at last to the main verb: "Sing Heav'nly Muse." And the invocation ends with a pair of inversions:

> . . . . *What in me is dark*
> Illumine, *what is low* raise and support.

Though much in Milton's ordering of words is Latin—or Greek, or Hebrew—much, too, is Italian. It is after Milton's Italian journey that this manipulating of English word order into some of the patterns typical also of Italian poets begins to show in Milton's verse.[1] A favorite device is placing adjectives both before and after the noun, the second one coming with a kind of delayed impact, as in "upright heart *and pure*"; or using two pairs of nouns and adjectives, the second pair coming in reversed order: *fabl'd Knights*/In *Battles feign'd*," "*fair large Front* and *Eye sublime*." It is by such arts that a straightforward statement like "Adam was formed for contemplation and valor"—a pattern clearly unthinkable to Milton—becomes by the slight trimming and balancing of ellipsis and inversion, a specimen in the authentic manner:

> For contemplation hee and valor form'd,
> For softness shee and sweet attractive Grace.

---

[1] See F. T. Prince, *The Italian Element in Milton's Verse* (Oxford, 1954), pp. 108ff.

It is too bad that these effects which Milton worked out with such loving pains should become a source of annoyance to readers unaware of their nature and purpose. Clearly, by distributing the terms so carefully throughout the sentence, adjusting them in their relation to associated terms, delaying or advancing them for climax or surprise, Milton gets a heightening of the ordinary sense similar to that which later poets—Hopkins, for example—secured by the same means two centuries later. He manages also, by this diffusing of the sense through slightly larger units, a toughening of the fabric of the discourse that makes it hold together over the large frame of the subject.

Related to the devices of ellipsis and inversion is a third: the fullness of style which is called, in the Greek, pleonasm. Milton is much more given to this device than his more innocent readers may realize. Whatever it may cost in space, and in the economy of attention, the gain is richness and weight; a relishing and reinforcement of ideas consonant with the grand style. At times it is mere tautology: "wrack and ruin" is a native instance, which we should not blame on Milton; but he develops it:

> . . . . and now all Heav'n
> Had gone to wrack, with ruin overspread.

In speaking of the flowers which Nature "pour'd forth profuse" in Eden, Milton is again being redundant, since the Latin and English terms mean the same thing. Indeed, it is only in connection with the last trait of Milton's style to be noted here, his use of words in their original and generally Latin meanings, that one sees Milton's real gift for tautology. The same pairing of English and Latin terms occurs in a phrase like *"illimitable* ocean *without bound,"* for example. For the process pushed one step further, consider the following, where Milton adds Greek to Latin and Old English roots:

> . . . . who shall tempt with wand'ring feet
> The dark *unbottom'd infinite Abyss.*

Which is to say—in three languages—a boundless boundlessness without bound. Thus, for the reader who can profit from it, pleonasm provides the gloss for Milton's etymologizing. It should be added, however, that no one who uses words as carefully as Milton will yield easily to the charge of mere repetition. Looked at closely some of these effects are seen to be ranged in a very subtle but distinct climax, as in

the phrase "erroneous there to wander and forlorn." Though "erroneous" now means little more than mistaken, and "forlorn" gives only a
mood, for Milton both terms keep their more literal meanings from
Latin or, again, Old English, so that the line moves in three stages to
its climax: to lose the way, to wander, to be utterly lost (*for-loren*).
The proportion of one Latin root (*errare*) to two English is interesting,
and not untypical. It suggests what criticism has begun to notice, that
Milton's diction is actually not so Latinate as has been thought. In
exploiting other languages, whether Greek, Hebrew, Latin, or Italian,
Milton did not neglect the native stock. We should still be alert, of
course, for moments when the Latin root does provide not only a con-
notative addition, but the whole of the intended meaning. Note, for
example, *prevent* used to mean "get there first" rather than "hinder,"
and *connive* meaning "wink at" ("close the eyes") rather than "conspire." The "diffidence of God" to which Samson refers is not timidity
but "lack of faith," and so on. It is clear how specific and imagistic
Milton's language can be by virtue of such diction. One may see, too,
how personal Milton was in his use of English, humoring his own taste
and his remarkably attentive ear.

Other details of Milton's style, many of them again borrowed from
the Latin, may be mentioned in passing, such as mixing concrete with
abstract terms, in combinations like "the vast abrupt," "the palpable
obscure"; or interchanging the parts of speech (note adjectives serving as nouns in the last two examples). Critics from Addison onward
have noted Milton's fondness for new words, sometimes of his making;
for the precise technical term, however unpoetic; for rare archaic forms
and the exotic polysyllables that name far places remembered from
books or from maps; and for the quibbles, quips, jingles, and half puns
that mark the Italianate taste in wit—"O Eve, in evil hour thou didst
give ear/To that false Worm . . . true in our Fall,/False in our promis'd
Rising." One may catch the echoing words in this small compass. But
for the more sustained interlinking of sound and rhythm typical of
the grand style at its height, one must consult a passage like Satan's
first Speech in Hell, "If thou beest hee; But O how fall'n!" (Book I, l.
84 ff.) This is not the occasion to examine closely the syntax of such
a passage; but speaking of ellipsis, it is clear that the omissions here
are on the larger scale of aposiopesis, where the thought is not only
trimmed, but left incomplete, the opening condition being resolved,
perhaps, in the exclamation that follows it, only to be renewed in a
new condition, "If he who mutual league . . . joined with me once,"

and so on toward another resolution more emotional than grammatical. If the reader doesn't founder on such syntax, it is because he is carried through the toils by the dramatic energy of the verse, running on with a motion constantly renewed like the obsessions that it conveys. The spectacle of Satan—or of Milton—wrestling with the language, putting words in, leaving them out, turning them around in redundant, elliptical, inverted expression is in itself a virtuoso demonstration of the grand style, which we can see moving toward a climax in one of Milton's most eloquent periods:

>   . . . . yet not for those
> Nor what the Potent Victor in his rage
> Can else inflict, do I repent or change,
> Though chang'd in outward luster; that fixt mind
> And high disdain, from sense of injur'd merit,
> That with the mightiest rais'd me to contend,
> And to the fierce contention brought along
> Innumerable force of Spirits arm'd
> That durst dislike his reign, and mee preferring,
> His utmost power with adverse power oppos'd
> In dubious Battle on the Plains of Heav'n,
> And shook his throne. What though the field be lost?
> All is not lost. . . .

Our attitude toward this writing may be mixed, conscious as we are both of the artifice it implies, and the eloquence it undoubtedly achieves. Still, if there is to be such a thing as a change in contemporary taste, once poetry has recovered from the effects of imagism, from its preoccupation with objects and its distrust of ideas, from its interest in prose effects and conversational inflections, it is difficult to see what alternative there can be, in the way of tone and rhythm, to a return to the grand style in some form. Milton, or someone like him, should be living in that hour, for we will need a poet of enough energy, strength, and resourcefulness to invent a new language for poetry. Should it come about, we may have once more the feeling that C. S. Lewis enjoys at the beginning of *Paradise Lost*, that "some great thing is now about to begin."

II

From what has been said about style, it is clear that there is a connection between what a poet has to say and the manner in which he says it. In turning from questions of style to consider some aspects

of Milton's meaning in *Paradise Lost,* we shall find, here again, that we
may distort the meaning if we mistake the purpose, or if we overlook
certain aspects of Milton's temperament which are reflected in the
content. One of these elements which will be discussed here is a tendency toward intensely personal expression, an insistent subjectivity which
has received its share of critical attention, but which there is some
danger of misinterpreting. The other thing to be noted is a conservative bias in Milton's style and thinking which has been frequently
overlooked. There is an interesting relation between these two things,
for they represent, if not opposites, at least somewhat opposed tenden-
ies. The self-preoccupation is reflected, as we have seen, in some of
the peculiarities of Milton's idiom, and relates to the problem of self-
expression, the indulgence of the ego; but Milton's conservative lean-
ings (which are also reflected in the style, as will be pointed out), show,
paradoxically, his inclination at the same time to connect his own values
to traditional modes of thought. We may devote ourselves briefly
to a discussion of these two elements of subjectivity and conservatism
in Milton; our concern being not so much to prevent a serious misreading of the poem, as to guard against the kind of misconceptions
regarding Milton's own nature which may throw misleading sidelights
on that meaning.

The strongly personal note which one hears consistently in Milton's
early poems is in keeping with their tone and subject; they are, after
all, predominantly lyric. It is the persistence of this tone in the later
poems which raises some question, for the subject is not at this point
ostensibly personal, nor the tone lyrical. Today of course we have
grown accustomed to expression of an extremely private nature—to dream
imagery, private symbol, and a general air of confession. Even such
longer poems as Pound's *Cantos*, Eliot's *Quartets,* or Williams' *Paterson*
function to some extent as repositories of personal comment and remi-
niscence. But the epic tradition called for objectivity, as an aspect of
decorum. There may have been precedent in Dante for coloring the
long poem with personal prejudice, but there is none in Homer, whose
values, as we derive them from the action, are public values, as Virgil's
are those of a national ideal. At one end of his range, of course, Milton
speaks for Renaissance and Christian values that are even more universal. But at the other extreme his poetry is conspicuously colored by
personal feelings. The invocations, of course, provide an occasion for
this at the periphery of the poem. Milton has, in fact, four or five
invocations. Either he is being exceptionally diffident, or he is making
the most of his chance to be thoroughly subjective, for each one is

full of his own concerns: the boldness of his subject, the difficulties
under which he is laboring—blindness, age, the sense of having been
born too late and in the wrong climate, or having waited too long: "on
evil days though fall'n, and evil tongues." There are times even in the
main narrative when one feels he is seeing the world of the Restoration
through Puritan eyes; as when the sons of Belial wander forth "flown
with insolence and wine." Such sideglances at his own times are harmless enough; but there are moments of pure ventriloquism where Milton's
own passionate feelings are given to his characters with little concern
for dramatic propriety. Milton's opinion of the populace is more than
strange on the lips of the Saviour in *Paradise Regained*:

> And what the people but a herd confus'd,
> A miscellaneous rabble, who extol
> Things vulgar.

When Christ rejects, vehemently, the whole tradition of classical learning in favor of Hebrew culture, one again wonders. Is it Milton again?
The suspicion dismays Douglas Bush, who winces to see Milton rejecting the lore of Greece and Rome to which he had devoted his life. Yet
if we assume the sentiments are Milton's, and take the hint from this
bit of subjectivity, we may learn something of Milton's mind that might
else have escaped us. It seems only natural, in the light of this passage,
that Milton should have spent so much time translating the Psalms, that
his imagery in *Paradise Lost* should be so steeped in Exodus, and
that after his middle years he should write on nothing but Biblical
subjects.

A more important misunderstanding concerns the celebrated question of Milton's misogyny. Though it may not affect major meanings,
it may color our view of Milton's temperament, and so indirectly affect
our reading of the poem, if we note how much of the woman-hater
there is in Milton's characters when they are being most ungallant, yet
neglect compensating notes of chivalry in less sensational places. It is
hard, for instance, not to identify Samson's situation, brought on by
a woman working on his sensual appetites, with Milton's own domestic troubles, or the bitterness of Samson's rejection of Dalila with feelings Milton may have had at one stage of his relation with Mary Powell.
So Belial's suggestion in *Paradise Regained* that Christ can be tempted
with women draws the scornful reply from Satan: "None are, thou
think'st, but taken with such toys." The same note of anti-feminism
on Milton's part is heard in the nagging of Eve before the fall, in

Adam's recriminations afterwards, and in the scathing indictment of marriage:

> [Man] never shall find out fit Mate, but such
> As whom misfortune brings him, or mistake.

What did Adam know of such problems? Yet if this is Milton's view of women, it is not his entire view; we must see the danger of neglecting less conspicuous passages that speak to quite different effect. Even the suggestion of Belial which Satan rejects is eloquent enough: "Set women in his eye, and in his walk:"

> . . . . Virgin majesty with mild
> And sweet allay'd, yet terrible to approach.

The same note of genuine romanticism occurs in Adam's account of his love, in Milton's description of the nuptial bower and of love before the fall, and in a conception of Eve herself which Byron might have envied: "For softness shee, and sweet attractive grace." That strain goes back to the first Latin elegy, where Milton rhapsodizes over English beauty. His experience in the seventh elegy of having been smitten by that beauty may have been innocent, but it is not necessarily theoretical, and it may explain the impulsive nature of Milton's affair with Mary Powell. It should be taken into account, in reading Milton's account of man's fall, lest it seem too sternly Puritan, too purely anti-feminist.

The second element that we have to discuss here, the element of conservatism in Milton's thinking, is even more seriously involved with the question of Milton's meaning than is the question of his subjectivity. Nor is it, incidentally, unrelated to the question of style. We have observed idiosyncrasies in the handling of stylistic elements amounting to what one critic has called "a systematic deformation of the language." One might suppose at first that the strategies involved in that process are those of a rebel against idiom, one who would remould the conventions of language to suit his own individual purposes. Yet from another point of view Milton's style may be seen not as a revolt at all, but as a regression, the result of a conservative bias that does not invent new usage so much as revert to outmoded ones. Though the effect is still strangeness, it is a strangeness that comes from preserving community with older traditions of language and culture than one's own —reaching from the Greek and Hebrew through Latin and Italian.

It is true that the image of a conservative Milton scarcely fits the notion of him one gets from the prose, where his attitudes are so often those of a liberal, and a vigorous one at that. The opinions expressed in his tracts against bishop and king sound much more like those of a revolutionary in politics, a sectarian, not to say heretical disputant in religion. Perhaps we should say simply that for the twenty years of the Civil War and the Commonwealth, Milton had one enthusiasm, writing, as his nephew recalled, "out of a pure zeal to the liberty of mankind." The same zeal informs the essay "Of Education," in which he wished "to principle the minds of men in virtue, the only genuine source of political and individual liberty." Even the essays on divorce, a subject on which Milton held views that were scandalously liberal in his day, were in the same cause, if we can believe him. And nowhere has the issue of free speech been argued so eloquently as in *Areopagitica*.

A liberal Renaissance humanism then stands out in the prose, imbued with the energies of war and reform, and with Milton's own immense appetite for action. When we come to the poetry, our tendency is to look for this same passionate individualism and zeal for liberty, and, if we do not find it in the form we expect, to assume that Milton is now too old, weary, and disillusioned to sustain his old enthusiasms. The present comments are aimed at preventing this kind of misreading, to which the fresh student of Milton is as liable as some of his more distinguished critics. It is a fair question, of course, how a man so dedicated to freedom and individualism should have written an epic whose subject is the sin of disobedience, whose most powerful images celebrate order and discipline in nature and society, whose tone is one of utter decorum, whose idiom is that of a language learned in school, and whose content has been called a monument to dead ideas. The answer to this paradox may be sought under the headings of politics, morality, and art. In each case it is a question of order, the need for some form of control that will release rather than contain the creative energies of the individual. In politics, the emphasis is on authority, the relation of the individual to external controls. In morality it is rather a question of discipline coming from within. In art, the two are, for Milton, combined; the artist achieves within himself an order analogous to that which he imposes on his material.

To take first the political side of the question; if Milton's respect for authority, for tradition, his need for and celebration of these things, appeared for the first time in *Paradise Lost*, one might assume it was a product of middle age, a concession to the practical. But one sees it in the poetry from the first. There is hardly a poem in the volume of

1645 which does not show the poet in the service of an ideal. In the
Italian sonnets, for instance, he addresses his subject in tones of loyalty
and humility, as if he were Petrarch himself. The poems are full of
veneration for figures of authority or age—the Earl of Bridgewater in the
Mask, Milton's own father, the great Task-Master of sonnets VII and
XIX—and for the military and political leaders addressed in the sonnets and prose tracts, like Cromwell and Fairfax. It is not, in other
words, the absence of authority that appeals to Milton, but the voluntary relation to worthy superiors. It is unwillingess on the one part,
unworthiness on the other that make for servitude and tyranny. In
Paradise Lost, for instance, the relation of the fallen angel to Satan is
one of servitude, of subjection to an unworthy master; that of the loyal
angels to Christ is one of elevation and joy. In Adam's relation to
God, Milton is no more concerned with God's worthiness as Father
than with Adam's willingness as servant:

> Our voluntary service he requires,
> Not our necessitated.

And the same is true, though it is hard for us to see it so, of Eve's
relation to Adam. The Biblical subjects that Milton tended to choose
are full of this theme of rule and subjection; an issue which seems, on
the surface of it, political. Samson's mission is, in its political aspect,
the freeing of Israel; Christ's mission, as Satan sees it in *Paradise Regained,* is the same, the freeing of his country from "Heathen servitude." Yet Milton's views in these matters have a strong conservative
flavor. Nowhere in his prose or poetry does he mention freedom
without equivalent responsibility. The servitude of Israel, or of victori-
ous Rome herself to a dissolute tyrant, is less important to him than
the moral character which has permitted it to exist. The definition of
tyranny for Milton is in fact the imposition of mechanical control from
without when the spirit within has failed in self-discipline. It is the
case with Rome, as Christ points out in *Paradise Regained*:

> What wise and valiant man would seek to free
> These thus degenerate, by themselves enslav'd,
> Or could of inward slaves make outward free?

And a similar failure causes the bondage of Israel, as in *Samson
Agonistes*:

> But what more oft in Nation's grown corrupt,
> And by their vices brought to servitude,
> Than to love Bondage more than Liberty,
> Bondage with ease than strenuous Liberty.

Here is the question viewed from its moral side. If Milton's doctrine of liberty is "strenuous," it is because it supposes a control of inner weakness by inner strength. The acquisition and the demonstration of that strength by Samson himself is the plot and theme of the tragedy. The failure of it in Adam is the subject of *Paradise Lost*. The vicarious reassertion of it by Christ is the subject of *Paradise Regained*. Such a concept of freedom, concerned with man's moral and spiritual rather than his political estate, shatters any notion of Milton as iconoclast, or mere regicide, and it should serve also as a corrective to the common misinterpretation of Milton's God as a tyrant.

If we neglect the conservative bent so clearly evident in Milton's worship of discipline, and think of Milton simply as a rebel, not only will we have trouble explaining the consistent strain of royalism that runs through the political imagery of *Paradise Lost*,[2] but it will be almost impossible for us to understand the combined moral and aesthetic fervor with which Milton contemplated the idea of Order in the universe. The vision of the world as one magnificent embodiment of a cosmic hierarchy, one grand chain of being from God on down, with each element in the system rejoicing in its relation to the whole, is one of those medieval and Renaissance ideas which kept for Milton the same overawing power it had for Dante and Shakespeare. Milton's passion for that idea is as much artistic as moral. It never fails to evoke his best imagery, and attendant music, wherever it occurs in the poems.

It is clear, then, that if Milton is a conservative in politics and morality, that conservatism has also its aesthetic dimension. Before leaving the point, it might be well to mention one other manifestation of Milton's conservatism that bears upon the art of his poetry. Whether it be coincidence or simply in the nature of things, the great creative geniuses seem almost always to stand at the beginning of their culture. Greek literature begins with Homer's epics, English literature with *Beowulf*. But when some of this first creative surge has passed, it begins to be replaced by the instinct to preserve proven forms and ideas,

---

2See Malcolm M. Ross, *Milton's Royalism: A Study of the Conflict of Symbolism and Idea in the Poems* (Ithaca, 1953).

rather than experiment with new. At its best, this later stage provides the rich resources of learning and the latest refinements of technique to bolster the individual talent. The marks of such an era are, in fact, artifice and learning, its inevitable symbol being the rich repository of classical manuscripts in the library at Alexandria. At its worst, of course, the art of such a period becomes bookish, imitative and sterile. It must be followed by a break with the past, and a plunge into newness. Perhaps it is because he comes between such movements—between the spontaneity of the Elizabethans and the formalism of the neo-classic eighteenth century—or because his own nature includes so much of both the creative and the conservative temperaments, that Milton's work shows the Alexandrian art at its most vigorous. In no other poet is so much energy and initiative combined with a Hellenistic thirst for knowledge, the true scholar's passion. Milton taught school, he wrote an essay "Of Education," he wrote a History of Britain, a grammar and Greek thesaurus, an explication of Christian theology. The results of this combined poet's and scholar's gifts are not always to our taste. If Milton is sometimes the pedant in his use of language, he is even more obviously Alexandrian in his appetite for books, his retention of his reading, and his inclination to use it in his verse. It shows in the fondness for proper names so clearly evident in the catalogue of fallen angels in the first book of *Paradise Lost;* in the way he gives alternate accounts of the location of Eden, because literature offers more than a single tradition; in the comprehensive vision of the world, and world history, in the last two books, and the hasty summary of cosmological theories given to Adam by Raphael in the beginning of Book VIII. All these represent the distillation of Milton's own wide reading in theology, myth, science, history, and mere lore. An example of Milton's method, his almost self-conscious importing of knowledge into the poem, is the list of winds that blow in Eden after the fall, a dozen or more drawn from some chart he remembered, or had read to him. Indeed it was customary for Milton to be read to in the evening and to compose *Paradise Lost* in the early morning, a routine which suggests how intimately knowledge was, for him, associated with the creative process.

These are some of the consequences of being a conservative in literature. The same conservatism is seen not only in matters of content, but in the respect Milton had for the conventional genres, all of which he fulfilled, consciously and completely, as they came to hand: the Italian sonnet after Petrarch; the pastoral elegy in the vein of Theocritus; the Latin elegy in the vein of Ovid; the mask; the epic. Even *Paradise Regained* represents a venture into a new genre, the short epic on the pattern of the Book of Job, as *Samson Agonistes* is modelled on Greek drama. The same respect for the conventions shows, by the way, in Milton's prosody. The Latin elegies follow closely the finest details of Ovid's versification. Even in *Paradise Lost*, where Milton prides himself on freeing English heroic verse from rime for the first time, he is careful to point to the example of Homer, Virgil, and "Italian and Spanish Poets of prime note." At the same time, his own blank verse, individual as it is, is scrupulously exact. In *Samson Agonistes*, where he claims the further freedom of a varying line length in what amounts to free verse, he relies explicitly on the example of the monostrophic chorus of the Greeks. Beyond these questions of content, genre, and prosody, there are a dozen devices of structure and technique that are equally conventional. The division of the epic into ten books, the redivision into twelve; the Homeric or extended simile that develops into a narrative-descriptive entity in itself; the beginning *in medias res*, the catalogues and episodes—for all of these there are literary traditions going back to Homer. To treasure these elements, to furbish them and put them to fresh use, is the mark of the conservative temper in art. The poetry that results from such an approach is not meant to be popular. Milton himself described the audience to which it might be expected to appeal as being both fit, and few. The qualifications for joining so select an audience have become no less rigorous with the passing of time.

It may be clear from these remarks on manner and substance in Milton that we cannot expect to read him with sympathy or intelligence if we ignore on the one hand qualities of style and language which he introduced quite consciously for his own purposes; and, on the other, qualities of mind and character that dictated the subjects he picked, and the treatment he gave them. Whether or not we like the style any better, we may at least make our objections on firmer ground. As for the content, here we must be on guard against more than a failure of sympathy. If we do the poet the honor of reading the poem with care, and in the light of traits too frequently neglected—his conservatism, his romanticism—we may see the absurdity of much that has been said of the poem: for instance, that the subject of *Paradise Lost*, with its respect for authority, its theme of obedience, did not really appeal to Milton at all, that he chose it because events were making against the choice of subjects he would rather have handled, so that he elected finally to write not of British heroes, and their struggle for freedom, but of Biblical matters, with their sometimes strangely passive heroes and their uncongenial emphasis on spiritual humility. In harmony with such misreading is the jibe, which has the merit of being entertaining, that Milton in the garden would have eaten the apple and written a prose tract on freedom of the will; or the even more absurd notion that has survived three centuries now, that the hero of *Paradise Lost* is not Adam but Christ, or God, or Satan, or Milton, or anyone capable of the energy and decision that appears wanting in Adam. Such views, it is suggested, represent much less than half-truths. They can be seriously advocated only by readers who re-write the poem to their own taste, seeing it through the veil of their own sensibilities—making Milton, for example, too much the romantic in his handling of Satan, too little the romantic in his treatment of women. The whole truth depends on our maintaining a more complete awareness of Milton's life and his purpose than has been shown by many of his critics; more, certainly, than the average reader, unwarned, is apt to bring to the reading of *Paradise Lost*.

Suggestions for Further Reading

Bush, Douglas. *English Literature in the Earlier Seventeenth Century.* Oxford, 1945.

————, *Paradise Lost in Our Time.* Ithaca, New York, 1945.

Lewis, C. S. *A Preface to Paradise Lost.* Oxford, 1942.

Stein, Arnold. *Answerable Style: Essays on Paradise Lost.* Minneapolis, Minn., 1953.

Waldock, A. J. A. *Paradise Lost and Its Critics.* Cambridge, England, 1947.

Willey, Basil. *The Seventeenth Century Background.* London, 1949.

Seymore Rudin

Molière and
The Misanthrope

⊷⊙❙⊙⊶

Rousseau was very hard on Molière's *Misanthrope*. He found beauty, laughter, and skill in it, to be sure, and he thought it—as have critics and audiences down the centuries—the playwright's finest achievement. But he did not doubt that his readers would agree that "the author's intention being to please a corrupt people, either his moral has a tendency to vice or the apparent good which it recommends is more dangerous than vice itself: because it seduces by a semblance of reason; because it teaches us to prefer the uses and maxims of the world to exact probity; because it makes wisdom consist in a certain medium between vice and virtue; because to the great conveniency of the spectators it persuades them that to be an honest man it is sufficient not to be a downright villain."[1]

Though Rousseau's strictures are not *per se* prophetic of twentieth-century judgments—they do not even represent eighteenth-century views adequately, and may indeed be regarded as evidence of one great Frenchman's spectacular misunderstanding of a great predecessor—they offer a useful way into a consideration of the meaning that Molière's masterpiece may have for present-day audiences. We look for multiple meanings these days, and one source of the special richness that we find in *The Misanthrope* is the sense that its protagonist is an ambiguous figure and that our reactions to and judgments of him may be curiously divided ones. To his contemproray audiences Alceste was—as his creator played him—a ludicrous character, foolishly at odds with the norms of society. To Romantic critics, he was a tragic hero, put to flight by the

---

[1]This and subsequent citations from Rousseau are from the text of the first English version of *A Letter to M. d'Alembert on the Theatre* (London, 1759).

corrupt world that he was unable to reform. To us, he may be both, or not quite either.

The use to which we may put Rousseau's moralistic castigation of the play is to see how it may illuminate the source of our divided responses even as we may question its assumptions and implications. Having sketched Molière's career as a series of attempts to please the public by ridiculing those who fail to share its debased values, Rousseau declares that "there remained only to try his talent on that form of the ridiculous which the world least of all forgives, that of virtue; this is what he has done in *The Misanthrope*. . . . The character of Alceste in this play is that of a fair, open and in short truly honest man; . . . the poet makes him a subject of ridicule. This, in my opinion, is sufficient to condemn Molière." We do not condemn Molière, but we may be moved to ask whether it is virtue that he ridicules, whether Alceste is truly honest, whether it is by the "semblance of reason" that we are seduced, whether we are indeed comforted by the demonstration that not being downright villains insures our honesty—or are indeed comforted by *anything* in the play. And if we ask such questions, we may find that answers are hard to come by, that *The Misanthrope* is a brilliantly slippery play, that its unresolved tensions look far ahead to the kinds of riddles that today's audiences expect to see propounded on our avant-garde stage.

Alceste's final flight from mankind is foreshadowed early in the play. In the first scene he is already raging to Philinte (in Richard Wilbur's deft and delightful translation): "Sometimes, I swear, I'm moved to flee and find/Some desert land unfouled by humankind."[2] Unlike his misanthropic successor Lemuel Gulliver, who loves his fellow men—or at least his fellow Englishmen—when we first meet him but is finally driven to the stables despite himself, Alceste has presumably found human society tolerable. Shortly before his reference to a "desert land unfouled by humankind," he has been informed by Philinte of society's established verdict:

> I tell you plainly that by being frank
> You've earned the reputation of a crank,
> And that you're thought ridiculous when you rage
> And rant against the manners of the age.

[2]This and subsequent citations from the text of *The Misanthrope* are from the translation by Richard Wilbur (New York, 1955).

The affair of Oronte's poem, the defeat in the lawsuit, the exposure of Célimène's perfidy, her refusal to join him in flight to the desert (what would he have done if she had agreed?)—all these, though they constitute a final series of blows, do not make a misanthrope of a once reasonable, sociable man.

Misanthropy may be called Alceste's humour—as it is a Jonson or a Marston character's; it identifies him, like his green ribbons. Though he has been courted by the Orontes for his connoisseurship, pursued by the Arsinoës for his manliness, even admired by the rare Eliantes for his integrity, he has always been the critic, the complainer, the outsider. And as such he has a hard time retaining the good will even of so complacent and even-tempered a compromiser as Philinte, who concludes the first act by shrugging off one of his friend's near-apoplectic rages with, "Oh, you're just joking. I'll keep you company." At odds with his beloved, his friends, his society, all mankind, he is—in a world where good conduct is evidently equated with accepting and abetting the established mode—a figure of ridicule, the dark object of a glittering world's scorn.

Does he deserve the scorn to which he is subjected by his fellows—and presumably by his creator? "The audience must be made to laugh," Rousseau repeats bitterly, as he argues that Molière has debased the play by exciting easy, thoughtless laughter at the spectacle of an honest man's loneliness and despair amid society's corruptions. The audience is indeed, on one level, expected to laugh, and there is a sense in which it is honesty and virtue that they are made to laugh at. But there is also a sense in which Alceste primarily embodies not these qualities but another which may ultimately nullify them. Like Orgon and Arnolphe—among Molière's other protagonists—Alceste is the excessive man, and an excess of anything can, in Molière, be the undoing of its possessor and his fellows. When Philinte asks, "Suppose you met with someone you couldn't bear;/Would you inform him of it then and there?" Alceste's answer is, "Yes," and he goes on to specify that he *would* tell Emilie that her elderly coquettishness is pathetic, and Dorilas that his bragging is a bore. To which position Philinte's rejoinder, some lines later, is:

> This world requires a pliant rectitude;
> Too stern a virtue makes one still and rude;
> Good sense views all extremes with detestation,
> And bids us to be noble in moderation.

If, however, Philinte, as Molière's *raisonneur*, offers a welcome re-
buke to Alceste's excess, it is noteworthy that he is not the author's
only spokesman. As Martin Turnell has observed,[3] Eliante—with her
greater generosity and humaneness, her realization that Alceste has justification for his anger and nobility in his extremism—adds a corrective
to Philinte's moderation. Eliante has been attracted to Alceste, though
in Act IV she unselfishly expresses the hope that his suit to Célimène
will succeed. What she has found attractive in him, she puts thus:

> The honesty in which he takes such pride
> Has—to my mind—its noble, heroic side.
> In this false age, such candor seems outrageous;
> But I could wish that it were more contagious.

Alceste's excessiveness is different from—say—Orgon's. The shams, the
inanities, the abuses against which he rails are real ones, and his revul-
sion against them must up to a point be shared by the audience. What
we are presumably not intended to share is his conclusion. We may
not see much reason for believing that Philinte's resolution at the
very close—"To change the mind of this unhappy man"—can be carried
out, but we presumably hope he will keep trying.

Gulliver's rejection of mankind was to be presented in ways that
prevent the alert reader from identifying it wholly with Swift's. In Alceste's case the complex interplay of theme, character, and language
produce a constantly intensifying sense of uncertainty as to Molière's
own position. From one angle, our hero begins as a noble opponent
of corruption, finds positive confirmation of his worst charges, and ends
with the heroically necessary act of total rejection. From another, our
foolish extremist, given from the start to the misanthropic humour,
persuades himself irrationally that the only course of an honest man
is the non-human one of total disengagement. And the uncertainty is
climaxed by our sense, at the final curtain, that nothing has been settled.
As Turnell observes, "His [Molière's] irony is turned on society as well
as on Alceste, and the play ends . . . not with the restoration of order,
but with something that is very like a mark of interrogation."[4]

If Turnell's comment implies, among other things, that comedy ordinarily ends with the restoration of order, it points to a fundamental
likeness in this respect between comedy and tragedy. And if *The Misanthrope*, which has often been described as coming closest to tragedy

---

[3]In *The Classical Moment* (New York, 1948).
[4]*Ibid.*

among Molière's plays, nevertheless resembles neither form purely, it does offer a comic protagonist with many of the tragic hero's lineaments. The play does not end with order, balance, reconcilation—as, on the one hand, the *Oresteia* and *Hamlet* and *Lear* do, and, on the other, *The Clouds* and *Twelfth Night* and *Tartuffe*. But it has offered a dense, profound examination of the extremist who is so often, in varying ways, at the center of both forms, the excessive man who in tragedy "commands our earnest good will" (in Oscar Mandel's formulation)[5] and in comedy evokes both our amusement and our censure. The time is out of joint, indeed, in the world of *The Misanthrope*, but Alceste was not born to set it right. In our delicately divided reactions to him, to his world, and to the conflict between them lies the source of the strange power and fascination of the play.

Alceste does not dominate the audience's attention so completely as these remarks may have so far suggested. Philinte, the reasonable conformist, and Eliante, the more humane moderate, have—as has been noted—their significant functions. It is in his conflict with Célimène, however, that Alceste comes to his crucial confrontation, the confrontation of a soul incapable of compromise with the charming embodiment of a society whose very soul is compromise. And the complexity of texture that Molière achieves in the play is partly a result of his subtle development of Alceste's inner conflict with respect to Célimène. Alceste finds that not only Philinte's reasonableness but his own lofty integrity are in jeopardy when the heart asserts its claims. Philinte and Eliante both find it puzzling not only that the sullen Alceste should be in love at all but that he should have chosen the worldly, flighty Célimène. But Alceste makes it clear in an aside (Act IV, scene 3) that his "heart's too faint and cowardly/To break these chains of passion, and be free,/To scorn her as it should and rise above/This unrewarded, mad, and bitter love." And in his self-reproachful cry to Philinte and Eliante, just before making his doomed last appeal to Célimène to flee with him, he admits the folly of his passion:

> And I shall prove to you before I'm done
> How strange the human heart is, and how far
> From rational we sorry creatures are.

He knows with Pascal that the heart has its reasons that "reason" does not know, and his helplessness before his passions is part of the humanity that we recognize in and share with him. When Rousseau

---

[5]In *A Definition of Tragedy* (New York, 1962).

argued that *The Misanthrope* "seduces by a semblance of reason," he presumably meant that Philinte's flexible reasonableness is unjustly held up as superior to Alceste's rigid honesty. But Philinte's philosophy is in fact shown up as inadequate to the realities of passion. Alceste rejects Célimène finally, but he does so after bitter internal struggle, and as a corollary of his total alienation from mankind. Alceste's solution to his amatory as well as his social problem is not recommended, but Molière does not seriously suggest that an adequate solution exists.

In its refusal to offer a solution to some of the eternal riddles that vex mankind, *The Misanthrope* differs from much of the rest of Molière, though its enigmatic tone is to a degree present in *Don Juan.* Indeed there is darkness—even savagery—in *Tartuffe,* but the radiance of the Sun King finally dispels even such terrifying hypocrisy as Tartuffe's, such monstrously wilful excessiveness as Orgon's. And Arnolphe's last anguished "Ouf!" in *The School for Wives* results from the triumph of young love, good sense, "reason" over vanity, wilfulness, excess.

No such triumph is achieved in *The Misanthrope.* Alceste flees, haunted and despairing, God knows where. Philinte and Eliante will presumably marry, though even this is uncertain; Eliante's last observation is only that *if* she were to offer Philinte her hand, it would probably not be refused. And what of Célimène, who has lost not only Alceste but the standing she has had in her own fashionable world? "We're off," Clitandre has declared in his parting shot, after the exposure of her duplicity, "to make the world acquainted/With this sublime self-portrait that you've painted." She has proved incapable of rejecting the world that has—for the time at least—rejected her: "What! I renounce the world at my young age,/And die of boredom in some hermitage?" She may or may not live to best other Arsinoës, attract other Orontes, Acastes, and Clitandres, dominate other fashionable circles. For all we know, her future is as dark and uncertain as Alceste's own. Unlike an Elmire or an Agnès, she has suffered humiliation and rejection by her peers as well as by the man to whom she has offered her hand. The "mark of interrogation" with which Molière leaves his audience is as applicable to Célimène as it is to Alceste and to the total meaning and effect of the play.

It was presumably Philinte that Rousseau had in mind in charging that the play "teaches us to prefer the uses and maxims of the world to exact probity . . . and makes wisdom consist in a certain medium between vice and virtue":

> This world requires a pliant rectitude;
> Too stern a virtue makes one still and rude;
> Good sense views all extremes with detestation,
> And bids us to be noble in moderation.

We may agree that wisdom of a kind, in Molière's terms, consists in maintaining "a certain medium between vice and virtue," but we may question whether the play is in any literal sense engaged in "teaching" at all—that is, whether so superbly ironic and elusive a work is describably in didactic terms. In any case Philinte is subject to correction by Eliante, and we are uneasily aware that Alceste's unpliant rectitude may be the highest and wisest corrective of all. The kind of "too stern virtue" embodied by Arsinoë does indeed evoke Molière's scorn, though it is perhaps her malice, rather than her prudishness, that is the principal target. But Alceste's sternness is not of the same order as Arsinoë's, and if Philinte's counsel may in turn be extended to Célimène, the question arises whether *her* sort of pliant rectitude is recommendable in any sense at all. "May I enquire,/" asks Philinte, "whether this rectitude you so admire,/And these hard virtues you're enamored of/Are qualities of the lady whom you love?" They are not, of course, qualities of Célimène, and the question whether they are not preferable to the qualities she does reveal—brittleness of wit, coquettishness, insouciance —is, in view of her final deflation—at least an open one.

Over forty years ago George Jean Nathan could write, "Sound art is never recondite. Molière and Shakespeare are as transpicuous as Maeterlinck and George Kaiser are ambiguous. That a great work of art is susceptible of many meanings, many interpretations, seems to me to be largely nonsense."[6] *Nous avons changé tout cela.* Long before Nathan, of course, audiences had found and appreciated many meanings in Molière and Shakespeare, as well as in Maeterlinck and Kaiser. But it remains true that Molière, at least, seems to shine—among the great dramatists—with a special bright clarity. Preciosity is transfixed in vividly luminous farce; the grotesqueness and irresponsibility of doctors are displayed with the sharpest definition; hypocritical piety, with its atmosphere of morbid sensuality, is exposed to hard light.

But *The Misanthrope* stands alone. And in no respect is its fundamental elusiveness so striking as in that of its hero's honesty. "A fair, open and in short truly honest man," Rousseau called him, and as against

---

[6]In *The World in Falseface* (New York, 1923).

the Célimènes and Arsinoës, the Orontes, Acastes, and Clitandres, even
—or perhaps particularly—the Philintes, he is so. His motivation, however, takes some questioning. "I choose, Sir, to be chosen," he is already
declaring in the first scene, "and in fine,/The friend of mankind is no
friend of mine." A bit later, in reference to the lawsuit that he, in effect,
knows he will lose through refusing to pull the necessary strings, he
reveals something of what prevents him from pulling them: "Oh, I
could wish, whatever the cost,/Just for the beauty of it, that my trial
were lost." He needs, thus, to suffer. And in the last act, when the trial
has indeed been lost, he brushes aside Philinte's suggestion that the case
could be re-opened:

> No, no, let the verdict rest,
> Whatever cruel penalty it may bring,
> I wouldn't have it changed for anything.
> It shows the time's injustice with clarity
> That I shall pass it down to our posterity
> As a great proof and signal demonstration
> Of the black wickedness of our generation.

Two considerations about Alceste suggest themselves. He is, for one
thing, the self-dramatizing sufferer, enjoying—as Dostoyevsky's Marmeladov was to enjoy—the humiliations that the world offers him, though—
unlike Marmeladov—not admitting that he in any sense earns them. And
he is, as Lionel Gossman has pointed out in a subtle analysis,[7] inexorably
committed to the world against which he rails, hopelessly dependent for
his self-realization on its good judgment even as he is obliged to flout
its ways, incur its bad judgment, and flee into total isolation. "I choose,
Sir, to be chosen"—to be esteemed, that is, for his special virtues. But
he is specially virtuous only in relation to the pliancy and compromise
around him. He wants to be chosen for the very qualities that inevitably
cause him to be rejected. And whether this constitutes "true honesty"—
in Molière's terms or in ours—is anybody's determination.

The Misanthrope remains a splendidly stageworthy play. The man
with the green ribbons, set against the glittering artifice of his world,
makes a consistently engrossing central figure. Oronte with his absurd
sonnet, the little marquesses with their ineffable vanities, Philinte and
Eliante with their graceful common sense fill in a rich background.
Célimène, not quite an antagonist, has her shadows as well as her
charms, and her scene with the powerfully drawn prude Arsinoë is

---

[7]In *Men and Masks* (Baltimore, 1963).

one of the most justly admired confrontations in comedy. The play's peculiar interest for us, however, lies not in its effective theatricality, its unflagging verbal adroitness (beautifully rendered, as far as is possible in English, in Wilbur's version), its neatness of construction. It lies in its theme of the conflict between individual and social imperatives, and in the ways in which its action makes us progressively less and less certain of how to pronounce on this theme. It does not teach us "to prefer the uses and maxims of the world to exact probity." It causes us, rather, to examine both the uses and maxims and the exact probity of their critics. It raises fundamental questions with grace and power. Less than any other work of its author's does it answer them or even suggest that they are answerable.

John C. Weston

The Satiric Purpose and Method
of <u>Gulliver's Travels</u>

Swift's main purpose in *Gulliver's Travels* is to make man less proud and complacent by causing him to see himself, even if but for a moment, as despicable, mean, foolish, disgusting; and to see his vaunted institutions as cruel, irrational, and fatuous. The book holds out no hope. It attacks and destroys. It comes close in the incident of the Struldbruggs (III, x) to rejecting the value of life itself. The shocking truth of Swift's destructive and harsh purpose could have been casually introduced into this essay, but we must unflinchingly face up to it, because the book cannot be understood without doing so. Most of the misinterpretations of the book come from kindly and gentle critics who, because they unconsciously recoil from Swift's savage indictment of humanity, invent interpretations to soften the indictment and thus to save the book for their admiration and enjoyment.

The book offers no hope. Even the passages that show obviously wiser societies or individual accommodations to life than our own or than those fanciful ones present in the book, are not offered as models for our emulation, as ways out of the melancholy position the book tells us we are in. These so-called utopian sections, which some critics claim reflect Swift's satiric norm, that is, the basis of positive values from which the attack derives, are not meant to offer a solution to our difficulties. Swift's purpose it to attack and destroy, not to offer encouragement and guidance to a bright future. He employs these sections rhetorically, as foils to foolishness or depravity; by contrast he wants to heighten our awareness of our meanness, not to solace us with a possible out. The cold and ordered primitive rationalism of early Lilliput (I, vi) increases our disgust for present Lilliputian cruelty and foolishness and by extension for our own. The restrained and commonsensical monarchy of the giants (II, vii) makes us aware of our failings and the truth of the Brobdingnagian king's indictment of us as "odious vermin." Lord Munodi's conservative, comfortable estate (III, iv) points up the idiocy of those who are destroying it, the scientists and inventors of Balnibarbi. And the society of horses in the last voyage (IV, viii, ix), similar to the ancient Lilliputian society but more extreme, is clearly a rhetorical device used to contrast with the Yahoos for the purpose of attacking by comparison what is most irrational and beastly in man, not of displaying a pattern for getting rid of our Yahoo qualities.

If the book offers no hope, why did Swift write it and why do people continue to take enjoyment in it? People like to be attacked for general failings more than they realize, at least better than they like being told what to do, especially if the attack is conducted by an artist with cunning, inventiveness, skill, and wit. George Orwell has suggested that we read this book because it speaks tellingly to that part of all of us which "stands aghast at the horror of existence." People read books less to improve themselves than to gain pleasure by satisfying needs, thus accidentally improving themselves in the long run. Swift's motives for writing the book, aside from those psychic ones, such as desire for fame and relief of anger, which are not directly relevant to literary analysis, were, first in importance, to humble mankind in general and, second, to make people think poorly of certain individual people, parties, societies, and institutions in England at the time. The humiliation of mankind can be seen as a necessary first step toward its improvement. Socrates said at his trial, so Plato reports, that a man cannot be wise until he first becomes aware of his ignorance; and just as Socrates' mission in life was largely negative destruction as a preliminary to improvement so we can look on Swift's mission in the same way. There is no reason why we cannot become better even though Swift points out no path; when we choose to get up and resume our journey, after we have recovered from the brutal mauling he has given us, we will choose a few new ways of our own and avoid a few of the now discredited ruts. But we will proceed on our way more slowly, more soberly, perhaps more tolerantly, and with less sanguine expectation about the possibility of all things. If this is unpleasant medicine for youth, particularly for a generation brought up on the cheerful, mindless optimism of Norman Vincent Peale, so be it. It does no good to soften the impact or disguise the purpose of this powerful book.

Swift's second purpose, his attack on particulars in his own society, need not detain us long. The more important contemporary references in these satirical passages are identified in footnotes of good editions of the book. Insofar as we can associate those items and people under attack in Swift's time with counterparts in our own, these satirical passages have added significance and point. For instance, we may find similarities between the High and Low Heels (I, iv; Tory and Whig) and our Republicans and Democrats, between Flimnap's dexterity in rope dancing (I, iii; the prime minister Robert Walpole's political skill) and a Washington senator's skillful fence straddling, between the use of the flying island of Laputa to put down rebellions on the continent of Balnibarbi (III, iii; England's harsh repression of Irish resistance) and Portuguese repression of rebellions in Angola, between the mad and useless zeal of the projectors in the Academy of Lagado (III, v; the English Royal Society) and many experiments in psychology departments of our big universities. We make these applications, of course, without the footnotes identifying the historical particulars. But by knowing the historical fact we can identify precisely Swift's purpose and point, and as a consequence we can select with more exact application analogous objects of dislike in our society. But most of the book is not particular satire and those portions which are can be generally understood and enjoyed to a large extent without consideration of historical context. Consequently, more important than to understand what Swift occasionally attacked in his society is to understand Swift's general methods.

His method, most obviously, is to place a single character into a number of fictional societies whose exaggerated correspondences or contrasts to real European society result in the condemnation or ridicule of the latter. Since he wants to present a great many such correspondences and contrasts, he invents a series of four voyages to widely divergent types of societies and a simple framework to connect them. Since Swift also wants other satiric hits to come from his voyager's reaction to the societies he encounters, he causes his character to tell his own story and not only to relate what he observed but to present his reaction to the adventures he has. This requires that his character must be such as to become involved in the various societies and experience them as a participator. Further, if the adventurer-narrator's reactions are going to be satirized, Swift must make him a typically faulty person so that he is vulnerable and so that we in identifying with him will also receive the thrusts he unwittingly sustains. But since Swift wants us to accept some of the narrator's reactions as true, he cannot make the narrator too much of a fool. The narrator must be a common mixture, pretty much an average man, like us, rather nice and bright but at times—also like us—somewhat ridiculous and blind. Most important, the narrator cannot be a very distinctive and idiosyncratic person, for he must stand for most of us. Such is the general scheme that Swift invented to use as a flexible and serviceable weapon to employ in his campaign of destruction.

Every quality of Gulliver's character can be explained as serviceable to the fiction of the travel book or to the purpose of the satiric attack. He is useful to the fictional device because he is afflicted with wanderlust and thus can go to various societies. He is a linguist so that he can learn new languages readily and soon become immersed in a foreign life. He is handy and inventive so that he can survive and so that he can amuse his captors; curious and interested so that he can present a full account; minute and exact so that it will be believably circumstantial and specific; decently educated so that it will be literate and allusive. He is comic and susceptible to satiric ridicule because he has a tendency to be satisfied with the surface of things, because he has no wit or sense of humor, because he has no general awareness or philosophical detachment, because he is overly proud and deferential to rank, because he is complacent about European institutions and mankind. Swift begins with the requirements of his satiric purpose and invents a person to suit it, in contrast to the modern novelist who begins with a vision of a person with a problem and shapes a series of events which that person would probably experience.

The satiric strategy of the first two voyages must be related because we perceive the obvious reversal of proportions: a six-foot giant among six-inch pigmies, then a six-foot pigmy among seventy-two-foot giants. Since pigmies are more than giants susceptible to attack and ridicule, Swift makes most of his points in the first voyage through the Lilliputians and in the second through Gulliver. We are to see our weaknesses first in the Lilliputians and then in Gulliver shrunk to Lilliputian size: "I reflected what a mortification it must prove to me to appear as inconsiderable in this nation [Brobdingnag] as one single Lilliputian would be among us" (II, i). Swift diminishes man's opinion of himself in these voyages by the most obvious tactic of shrinking him in physical size. And thus we are made to see our posturings and pretensions in ridiculous contrast to our real puniness, helplessness, meanness, and insignificance.

The attack in the first voyage is mainly on man's political behavior as seen in the institutions, conventions, political types, and occurrences of the imperial court of Lilliput. The leaping and crawling for favor, the senseless animosity between the High and the Low Heels and between the Big- and Small- Endians, the persecutions and proscriptions, the cabals and intrigues and backbitings, the self-seeking maneuverings to stay in office—all of these have application to the political life of all countries too apparent to labor. But Swift broadens his attack to strike at less particular failings of ours. We at first tend to admire the Lilliputians for their bravery, ingenuity, and energy. But we soon begin to feel that they are a bit ludicrous. The officer who awakens Gulliver by thrusting a pike half way up his nostril impresses us as senselessly curious, like a small monkey. The few guardsmen who shoot arrows at him without any cause, seemingly to while away the time, remind us of our own malicious and causeless flirtations with danger through boredom. The bravery soon appears more like idiot recklessness, and their enterprises—at first remarkable in creatures so small—soon appear trivial in all their bustling self-importance. The emperor's strutting pride becomes absurd. It is not long after Gulliver's capture of the Blefuscudian fleet that the miniature picture darkens and we see these prideful midgets as conniving, secret, cruel, ungrateful, treacherous, and hypocritical, in short odious and disgusting, and only not monstrous and fearful because they are so minuscule. Swift makes us like giant spectators of our own race, who at first wonderingly admire but increasingly become aware of its failings. His technique is gradual revelation.

Swift's satire is always complex in that he does several things at once. Even though the Lilliputians are the main vehicle of his attack on us, he also pokes fun at the giant Gulliver, along the way, with the purpose, of course, of satirizing corresponding qualities in us. Gulliver is so impressed by rank that he describes the tiny emperor as "majestic" (ii) and informs us with intense satisfaction that the pigmy race has conferred upon him the title of Nardac (v). He repeatedly shows his humorless lack of a sense of proportion, for example when he defends a Lilliputian lady with elaborate arguments and indignant righteousness against the charge of having had adulterous relations with him (vi).

The narrative of the second voyage is more comic than satiric because the object of attack is mainly man's generic rather than historic weaknesses and follies and because there is relatively little reference to his darker crimes and mortal errors. The technique is mainly comic ridicule. The object of the ridicule is our puniness, our physical inadequacy, our dependence, and withal our inappropriate sense of dignity and merit. The vehicle is Gulliver, the helpless pigmy among a race of giants. Gulliver narrates, with a straightfaced lack of awareness that increases the comedy, how he fares among his amused and tolerant titan keepers. The scholars at the king's court discuss at length his physical inadequacy: "They all agreed that I could not be produced according to the regular laws of nature, because I was not framed with a capacity of preserving my life" (iii). And his dependence and frailty are shown by a wealth of humorous adventures. He is attacked by rats, birds, flies, wasps, a toad, a spaniel, a monkey. He is treated like a baby and a doll by his teenage nurse, Glumdalclitch, who dresses him, pets him, keeps him in a doll house, comforts him. His very behavior is childish, as when he becomes bemired by falling into a mole's hole and invents a lie to tell to his nurse for fear of a reprimand or when he is confined to his travelling box for a time as a punishment for leaping into a pile of cow dung (v). He is made ridiculous with adventures which show Swift's comic inventiveness: he is held aloft by a boy (i), wedged into a marrow bone and dropped into a pitcher of cream by a dwarf (iii), dangled on a pin of a lady's bodice (v.) Gulliver is forced into the role of a freak, a court jester, an entertainer, an expert in buffoonery. His posturing and gesticulation, his eagerness to be amusing, pleasing, and understood would be touching and pathetic if they were not so ludicrous. After one such bout of swaggering self-importance, Gulliver must endure the King's condescending and amused expression of curious interest as to whether such a "diminutive insect" as Gulliver were a Whig or a Tory (iii).

Besides this ridicule of man's pompous puniness, there are a number of other supplementary objects of satire. Most important, Swift satirizes governmental institutions of England by the summary account Gulliver gives of his several conversations with the king (vi, vii). This section has three parts, each with its own satiric device of indirection. First, Gulliver describes with lyric hyperbole the government of England; the description is ironic because Gulliver unlike the reader does not know he is overstating his case. Second, the wise and benevolent King cross-examines Gulliver, probing below Gulliver's panegyric to discover the ugly truth and concludes with the famous indictment of man, "the most pernicious race of little odious vermin that nature ever suffered upon the face of the earth"; the technique is ruthless exposure but indirect because Swift hides himself behind the character who utters it. Finally, Gulliver, out of patriotic motives, attempts to impugn the King's testimony by asserting and then proving his stupidity, prejudice, and incompetence; but the attempt is ironic because his very proof—the King's refusing the gift of gunpowder—redounds and proves the contrary of the King but the truth of the assertion when applied to mankind, with the additional charge of bloody and senseless cruelty. This last part of the series shows Swift's genius at squeezing the last drop of ironic potential out of a situation to our surprise and delight.

Just as Swift used Gulliver for supplementary ridicule in Lilliput so in this voyage, with its reversed proportion, he uses the Brobdingnagians for the same purpose. Gulliver's first owner, the farmer, is used to show the cruelty of men caused by their insatiable greediness (ii), and the maids of honor, women's frivolous lasciviousness (v). But most important Gulliver's microscopic eye again and again exposes the physical horror of our bodies and their functions: the monstrous breast of the nurse in the farmhouse (i); the nauseous eating habits of the dainty Queen (iii); the lice, tumors, and wens on the bodies of the beggars who crowd around Gulliver's coach (iv); the foul body odor, hairy moles, and copious urinating of the maids of honor (v). Swift, in the interest of a destructive purpose which offers no quarter, wants to make us loathe our bodies so that we cannot find solace in them after he has destroyed our good opinion of our moral and intellectual parts.

The third voyage departs in obvious ways from the subject and technique of the other three. Gulliver visits a number of societies, not just one. Whereas in the others, after we accept the terms of the fiction, great accumulations of minute detail create a sense of reality, in this voyage, because of the short space devoted to each of the four societies, there is far less such realistic detail. In this voyage alone Swift presents the use of magic performed by magicians (vii, viii). The interaction of the character of Gulliver with the fabulous societies he inhabits is little used in this book as a device of satire, Gulliver often becoming simply Swift's spokesman—as occasionally he does in the other voyages. Finally, Swift attacks historical contemporary particulars in this part more than in any other: current tastes for abstract science and the scientific method applied to moral subjects like politics; theories of music; Sir Isaac Newton and his principles; the Royal Society and technological experimentation; England's repressive laws against Ireland and the Irish resistance to Wood's copper coinage; the two first King Georges and Whig politicians and their activities; projects for a universal language; controversial philosophical theories like those of Descartes; the veracity of modern historians and the progressive view of history; and the Dutch. This list is by no means complete. Annotation to good editions and some separate studies (see the book by Case in the list at the end of this essay) identify contemporary objects of Swift's displeasure on almost every page. Swift seems to have chosen to reserve for this voyage almost all his practical and particular antagonisms which he could not fit into the general satire of the rest of the book, inventing a number of societies to embody them in all their miscellaneous diversity, and hurrying Gulliver through these societies as a reporter and wise commentator.

But parts of this impression require qualification. Quite often Gulliver is foolish and obviously not Swift's spokesman, as when Gulliver admires the idiotic book-writing machine (v) and when he demonstrates his impious and absurd desire for endless life and his penchant for utopian dreaming in his vision of the future with the community of immortal but aging Struldbruggs. Also, the seeming miscellany of satiric objects has a loose kind of thematic unity, at least in the first three of the four societies described in the voyage: Swift in these generally attacks abuses of reason and learning. In Laputa (ii-iii) he attacks excessive abstraction and political science; in Balnibarbi and its capital Lagado (iv-vi) he attacks reason misapplied to useless technology and to the technologizing of humane subjects; and in the Isle of the Sorcerers (vii-ix) he mainly attacks the errors of literary scholars, of philosophers, and of historians.

Gulliver when he leaves Japan for home after his third voyage is the same Gulliver who left England at the beginning of the book. His vision of the world and his qualities of mind have not changed at all. After all his experiences which should have led to his disillusionment, he still naively falls for the unkind joke set up for him by his Luggnaggian hosts (III, x) and demonstrates his unrealistic idealism. He is still a man who has, he says, "been often apt to amuse myself with visions of what I should do if I were a king, a general, or a great lord." Near the very beginning of his experiences in Houyhnhnmland, after all his exposure to man's perfidy, he asserts that even though he found Yahoos detestable, "there were few greater lovers of mankind, at that time," than himself (IV, ii). But both of these descriptions of Gulliver's mental condition are interjected quite by the way and serve an immediate satirical purpose rather than a characterizing one: in the first, to show mankind's weakness for illusory dreams of impossible perfection; and the second, to help create the relation of Yahoos and European man and to add to the loathesomeness of the former. The revelation of Gulliver's character is always secondary and implemental to the specific satiric task at hand. Gulliver's character is a flexible tool of satiric attack and does not exist for its own sake. This often neglected fact can be demonstrated in another way. Even the superficial reader will soon discover that Gulliver's character is inconsistent. A few examples among dozens will suffice: after refusing to bring all Blefuscu under the domination of the Lilliputian Emperor because he "would never be an instrument of bringing a free and brave people into slavery" (I, v), he cites the

Brobdingnagian King's refusal of the knowledge of gunpowder, which he said would have made the King "absolute master of lives, the liberties and the fortunes of his people," as proof of prejudice and narrowness (II, vii); he rejects utopianism in the Academy of Lagado (III, vi, first paragraph) and shortly afterwards demonstrates his propensity to it by his fanciful dream in Luggnagg of a perfect society (III, x); he rejects the theory of the decay of nature formulated in the Brobdingnagian "little old treatise" (II, vii) but in the next voyage we find him speaking of "that continual degeneracy of human nature so justly complained of in all ages" (III, x). But each of these shifts serves changing satiric requirements, and discovering such discrepancies is useless and ought not to make us triumph. Swift did not care about them at all. In this satire, the main character is made to change to suit the passing satiric requirements in contrast to a modern novel where the character is believably consistent and developing. It is a great mistake to impose upon this satire in the form of a travel book the characteristic features of an entirely different kind of book.

But if Gulliver does not develop in the first three parts, he obviously does in the last. He begins his sojourn among the Houyhnhnms (pronounced WHIN-ums) with about the same character and attitudes toward life as he displayed in the previous voyages, but by his gradual identification of himself and European man with the disgusting Yahoos, he becomes completely alienated from mankind to the degree that at the end he is little short of insane. He learns to despise mankind so much that when he is expelled from the society of horses, he at first seeks the isolation of a hermit, then when that is forcibly denied him attempts suicide, and finally when dragged protesting back to Europe lives in a stable and only suffers the presence of his family if his nose is well stuffed with tobacco. We see him at the very end pampering English horses as a kind of tribute to his old Houyhnhnm master and, in the interest of some day finding the society of his countrymen "not insupportable," publicly banishing from his presence all those *tame* Yahoos, that is Englishmen, afflicted with pride.

The satiric strategy of the last voyage appears clear enough. Swift attacks mankind by describing at great length the Yahoos, that most disgusting race of creatures ever invented by the mind of man, and then demonstrating that Europeans taken as a whole have all of the disgusting faults of the Yahoos (vii) and what is more have many additional, unnatural vices created by the misuse of the reason absent in Yahoos. Swift seems to agree with Gulliver's master in believing that man is "a sort of animals to whose share . . . some small pittance of reason had fallen, whereof [they] made no other use than by its assistance to aggravate [their] natural corruptions, and to acquire new ones which Nature had not given [them]" (vii). Further, Swift seems to aggravate this view of man as worse than Yahoos by contrasting to it a superior creature and its society, the clean, reasonable, noble Houyhnhnms and their peaceful and ordered anarchistic society of primitive rationalism. Swift seems to cause his narrator to see the horrible truth about mankind thus presented and as a result to go mad.

Up until about twelve years ago this view of Swift's misanthropic purpose was universally accepted. But since then a radically different, and I think erroneous, interpretation of the last voyage has gained such wide acceptance among American critics of Swift (see, for example, essays by Monk and Winton in *Casebook*, ed. Foster, listed at end of this essay) that it requires analysis. According to this new comic or ironic or Christian view, as it is variously called, Gulliver is always a satiric mask and never reflects Swift's view directly; consequently, Gulliver's vision of man as worse than a Yahoo is not at all the one Swift intends his reader to have. The Houyhnhnms are impious deists because they believe that "reason alone is sufficient to govern a rational creature" (vii) whereas orthodoxy also requires faith in prayer and in revelation. The Houyhnhnms are therefore ridiculed: we see them solemnly pulled on sledges by Yahoos and ludicrously threading needles, milking cows (ix), and cutting oak wattles with a stone-age axe (x). Gulliver is grievously wrong, so runs this argument, not only in accepting the Houyhnhnm society as a perfect pattern for man, but in his consequent rejecting man as a rational animal who only uses his reason to increase his vices. Gulliver should have known, these critics claim, that man is not a rational creature but according to the Christian view a creature *capable* of reason and thus not to be rejected for failing to live up to a nature he never possessed. Further, Gulliver demonstrates more pride in his sinful isolation than the worst of men. And, finally, Swift shows that European man is not worse than a Yahoo by presenting Don Pedro, the Portuguese sea captain, as benevolent, wise and tolerant.

But it seems unlikely that Swift would allow the meaning of the final voyage to hang on a point of Christian doctrine never mentioned in the book and that he would attack man savagely in the first three-quarters of the book only to reduce the severity of the charge and give him the solace of a way out at the end. We have seen that Gulliver is a flexible device and when the satirical occasion demands can reflect Swift's view. Thus the vision Gulliver sees of man can well be the one Swift sees and wants us to see. The Houyhnhnms are not really ridiculed: their occasional amusingly impossible activities are intended to remind us of their horsiness—even a horse, Swift seems to be saying, can be a better creature than man. The Houyhnhnm culture—on the grounds of the facts alone, independent of Gulliver's testimony—is obviously meant to be better than the vision of the European one presented in the book (v-vi). This being a satire, the Houyhnhnm culture is not presented as a solution for man's difficulties, as a practical pattern for his emulation, any more than the other superior societies in the book, but it is presented as a theoretical ideal for the purpose of rhetorical contrast to point up the extent of man's departure from it. And as to the reason for the goodness of Don Pedro, Swift seems to be dramatically demonstrating the impact of Gulliver's vision: even such a good man as Don Pedro has little effect on it. Besides, Swift attacks mankind in general and does not disallow particular exceptions to the indictment.

So without accepting as proper Gulliver's *response* to his discovery of of man's depravity (satire seldom recommends positive responses), we must accept as Swift's the truth of Gulliver's *vision* of man, that is, as essentially like an unspeakably repulsive Yahoo only worse because he misuses his reason. In the last voyage of his *Travels*, Gulliver, like Swift, went up to the abyss and peered tremblingly down. He recoiled in horror. Swift wrote a book to make us do likewise.

Suggestions for Further Reading

Case, Arthur E. *Four Essays on "Gulliver's Travels"* (1945). For learned discussion of contemporary references in the *Travels*.

Foster, Milton P., ed. *A Casebook on Gulliver among the Houyhnhnms* (1961). A collection of important essays centering on the interpretation of the last voyage.

Price, Martin. *Swift's Rhetorical Art* (1953). A brilliant analysis of the structure, symbolism, techniques of Swift's satires.

Rosenheim, Edward. *Swift and the Satirist's Art* (1963). The above essay is indebted to the view of Swift's art presented in this book, more, perhaps, than any other.

Hermann J. Weigand

Goethe's
Faust

The history of Doctor Faustus, the celebrated magician who sold his soul to the devil in return for a stipulated term of personal services, the revelation of occult mysteries and diversified entertainment, was a thrilling horror story with an edifying moral. First published in 1587, it was sold like other "chapbooks" at country fairs year after year, undergoing a variety of versions. Without any pretension to literary form, it catered to the undiscriminating taste of a growing middle class reading public in an age of printing, discovery and religious controversy. It was immediately snapped up by Christopher Marlowe and turned into a play for the Elizabethan stage. Before long the theme supplied one of the lasting attractions with which troupes of travelling puppet players diverted their audiences. In the third quarter of the 18th century, young Goethe made the acquaintance of both the chapbook and the puppet show. Child of an age that experienced the world in terms very different from those of the age of the Reformation, Goethe sensed that the theme of Doctor Faustus harbored unlimited possibilities for expressing the altered and expanded aspirations of the human soul. In the early 1770's he began to toss off the first scenes of a projected *Faust* play. The complete work was given to the world sixty years later. *Faust* has become the legacy of a lifetime. It embodies the most mature distillate of the wisdom of Germany's greatest poet.

The age of the Reformation saw the career of Faust as an object lesson and a warning. To the age of Goethe it was natural, on the other hand, to look upon the doctor-magician as a blurred and distorted prototype of man's ideal aspirations. This is the premise that explains Goethe's abiding attraction to the theme. Faust appealed to Goethe as a symbol of man's emancipation from authority. Regardless of whether Faust's path would eventually lead him to perdition or to salvation, his courage in daring to trespass upon the realm of the forbidden makes him a heroic figure charged with positive value. This is the age of the enlightenment, and obedience is not one of its watchwords. The Judaeo-Christian pattern of thought continues to persist as the general framework of the philosopher's speculations and the poet's imaginings, but for the free spirits of the age it has lost the sanction of any ironclad dogmatism. A century earlier, Milton still founded his great poem of *Paradise Lost* on the theme of "man's first disobedience." This involved the axiomatic acknowledgement of divine arbitrary authority. The 18th century, on the other hand, was set to challenge all arbitrary authority, in the spiritual as well as the secular sphere. Mere power as such could compel submission but not induce reverence. Thus what had been branded as sin could take on the aspect of a higher glory. The criterion of moral value must now be sought in the essential nature of reason. Thus Schiller, lecturing to his students on the fall of man with the Biblical story as his text, is ready to concede that the fall precipitated a catastrophe. But he takes pains to point out that the fall was also an absolutely necessary first step in the higher development of mankind. With the fall, the mind of man embarks on the realization of its limitless potentialities, and autonomy as the premise of human dignity was never more pointedly formulated. Autonomy involves pride, and pride, we remember, was the cardinal sin of the fallen angels. Their rebellion sprang from "superbia." But even Milton could not refrain from endowing Satan, Archfiend and seducer of man, with qualities of strength, steadfastness, and endurance that lent him more than a tinge of the heroic. Faust also exhibits a pride that the Church would have branded as sinful, though it is by no means nihilistic in its aim. All in all, the situation conspires to make us approach the personality of Faust with a highly favorable prejudice.

Let us go afield a moment longer before entering the portals of Goethe's poem.

The spirit of Faust stops at nothing in its quest for self-realization. An exponent of this spirit, Faust, the individual, assumes symbolic significance as the extreme exemplar of the deepest drives of western civilization. Self-realization, properly considered, is a program without inner or outer limits. It is the spirit of total experiment probing the recesses of the individual soul, the relation of the individual to society, the relation of man to his terrestrial environment, the relation of man to the universe. The hazard of self-destruction in the pursuit of this quest is a risk to be faced. In a supreme moment of his career Faust exclaims: "Dasein ist Pflicht, und wär's ein Augenblick"—Total self-realization is imperative, even if it were only for a moment." This is the drive that made Nietzsche speak of himself as the flame that glories in consuming itself. It is the drive that Oswald Spengler, in his *Decline of the West,* saw as the central force that distinguishes the present cultural sphere from those of all former ages. Without question, Goethe projected in the personality of Faust a sublimely noble aspiration of the human spirit. This does not mean, of course, that Goethe glorified Faust uncritically. That he was not blind to his dark and sinister side no thoughtful reader of the play can overlook. Even before his association with the Evil One Faust is labelled a "superman" in a deeply ironical context.

After these preliminaries are we ready to enter the portals of Goethe's dramatic poem? Almost, but not quite. Like a stately edifice, the *Faust* drama has a gate, a portico, and an elevated platform which we must traverse before passing into the interior.

The gate takes the form of a poem in which the poet, at an advanced stage of his life, invokes anew the airy shapes that haunted the young man's imagination and now press in upon him demanding that he endow them with substance. While the poem is cast in a melancholy mood, the portico, entitled "Prelude in the Theater," treats us to a spirited improvisation in which the director, the poet, and the clown discuss the impending production from a variety of angles, mixing business sense, seriousness and fun along with satirical shafts aimed at the expectant public. We pass right on to the elevated platform, the "Prologue in Heaven." Here we pause, to note the scene, the songs of glory, and the ensuing dialogue with the utmost care, for this is our initiation, in the heavenly regions, into the action that will take place on earth. The Prologue at once characterizes the *Faust* poem as epic drama, for as in the epics of the ancients, Homer, Virgil, Statius and the rest, down to Dante, Milton and Klopstock, the terrestrial action has its counterpart in the councils of the supernatural powers.

The Prologue is a brilliant stage scene revealing the heavenly powers in the best anthropomorphic tradition—the Lord, flanked by three archangels, with the lesser hosts in the background. The paeans of praise deserve the student's closest attention in their blending of the old and the new astronomy (the sun and the lesser planets revolving around a motionless earth, and the earth in rotation), their Pythagorean reference to the music of the spheres, their simple mythology (the setting of the sun as journey's end), their literary synaesthesia (the rendering of light in terms of sound), their references to the forces of the tides and meteorology, and finally their climactic allusion to the still, small voice of the prophet Elijah's vision (I Kings 19:12). The setting is solemn and dignified, but the ensuing dialogue is at once shot through with satire and humor.

We see the Lord of the universe engaged on an inspection tour that has brought him to the vicinity of the earth. Closely following the analogy of the Book of Job, Satan-Mephisto, the wag ("der Schalk"), the least distasteful to the Lord of all the spirits of negation, comes to pay his respects to the Lord with guarded mock reverence for the Almighty, with jibes at the "domestics" ("das Gesinde") and a parodistic echo of their strains of praise, and he launches into a tirade of criticism levelled at man, the little god of creation, and at the creator for having endowed him with the ambiguous gift of reason. When the Lord interrupts with a reference to Faust, the most exalted exemplar of the breed, Mephisto gives full rein to his satirical vein, characterizing Faust as mad and proposing a wager to the Lord that, granted permission to ply him with his arts of seduction, he will succeed in deviating this soul to his own ends. The Lord, with great tolerance and unperturbed confidence in the sound kernel of Faust's soul grants the desired permission for the duration of Faust's sojourn on earth, implying that there is more to come. The Lord's generalization about "a good man," with obvious application to Faust, his "servant," shows that his concept of the "good" transcends the standards that associate the term with divinely and socially sanctioned norms of moral behavior. His unfathomable tolerance of the self-assertive spark differentiates him radically from the Biblical Jehovah whose wrath doomed disobedient man to perdition.

Inasmuch as the Lord of the "Prologue" must be taken as the source of infinite goodness, power, foreknowledge and wisdom, there can be no doubt as to the ultimate discomfiture of Mephisto. That Faust will be saved in the end is programmatically certain. It may be puzzling in terms of this view that Goethe entitled his poetic drama a tragedy. Would not the outcome have justified the title of comedy in the sense used by Dante? But the solemnity of the action, in analogy to Greek drama, may have been decisive in warranting this label. This, however, is a question that the reader of the whole drama may be left to ponder.

The first four scenes of the human drama, a unified sequence spanning one night and two days, show how the impatient, frustrated idealist is induced to enter into an association with the "spirit of negation," that is destined to cast its shadow over the rest of his earthly life. The first scene develops Faust's situation and his personality in a dazzling variety of facets. It unfolds chiefly by way of a very extended dramatic monologue, interrupted by dialogue passages that allow no monotony to develop—the apparition of the Earth Spirit, the dialogue with his assistant Wagner, and the pealing of the bells and the chorus of Easter voices at the climactic moment. On stage the dramatic monologue usually suffers drastic cuts. Its extreme length and subtlety overtax the capacities of both the average theater audience and all but the greatest actors. But for the reader who yields to its spell every line carries its own emotional charge born of Faust's situation and the visible and tangible associations that stream down from the clutter of the high, musty study. With two exceptions: (1) the opening paragraph is a deliberately archaic piece of exposition, evoking the age of the Reformation and the verse form of its most popular poet, Hans Sachs, by its prosy diction and the mechanical rhythm of its four-beat couplets. (2) Later on we come across one more passage where Faust, in the trough of the emotions that tossed him, reflects in general terms on the theme of anxiety as the most corroding affliction of the human race. This does not seem to relate to his immediate state of mind, but we are forewarned of what is coming when Anxiety, in the guise of a spectral sister, confronts Faust on the last night of his life as his most sinister assailant. But apart from these two passages all the rest of Faust's monologue has the compelling power of spontaneous improvisation. This effect is achieved by a most felicitous blending of form with content that has been the despair of all translators. The lyrical pitch of the diction, vocabulary, and sentence structure varies from mood to mood. The lines are not of a set length but swell from four to five and six-beat waves to return at will to lesser undulations. The rhyme scheme operates with equal freedom, now joining lines in couplets, now looping two pairs, now circling an inner by an outer pair, now binding triple lines or triple pairs together, employing a free alternation of one-syllable rhymes with those of two. These few remarks on form must suffice. They apply in large measure to the whole of Part One of the drama. In Part Two the problems of form are far too complex even to be touched upon here.

The middle-aged scholar, who recapitulates his career in the opening lines, is a man wearied and exhausted to the breaking point. He has mastered all the substance and all the techniques of the total medieval university curriculum. The intangible abstractions of logic, metaphysic and theology have left him disillusioned. He is equally fed up with the procedures and yields of the practical professions, law and medicine. The satirical colloquium to which Mephisto treats the eager freshman in a later scene merely transposes all of Faust's feelings on these matters into a humorous key. Faust is in deadly earnest. Words have assumed a hollow ring. Words are a device to conceal fundamental ignorance. Words provide no tool for a breakthrough from the world of appearance to the world of essence. In scene after scene Faust harps on this central fact. This is his frustration. He conceives of the world in terms of a pantheistic reinterpretation of Scripture. Creation (God, Nature) is a divine, eternally emerging process. He affirms it with all his soul. Is he not cast in the creator's own image, part of his essence? Is it not his birthright, then, to participate consciously in the sublime dynamic process? Is he not higher than the angels—mere ministrants they? This is the repeated starting point of his broodings after his rejection by the Earth Spirit. Meanwhile, in the opening passage, he gives only a passing glance to the thought that riches and honors, attending the pursuit of worldly success, have passed him by. In his frustration he has taken recourse to magic as a possible shortcut to the spiritual revelation he longs for with every fibre of his being. Impatience dictates this bold and forbidden course, a fever pitch of frenzied affirmation. At this stage the spirit of negation is utterly foreign to him. Faust is a rebel only as regards the barriers of sense that keep him from communing directly with the divine spirit. Philosophically speaking, he storms against being hemmed in by space, time and causality. Rationally considered, Faust's behavior is quixotic, yet, even while overreaching himself, Faust tempers his folly with some discretion. Contemplating the magic symbols drawn by the renowned master's own hand, he turns from the figure suggesting the workings of the universal spirit as too vast for his comprehension. He hails the Earth Spirit, the lesser deity that dwells in the earth like the soul of man in the body, as the more fitting object for his empathy. His ardor is rewarded by a manifestation. Recoiling in terror from the insupportable light, he hears himself gently reassured and chided with mild irony. Then, with a superhuman burst of courage Faust rises to the challenge of the unique moment to proffer himself to the apparition's embrace, only to find himself put in his place by a terse, definitive rejection. But before Faust has time to come to terms with his humiliation his assistant's knock at the doors dispels the mood.

Faust dislikes and despises Wagner's fawning airs and his careerist aspirations. That he reveals no trace of these personal feelings either in the midnight discourse or on the next day's afternoon walk, bears testimony to his generosity and humanity. Faust is no cynic. He does not vent his pessimism in taunts and sarcasms levelled at his fellowman. He strives to educate by example and precept. Throughout the dialogue, the issue is sharply drawn between sincerity and scheming, simplicity and pretension, dedication and self-seeking, between earnest self-examination and easy complacency.

After Wagner has left, Faust's mind returns to the vision, to assess its impact. His ego has suffered an annihilating deflation. His buoyant feeling of participating in the creative pulse, on a par with the gods, has been cruelly exposed as brash presumption. Sharp despair yields to the softer hurt of selfpity, inducing a mood of quieter, almost impersonal meditation on the theme of anxiety. But his brooding soon reactivates the sting of his having been called a worm. He indulges in self-laceration as he develops the parallel between the worm grovelling in the dust and his own life. Now the paraphernalia of his cluttered study meet his eye to mock his existence. Item after item—the stacked books and rolls, the grinning skull, the obsolete and useless machinery on which his misguided father pinned his faith—stare him in the face as so much dust. But when he spies the vial that harbors the potent poison that he has decocted, his mind veers to a different tack. In a twinkling he has rebounded from his despair to salute suicide as the most thrilling of all adventures. His imagination straightway paints the exploit in the most glowing poetic colors. But the Easter bells and chorus stay his hand. Though they cannot rekindle his faith in the miracle of the resurrection, memories of the fervent piety of his childhood crowd in upon him. His mood is softened, and the momentum for taking the irretrievable step is lost.

The scene of the Easter walk reinforces some important aspects of Faust's personality that were only lightly touched on in the initial scene. He mingles with the simple folk and receives the tribute of their love and respect with unaffected modesty. Their praise of his dedication and success during the plague he counters with the admonition to give credit where it is due, to the helper above. To infect them with irreverent skepticism is the last thing he desires. But most important, the allusion to the plague has touched in Faust's soul a complex of confused and bitter grief. He confesses the young man's importunate piety, the ascetic zeal with which he tried to bend the will of heaven to his desire. Evidently Faust is of the stuff that great saints are made of. Then he speaks with guarded criticism of his father as having been deluded into the blind alley of alchemy: Dispensing his nefarious concoctions in good faith, he and his colleagues perpetrated wholesale murder surpassing the ravages of the plague. The honest intent may exonerate his father, but it cannot efface a deep sense of guilt on Faust's own part. And the extreme emotional outburst about "the impudent murderers" helps us to see two enigmatical lines of Scene One in perspective. The lines, "what you have acquired from your forefathers, assimilate it in order to possess it," had seemed to interrupt the expression of a desire to be rid of all that had been handed down to him, with a puzzling non sequitur. Those lines make sense as the quoting by Faust of a familiar adage. But in his mouth the adage has the ring of bitter irony as the repudiation of his traditional heritage.—The end of the scene introduces the poodle in the guise of which Mephisto is to make his debut.

Returned to the study that on the previous night had twice seen the superman poised on the brink of annihilation, Faust is about to make the acquaintance of his satanic companion. Scene Three, a theatrical showpiece, unfolds in three stages—the problem of scriptural translation, the exorcism, and Faust's dialogue with the travelling scholar. This scene shows Faust at his best. Having bathed in the fresh air of the woodland hills, he is cleansed and tranquil, at peace with himself and aglow with the love of God and his fellowmen. In this mood he yields to the impulse to translate a New Testament passage from the Greek. No believer in the dogma of the Church, but in search of revelation everywhere, he finds its purest spring in the New Testament. Characteristically, he turns to the opening chapter of the Gospel according to Saint John which, in contrast to the three "synoptic" gospels, exhibits a blend of Hellenistic mysticism with the Jewish ideas of the promised Messiah. The very first verse stymies Faust's efforts: "In the beginning was the word." The word, the "logos," a term of the most elusive connotations, is not fit to be rendered by the prosy German equivalent, "das Wort," an empty husk against which he had railed bitterly. He casts about for a term that might more adequately spread its aura over the page. In this effort he appears as the double of Martin Luther who set his aim to render the spirit of the gospel rather than the letter. Faust's concentration is disturbed by the antics of the restless poodle.

When repeated attempts to quiet the animal fail, Faust senses that there is something wrong, and the transformation of the dog into a monster presently confirms his suspicion. He proceeds to smoke out the spirit with a systematic series of exorcisms.

When they all fail to work, Faust changes his diagnosis: Since this is not a neutral elementary spirit, it must be a demon out of hell. This calls for more potent incantations. Working himself up to a fever pitch of excitement, Faust cudgels the recalcitrant monster with spells that circumscribe the mystery of the eternal Only-Begotten and his passion. These, and the threat of the irresistible Trinitarian thunderbolt, take effect: In place of the shapeless monster there stands the harmless figure of a travelling scholar.

Do we find this confusing? This man, who had dismissed hell as figment of morbid fantasy, this man, who had expressed his disbelief in the glad Easter tidings—this same Faust has now worked a miracle with magic spells that derive their potency from the assumption of the Christian mysteries as valid realities! This is paradoxical. We note this only in passing; for Faust is not the man to solve the riddle of the Beyond. His mind dwells in a kind of Limbo swarming with mutually contradictory images and concepts. For the moment he is completely occupied with his visitor.

What strikes us throughout the ensuing dialogue is Faust's composure, his superior control in the presence of the infernal emissary. To the spirit of negation he opposes his deep, positive reverence for the eternal mysteries of Nature's creative works. The professor even lectures the devil on the folly of his impotent negativism and admonishes him to mend his ways.

To his surprise Faust discovers that the devil has allowed himself to be caught in a trap. The handling of this all but incredible situation (against the background of the folk image of the devil as an essentially stupid fellow, easily tricked) shows a most ingenious interplay of chance and design: The poodle, evidently bent on no more than a bit of preliminary reconnoitering, has been forced to show his hand prematurely. Faust's self-confidence is heightened by the discovery that he has the visitor in his power. When his prodding questions bring out the fact that demons who invade the human realm are governed by strict rules of behavior, it is Faust who takes the initiative in broaching the idea of a pact, and it is Mephisto, caught off guard, who has to resort to a delaying action. Eventually Mephisto, apparently resigned to the situation, puts his captor to sleep by a ruse and makes his escape. Faust awakens in a state of redoubled frustration.

The next scene brings the great showdown, Faust's wager and pact with Mephisto. The time, the morning after; and Faust in a morning-after mood, a colossal hangover after the series of emotional shock waves that had battered him continuously for two nights and a day and have left him at a dead center of total exhaustion.

On this morning the tables are turned. The initiative has passed to Mephisto. Even before the smart cavalier enters the study, Faust's irritability is established as he is made to repeat the invitation to enter three times. He is in a devastated mood. There is no fight left in him. He is querulous, petulant, whining. His emotional tone is slack, unstrung. His harping on the theme of renunciation, his complaints about the staleness of his days and the terrors that haunt his nights mark him as the victim of an anxiety neurosis in the making. His attempts to wax lyrical in his laments appear forced, reminding us of the distorted tones of a wornout record. Each of Mephisto's amused taunts and jibes makes him wince. Before long he flies into an uncontrollable rage that finds expression in a tirade of curses so all-inclusive as to leave no value intact. With these curses Faust, so positive heretofore in his reverent affirmation of the creative process as divine, has yielded to the spirit of negation. His curses are an echo of the tempter's nihilism. They mark a turning point. Henceforth the infection of radical evil festers in Faust's blood.

Naturally, this violent swing of the pendulum provides for its own correction. In the remainder of this inexhaustibly rich scene Faust soon regains his balance. When Mephisto approaches him with a concrete proposal for their permanent association, with the forfeiture of Faust's soul in the Beyond as the price, Faust counters with a wager that shows him an alert and shrewd bargainer. The substance of the wager on which he conditions the pact is that Mephisto will never succeed in extinguishing the restless urge that makes Faust forever reach beyond the illusory satisfaction of the moment; that Mephisto will never succeed in lulling him into a sense of ease and contentment. "If you ever hear me say to the passing moment: Do linger, you are so beautiful!, then you may clasp me in fetters, then I will glady perish. Then may the funeral bell toll, then your term of service is done. Let the clock stop, the hour hand fall. Let my time be over!"

Two lines, that formulate the condition, are followed by seven swift, short sentences that draw the conclusion. The four times repeated "then" reverberates like the measured strokes of a gong. Mephisto underlines the significance of the pronouncement with the reminder to Faust: "Mark your words well. *We* shall not forget!" There is superb irony in the fact that, when Faust has breathed his last, Mephisto misquotes a crucial word and has to stand being corrected by his minions, who have remembered the exact wording.

After Faust has reluctantly gone through with the "farce" of signing the contract with a drop of his blood, he expatiates in a series of swiftly changing moods on the meaning of the momentous step he has taken. Dejection and elation spell each other off. The immediate vista is a mad, pointless whirl of dissipation. A moment later his energies rebound with the resolve, now that all prospects of an intellectual breakthrough have gone sour, to encompass in his individual person the totality of *experience* open to mankind, the whole gamut of the emotional life of the race, all its joys and pains, with ultimate annihilation as the end. Mephisto finds amusement in pointing out to him that he still persists in his aim to unite incompatibles, and once more Faust wallows in the trough of dejection. The impasse is broken by Mephisto's arrangements for the two of them to set out at once on a life of adventure in the world, leaving the musty study behind. As Faust goes to gather up some necessaries for the trip in the magic cloak, Mephisto regales the eager freshman with his satirical wisdom.

Now follow the scenes of Auerbach's Cellar in Leipzig that night, and the visit next day to the witch's kitchen to accomplish Faust's physical rejuvenation. They need not detain us long. The roisterous atmosphere of the wine cellar, where Mephisto befuddles the drunken students with his magic tricks, may bring to mind the grosser aspects of Shakespeare's Falstaff scenes. It is entertaining in its triple perspective of the students' coarse antics, Mephisto's delight in leading them by the nose, and Faust's bored impassivity throughout.

In the witch's kitchen the situation is similar: Mephisto has a wonderful time enjoying first the grave nonsense of the animals that watch the boiling cauldron in the absence of their mistress, then in relishing the hysterical fury of the witch making her way down the chimney, and her consternation in recognizing the intruder as her master. Faust shows not the slightest interest in all the nonsense and obscenity. Only one thing catches Faust's attention, a magic mirror. It dazzles him with the elusive shifting image of the most beautiful woman the world has ever seen, Helen of Troy. He reluctantly leaves it to submit to the ritual hocuspocus of the potion that is to rekindle in his veins the sexual fire of adolescence.

The stage is now set for the Gretchen tragedy, the absorbing theme of the last third of Part One. In the overall drama of *Faust* the Gretchen action is only an episode, but it is developed with a spontaneity, a richness of delineation as regards the personality of Gretchen and her

milieu, a depth of feeling, and a poignancy of tragic ruin that no sensitive reader is proof against. Thanks to Mephisto, who engineers the
seduction, many of the scenes sparkle with infinite vivacity and humor.
As a matter of fact, Mephisto's initiative and resourcefulness make him
more and more the star performer, eclipsing the hero, whose unresolved
tensions, unfolding in new situations but without major surprises, reduce
him, dramatically speaking, to a more passive role. (This tendency, in
fact, prevails throughout the greater portion of Part Two. Only at relatively brief intervals of special intensity does Faust come to the fore
and take the lead. And it is only in the final act that Faust fully regains
the undisputed summit of the dramatic protagonist.)

The Gretchen action develops swiftly. In the space of a few days
Faust, fluctuating between carnal desire and adoration, has won the
love and unquestioning trust of the artless girl. From now on we lose
track of the passage of time. When the lovers meet again, Faust is put
on the defensive by Gretchen's insistent questions about his religious
beliefs, showing her concern for his salvation, and by her undisguised
aversion for his companion. Gretchen's plain speaking is one of her most
endearing qualities. In the matter-of-factness of her approach she is
prosy and unimaginative, quite unlike the sentimental "romantic" hero-
ines commonly met with in fiction. Faust is prompted to express his
undogmatic pantheistic faith in exquisitely lyrical language, and Gretchen
is half reassured. He is less successful in his embarrassed defense of
Mephisto. The meeting ends with Gretchen's agreeing to doctor her
mother's bedtime drink.

When the curtain rises again, events have taken their inevitable
course. At the well Gretchen becomes reflectively aware of the harsh
condemnation her own social class metes out to any girl caught straying
from the straight and narrow path, and the double standard that prevails
regarding the man's part in the affair. Before the icon of the Virgin
she bares her prostrated soul. The next thing, her brother, stung by
the wagging of loose tongues, ambushes the strangers serenading the
sister whose beauty and virtue he had idolized. He is killed, and his
dying words strike the poor girl's heart with fiendish cruelty. The killers
have fled, the idyl is over. From the scene in the Cathedral we learn
that her plight has infinitely worsened since her brother's death. Not
only that the first stirrings of pregnancy fill her with forebodings, she
bears a crushing burden of guilt on her mother's account, who faces
a long period of purgatory, having died in her sleep (like Hamlet's
father) without the ministrations of the Church. There can be no doubt

about the circumstances: A precautionary overdose of the sleeping potion must have proved fatal to her mother—this on the very night of Valentin's murder. Had it occurred earlier, the fact would have had to be brought out in the play, and Gretchen's overwrought conscience would have made a later tryst unthinkable. Goethe did wisely in sacrificing the chronological sequence to the continuity of mood of the Gretchen action. The nine months of anguish that undermine her sanity are shrouded in obscurity. We see her for the last time in chains in a prison cell. Her mind is unhinged. She has done away with her baby. The executioner's sword awaits her at the dawn of day.

After the Cathedral scene, a violent shift of mood and locale takes us to the witches' rendezvous on the Brocken with Faust and Mephisto as spectators and participants in the tumultuous annual convocation. This is a virtuoso performance of poetic genius. The language is strained to evoke a bewildering medley of eerie sound, light and movement in the surge of the demonic elemental forces. Faust and Mephisto, their way lighted by a will-o'-the-wisp, are caught in the tugging updraft and the crush of the flying hosts and detached individuals all straining to reach the summit for the celebration of the black mass. The modern theater, and particularly the film, finds a challenge in translating this feast of the imagination into a spectacle for the senses, but in accomplishing this it inevitably reduces the suggestive magic of the poetic word to a mere shadow.

In the carnival of obscene animal energy we never get to see the climactic performance on the summit, presided over by "Herr Urian." Mephisto's caprice shunts Faust away from the upward surging throng into the quieter byways of a camping area. At this sideshow we meet a group of motley characters, oldsters, has-beens, who got bogged down in their flight because the vital spark failed them. These impotents expatiate nostalgically on the good old days when they called the tune, and Mephisto gleefully apes them. From general satire, directed against types, the focus disconcertingly shifts to personal satire: Goethe lampoons a literary enemy, Friedrich Nicolai, the old warhorse of the German enlightenment. The many topical allusions were relished by contemporaries in the know but are pointless without a detailed commentary today.

And what of Faust? He had felt the stiff climb among the knobby crags as a zestful challenge. To his inner eye the mountainside had unveiled itself as a living matrix of treasure in the making. Eagerly looking forward to the main spectacle, he had been drawn off to a sideshow. He had danced with a young witch but lost appetite when a red mouse slipped out of her mouth. Then he had spied the wraith of a girl, and Mephisto's warning to avert his eyes from the "Gorgon" had only served to rivet his gaze on the wide-open dead eyes and the gliding gait of the apparition. More and more it had taken on the semblance of Gretchen, and a red line, no wider than the back of a knife, circling her throat, had loomed as a portent of her fate. There we leave Faust, to turn to the anticlimactic conclusion of the *Walpurgisnacht* scene, with some final jibes against halfbaked plays and amateurish performances.

Very abruptly the end of the Gretchen tragedy is now enacted. The discontinuity is extreme, as regards both the time and the form. The gap of nine months in Faust's life since his flight after Valentin's murder is a blank. Somehow Mephisto's magic must have succeeded in blocking Faust's memories of Gretchen and in stifling the voice of his conscience regarding her fate until the last night of her life. Then, learning what has happened to her and what awaits her, Faust breaks into violent recriminations against the satanic seducer, only to have his own guilt spelled out to him with pitiless matter-of-factness. The medium of this scene is prose—the rhetorical, exclamatory and at the same time long-winded prose of the "Storm and Stress" movement of the 1770's. Goethe left the scene "Bleak Day. Field." intact as a relic of his earliest work on the subject of *Faust*. The reference in the scene to the dog who amused himself during Faust's nightly strolls with playing practical jokes on harmless wanderers must belong to a phase of the composition before Goethe had hit upon the happy expedient of the exorcism scene as the means of introducing Mephisto to Faust.

Part One of *Faust* ends with the scene of the attempted rescue, an overwhelming finale. The personality of the wretched girl in the prison cell is completely shattered, but every fractured piece suggests the one-time perfection now irretrievably destroyed. In the wandering of her unhinged mind she bears a striking resemblance to Shakespeare's Ophelia, but with this difference: Ophelia, innocent victim of a cruel fate, evokes a mood of pure pathos, while Gretchen, involved despite herself in fearful guilt, is a truly tragic victim. Physical dread and a desire to atone rend her bosom. Instinctively she senses the sinister aura of her onetime lover and shrinks from his touch. In a final flash of lucidity she throws herself upon the merciful judgment of God, and a voice from the Beyond proclaims her salvation.

The Gretchen episode was the first stage of Faust's career in the world of man outside the confining walls of the study. For Faust, the pure love of Gretchen will be forever imbedded in his memory as the deepest spiritual blessing vouchsafed to him by a kindly Providence, and as the ineradicable reminder of his darkest hour. When he finally departs from the earthly stage the intercession of Gretchen will weight the scales in the achievement of his redemption.

————————

Part Two strikes the reader rather as a new beginning than the continuation of the *Faust* drama. The method, the perspective, the focus, the form in all its aspects, are radically new. Psychological drama, though not abandoned, is subordinated to symbolical drama. The Faust of Part Two is more a representative of mankind in its strivings and errings than an individual. The action is divided into five acts of such length as to preclude presentation on the stage in a single evening. The development is epic rather than dramatic. Instead of a forward movement focussed upon the outcome of Faust's association with the forces of Evil, the scenes are crowded with pageantry and spectacles in many of which Faust's presence is unobserved or he is off stage altogether. The versification is subtle and experimental in the extreme. The poetic style and vocabulary are full of innovations that it took German poetry generations to assimilate. The time of Part Two ranges over half a century. Yet of this total span only a minimal portion is accounted for by the action presented. In the present sketch the most fleeting glance at all but the final act must suffice. Only then, on the final day of Faust's life, does the dramatic action resume its forward thrust.

The first scene of Act One shows us Faust asleep at the approach of sunrise in a smiling spring landscape. Ariel and his elfin host guard Faust's slumber. Their song helps to banish the images of horror and anguish from his memory. After this symbolical opening Faust awakens. His reaction to the sunrise translates itself, in his reflective consciousness, into a grandiose symbol of the new approach to life on which he sets his course. The barren quest of the absolute is renounced in favor of the more profitable pursuit of exploring the infinite variety of the world of phenomena. Insofar as this insight is Faust's, it is one of those momentary flashes of heightened realization that illuminate the landscape of the mind for a fleeting moment, only to be pushed into the background by the preoccupations of daily life. (Strangely enough, there are moments in Part Two when even the voice of Mephisto loses its negativism and becomes indistinguishable from that of Goethe, as in the definitely goodnatured send-off given the Baccalaureus, who storms ahead on the very quest of the absolute renounced by Faust and with the imagery of light and darkness employed in reverse.) This is only to point out that the champions of strict consistency are hard put to it in their interpretation of *Faust Two*.

The scene now changes to the Imperial Court. There is a pleasure-loving young emperor, whose realm is fast drifting into a state of chaos. Mephisto's advice solves the most pressing problem of the moment—that of the exchequer. On the flimsiest security, indeed a phantom security, he gets the treasury to issue an unlimited supply of paper money. Henceforth nothing is allowed to interfere with the carnival mood. His appetite whetted by the quality of the entertainment, the emperor asks Faust to conjure up Paris and Helen from the underworld as a spectacle for his court, and Faust, trusting in his companion's infinite resourcefulness, promises that it shall be done.

Dramatically speaking, the lavish pageantry of the night before is an elaborate device to trigger the main business of Acts One to Three. This is nothing less than to reenact one of the major episodes of the 16th century *Faust Book* and achieve so staggeringly impossible a wish-dream as the physical union of Faust with the all-time paragon of beauty, the fabulous Helen of Troy. Goethe seized upon this theme to symbolize the passionate dedication to the quest of beauty as one of the supreme drives of mankind. At the midpoint of his earthly career, Faust, dynamo of insatiable energy, is kindled with the passion to achieve in the here and now of the world of sense a union with the phantom of absolute beauty that resides in the shadowy world of Hades or in the realm of Platonic ideas. By a singular grace of the Powers his dream is vouchsafed fulfilment for one brief moment. The realization of the absolute takes tangible shape in the offspring of their union, the radiant boy Euphorion. He is the incarnation of the poetic spirit. But, sired by absolutes, he, in his turn, is bent on the impossible. Bounding aloft from the cliff to try his wings, he plunges to his death, another Icarus, and Helen slips from Faust's embrace to rejoin her child in the underworld.

Three long acts develop the story. In Act One, Faust, coached by Mephisto in a scene of wondrous awe, penetrates into the realm of the "Mothers" and brings back the famous couple. As they are subjected to admiration and criticism by the court, uncontrollable jealously and passion for her possession make Faust touch the phantom Helen. He is knocked unconscious by an explosion and carried off by Mephisto to be deposited in his old study.

In Act Two there is first a superbly humorous interlude: Disguised in Faust's old mantle, Mephisto has a spirited colloquy with the erstwhile freshman, now a sophisticated philosopher sporting a bachelor's degree. This scene reactivates our time sense. It places the action of Acts One and Two, along with the "timeless" moment of Act Three, at a point several years beyond the close of Part One. Together with Act Four, all the Second Part except for the last act may be supposed to transpire in a single season.

We next follow Mephisto into an adjoining laboratory where Wagner, Faust's former assistant, now a professor with an enormous reputation, has been laboring for months on end to produce an artificial man, a homunculus, by the art of alchemy. Thanks to Mephisto's presence the miracle comes off: a sprightly mannikin in a test tube slips from Wagner's grasp to hover, weightless, in the atmosphere and greet daddy Wagner and cousin Mephisto with merry chatter. Hearing of Faust's plight, the little creature slips through the doorway to gaze on the unconscious form, and his supernatural intuition spells out the sleeper's vision—the divine swan embracing Leda to sire Helen. He knows that if Faust were to awaken in the study the shock would kill him. But the resourcefulness of our mannikin is equal to the emergency. It so happens, he says, that this very night is the classical counterpart of the witches' sabbath. All the creatures of classical myth are now gathering for their annual rendezvous in northeastern Greece. Let Mephisto carry Faust on his magic cloak, and he himself will lead the way. Straightway they are off, leaving Wagner to attend to his laboratory. By this ingenious device Faust is transported to Greece. As soon as he sets foot on the sacred soil he awakens. His first words are: Where is she? He is possessed of only one thought, to find her. The three now strike out on separate paths to explore the inexhaustible world of wonders. Following each of them in turn, the reader is put through a most thoroughgoing refresher course in classical mythology. As for Faust, he learns from the sphinxes that the celebrated centaur Chiron is abroad and most likely to be of help in locating Helen. Luckily Faust encounters Chiron and, astride on the restlessly trotting monster's back, he ventures to report his quest. The genial centaur, infinitely amused at this mortal man's harebrained whim, nevertheless takes him to the priestess Manto, who guards the approach to the underworld at the foot of Mount Olympus. She hears Faust's plea sympathetically and promises to lead him down to the great goddess Persephone, who alone can grant it.

In this way it comes about that in Act Three Helen has actually been released from the underworld to live again for a timeless moment. Faust's and Helen's exchange of greetings turns into a duet of mutual homage. Helen's union with Faust symbolizes a fusion of the genius of the Germanic north with that of Greek antiquity. The whole act—a phantasmagoria Goethe called it—is a *tour de force* of the poetic imagination without a parallel in Goethe's work. As anticipated above, the mirage of perfection is shattered by the death of their offspring, Euphorion.

If Acts One to Three were focussed upon the experience of beauty—the aesthetic sphere—as a momentous enrichment of Faust's (and mankind's) expanding development, Act Four introduces a new theme to engage man's restless imagination. It is the challenge of the physical environment, the will to understand and control the forces of nature. It is man's will to power in the face of the inert or hostile elements. Borne aloft by the garments Helen has left behind, soaring with the clouds over mountain and sea, Faust's gaze is arrested by the spectacle of the tides, their ceaseless ebb and flow. It impresses him as a symbol of enormous power wasting itself in futile repetition. There dawns upon him the idea of a task, a project: to curb the sea, to reclaim a vast expanse of shore line by a network of dikes. This is a challenge to appeal to his own indomitable energies that have been idly wasting themselves. This is a job for Mephisto and his minions to execute.

Most of Act Four is taken up with the machinery for acquiring the rights to the shoreline as a sovereign fief from the Emperor whom Faust had served. This cannot concern us here. But the Faust we meet again in Act Five has devoted, we must suppose, half a lifetime to this constantly expanding project. Faust has now become a great lord. His eye roams over a limitless expanse of newly created land, flourishing with human habitations, gardens, and woodland. He has built a palace with a high observation tower, and his fleets gather in a distant harbor from which a canal extends to the palace. To judge by Faust's and Mephisto's words, Faust's realm encompasses the world. We cannot suppress an uneasy feeling that this is more than a slip of rhetorical exaggeration: Has Mephisto's new obsequiousness of manner deluded Faust into a state of megalomania? But there is one feature to mar Faust's pride of absolute rule: On a high dune a very ancient couple with rights antedating his have refused his offer to sell on advantageous terms. Day after day the tinkle of their chapel bell exasperates him. Does it awaken uneasy echoes of the church bells that made him set down the poisoned chalice on that first Easter morning? Be that as it may, the tiny knoll sets limits to his craving for absolute sway. The order for their dispossession results in unforeseen circumstances: The old couple die of fright as the door is battered down. Faust is seized with remorse. Once again his impatience has got the better of him. Was not impatience his cardinal sin? On the day of the wager and pact, when in his bitterness he had uttered his all-encompassing curse, had he not saved up the curse on Patience as the final line of his tirade? But he persuades himself to take the calamity lightly. Of course, Faust had not intended the consequences of his rash command, but he might have anticipated them if his sense of frustration had not blinded him, and in any case he had committed a deliberate violation of human rights. Such unscrupulousness as to means is typical of persons who are accustomed to the exercise of great power. The bloody deed leaves a stain on Faust's great achievement. To dismiss it as a trifle in view of the immense benefits accruing to mankind from Faust's titanic project, would be idle because these benefits were incidental to the exercise of his energy. Faust was no philanthropist. He envisioned the task as a great means to express himself. There was no altruistic motive, for better or worse, to color the project of that great egoist. But, first appearances to the contrary, Faust did not dismiss his responsibility lightly. His brief soliloquy, dwelling on his inveterate impetuosity, shows that his conscience is deeply troubled. And now as he is about to be assailed from another quarter, we see him give evidence of an ethical resilience that more than reconciles us to his faults. "Geboten schnell, zu schnell getan." ("Ordered quickly, done too quickly.") Faust's repentance is sincere, but he does not waste his energies in morbid brooding over an act that cannot be undone.

Now comes the visitation of the four weird sisters, spectral apparitions that personify Want, Distress, Debt or Guilt ("Schuld" stands for both), and Anxiety. The first three find their entry to the palace barred. They have no power to molest a rich man. Not even *Schuld* in the sense of guilt; for objective wrongdoing must have an acute sense of wrongdoing as its subjective counterpart, to be troublesome. Anxiety, however, can slip through the keyhole, where other potential disturbances of tranquillity are barred. As the three depart, they hail the approach of Brother Death in the background. Frail as Faust is, at the outermost edge of the human life span, his mind, forever active and restless, finds the thought of death repugnant. "I have not yet fought my way to freedom," he protests. Now (like the Sorcerer's Apprentice) he finds himself irremediably entangled in a web of apparitions and portents, a prey to forces he cannot control. At this moment his soliloquy becomes a dialogue with the spectral sister of whose entry he has become aware. He tries to dismiss her with an imperious command, but she refuses to budge.

He reacts violently, but, about to have recourse to the magic powers with which he has saddled himself, he checks himself with the soft spoken admonition: "Take care, do not speak a magic word."

This line, spoken under his breath, is the significant turning point in Faust's psychological drama. Though ever so late, with death at his door, for once he has not yielded to that impatience which was the fatal flaw of his personality. He has taken a first step to reverse the pattern of his responses to life. This is decisive. This is a metaphysical act in terms of Schiller's dictum: "The first step upward, ideally considered, is equivalent to traversing the whole road to the goal."

Now the weird sister announces her identity, and in three long passages of a whining, monotonous, staccato rhythm that suggests the wheedling persistence of a mosquito buzzing about the ear, she assaults the fortress of his will, hoping to reduce him to a bundle of nerves, prey to an anxiety neu.osis. Three times he stands up to her assault maintaining the integrity of his personality in passages that rank among the finest in the play. His control never slips. He gives a thumbnail sketch of the course of his life, pronouncing an agnostic credo as to the beyond, lasting out against the crooning tormentor, writhing under the pain of her relentless hypnotizing drone, but the integrity of his will is proof against her assaults. Let us not imagine for a moment that this is simply a rhetorical confrontation. The danger to Faust is very real. We turn back to the very first night of the *Faust* drama, where Faust, during one of his fluctuations between ecstasy and despair over his having been vouchsafed the vision of the Earth Spirit, lapsed into reflections about the power of "Sorge", Anxiety, to torment man with apprehensions of ills that never come to pass. That, to be sure, was the one passage among all those memorable first night monologues, which seemed least prompted by his personal desperate situation, approaching, rather, in the ring of its tone a mood of general reflection on human life. But two days later, at the time of Mephisto's second call that led to the wager and pact, Faust had exhibited a facet of his temperament that differed from anything we had observed heretofore. Whereas, on the preceding evening, he had replied to the riddling and the tantrums of Mephisto, the travelling scholar, with composure, superior raillery and the active curiosity of a man in full command of that startlingly novel situation, this time he is completely out of sorts, he is petulant, querulous, whining, unnerved, pouring out lamentations about the emptiness of his days and the haunting, affrighting dreams of his nights, and bridling at Mephisto's jibes. The Faust of that mood, when at last provoked into uttering the all-embracing curse, showed all the symptoms of an anxiety neurosis. This lassitude, the show of a personality quite unstrung, was very different in kind from the bold superhuman gesture with which he had hailed the "Earth Spirit", the dark, tense despair of his brooding after having been rejected, and of the euphoric serenity with which he had grasped the poisoned chalice. We see then that the danger of his succumbing to a neurosis that would have left him at loose ends, was very real. It is in these terms that we must evaluate Faust's triumph over the specter of Anxiety on the last night of his life.

Anxiety is routed. Unable to enter the inner fortress of Faust's personality, she departs from the palace but in doing so she exhibits her demonic power: She breathes upon him and casts a spell, making Faust go blind. "The run of men are blind all their lives," she comments; "now, Faust, it is your turn to become so at the end."

As a rule, commentators have tried to read a deep symbolism into the spell that reduces Faust to blindness, such as: Having been a man of clear-eyed determination all his life, he falls a prey to delusion in the end; he loses his faculty to appraise mankind realistically and surrenders to a utopian optimism. I think the whole attempt to read a symbolical meaning into Faust's blindness is a mistake. Rather, a mythical interpretation is in order. All is then both simple and humanly moving. Faust has matched his energies against an assailant from the non-human, infernal regions. Astonishingly enough, he has come off the victor. But is it customary, we ask, for a mortal to emerge from so unequal a contest unscatched? No, indeed, this would run counter to all tradition. He bears the mark of it on him for the rest of his life. The first analogical example that comes to mind is the Biblical story of Jacob wrestling with the angel. Jacob triumphs, but his halting walk ever after serves as a reminder that the angel had touched his hip. Like everything Biblical, the story of Jacob was so familiar to Goethe that he may have counted on the awareness of the analogy to come to mind automatically. In the case of Faust a peculiar pathos attaches to his being stricken with blindness as a compensatory penalty of his victory over the Demon: It happens to him at night, in the last hour of his life, and in the small span of time left him he possibly never registers any awareness of what has happened to him. The night closing in about him simply acts as a stimulus to heighten his fervor for pushing the task to which his life is dedicated.

We summarize: On this last night of his life, Faust has again been carried away by an excess of impatience to the perpetration of a high-handed act of injustice that resulted in destruction and murder. He

has subsequently repented of this abuse of his power. Then, when
assailed by the spectral demon of Anxiety, he had, in the nick of time,
remembered to check his impatience. The hypnotic crooning had prompted him to pass his life in review and, in full acknowledgement of early
decisions irretrievably made, he had deeply repented of his cardinal sin
of impatience that led to his all-embracing curse and his involvement
with the powers of darkness. In this he had successfully countered the
Demon's assault, but the victory that left his personality whole has left
its mark on his body.

     During the few moments of life left him Faust continues to grow.
A moment ago we saw him reject—in principle—his lifetime association
with magic and the infernal powers as a mistaken approach. Now a
breakthrough of another kind occurs. Whereas the earlier one concerned
his relation to Nature and the mystery of the universe, this one concerns
his relation to mankind. Faust's social sense had not been developed.
Social relations have played a small part in his experience. Except for
Gretchen, whom he both worshiped and abandoned, he has never been
close to any human being. He has never had a friend or felt the need
of one—a strange lack indeed for a man who had programmatically set
out to encompass the whole range of human experience in his person.
He had been a great benefactor to mankind, but all the benefaction
accrued as incidental to his sense of self-realization. It is in this regard
that Faust's final utterance achieves a new breakthrough: For the first
time he no longer thinks of man in terms of rule and obedience. He has
a vision of a self-contained human society of free men, animated by
the balanced operation of the two basic principles of competition and
cooperation—competition as the drive directed against the non-human
element, cooperation in the effective exercise of that drive in a society
actuated by a common zeal. This is an idyllic vision, to be sure, an
extreme simplification. The forces operating in human society will never
range themselves to conform to so neat a design of polarity—certainly
not in a democracy as we know it, and even though Goethe's eye dwelt
with fascination on the new order taking shape in America. To a new
direction, rather than to a goal achieved, Faust sets his sights. This is
for him, at the last moment of his life, the embodiment of wisdom, the
spirit that gives the stamp of value to collective human activity. Having
outlined this creed in a phrasing which echoes the central formulation
of the wager scene, though translated from statement to contingent
hypothesis, Faust falls dead.

In breathing his last, Faust has uttered the key phrase of the wager that conditioned his pact with Mephisto. In the thousands of lines intervening, that situation had never again been alluded to. Does its recurrence now stir an echo in Mephisto's ear? If so, he betrays no sign of it, as he shakes his head bemused by the unaccountable taste of this mortal. He admits, moreover, in plain words: Me he withstood so valiantly, now Time masters him at last. Then, after further multiple echoes of the pact's phrasing, he concludes: "Es ist vollbracht," it is accomplished. The German *vollbracht* is a parodistic echo of Christ's last word on the cross. Does the word here signify a burst of exultation or a sigh of relief? Be that as it may, the spectral gravediggers cut in with a correction: "Es ist vorbei." Let time be past, over, done for me, were the words with which Faust concluded the rhetorically ringing lines of his wager. This correction touches off a tantrum of nihilistic rage in Mephisto in which he rings the changes on that senseless word *vorbei.*

Having recovered himself, he stakes his confidence on Faust's signature. He orders the hellish host that has gathered to keep a sharp lookout for the precious soul and snatch it at the moment it leaves the body. There follows a scene of magnificently farcical humor. Hosts of angels are circling above the grave; they sing and scatter roses that, falling on the devils, pain them with more than hellish fire. They take flight. Worse still, Mephisto's lascivious appetite is beguiled by the pleasing forms of the boy angels, and, his attention distracted, the soul is snatched and borne aloft.

The postlude that ends the drama with magnificent recourse to Catholic imagery lets us glimpse various levels of Purgatory—Purgatory, not as a place of torment, but as the unending process of purgation and purification on the part of individual souls and groups dedicated to the deepening contemplation of the divine mysteries. We hear the fervent chants of various fathers of the Church, bearing exalted names. We hear the voices of the very young, who come into mortal life only to leave it again at once. We hear a chorus of penitent women adoring the blessed Virgin, and in their number there is one that bears the features of Gretchen. Her voice thrills with gratitude to the divine Mother for having heard her intercession for her wayward lover. All of this scene is designed to be executed after the manner of a richly orchestrated oratorio.

Faust's salvation is a highly unorthodor affair. Let the Lord make a defense of his tolerance to the theologians. Arrogantly erect to the last, no humble penitent sinner suing for mercy, Faust is nevertheless rated a sound and perfectible substance by the divine arbiter. On his credit side is his ceaseless striving to expand his personality, despite his constant lapse into error. Perhaps the realization of the part played by Gretchen in his redemption will temper his nature with a little of that sweet humility which is both a gift of divine grace and a visible sign of its bestowal.

Peter Heller

Faustian Striving:
An Essay on Goethe's <u>Faust</u>

I

Whatever the genre may be that will fit Goethe's attempt to express the quintessence of the fragmentary and questionable experience available to man in the course of his questionable and fragmentary life, his *Faust* is, above all, a triumph of poetry. Every line is alive. The angels proclaim the eternal radiance and vital splendor of the universe, as fresh even now, as unworn by time as ever. The devil pokes fun at the abject condition of man who pretends to aspire beyond the dust but to fall flat on the ground and to crawl along his way in the perennial rut and inextricable mess of all things human. But whether the mood and message are affirmative or despairing, the freshness, the radiance, the vital elan win out by virtue of the vigor, the simplicity and winged accuracy of a poetic diction ever unembarrassed and unconstrained, a power of vision which celebrates its victories as readily in the catalogue of curses which the frustrated Faust pronounces to vent his resentment on all the blessings of life, as it does in the mystical choirs which accompany the ascent of his spirit into a realm beyond the range of both human curses and human enthusiasms in order, finally, to pronounce the transfiguration of all things human into a symbol of the ineffably divine essence.

Yet the prime manifestation of Goethe's poetic spirit in the very texture of his great text has resisted so far all attempts of English translators. What remains is, at best, the epic, the dramatic and the philosophical substance, and, particularly, Goethe's conception of Faustian striving as a symbol of the grandeur and misery, the intellectual and emotional drive, the dynamism of modern man. And at that, even the

story and theme seem on first sight rather odd and quaint, quite uncon-
temporary and unmodern.

Goethe's long life spanned the second half of the 18th century and
the first third of the 19th, a period of more than 82 years. Ever since
his student days and into his eighties, he was, on and off, at work on
his *Faust*. Why, Goethe is very nearly a contemporary of ours! A well
preserved gentleman once told me that his own father had still seen
the old man pacing up and down his garden at Weimar putting the
final touches to the second part of *Faust*. But however contemporary
Goethe may be—even his efforts in the natural sciences, in botany, in
the theory of color are still considered to be of some interest—his *Faust*
certainly points to an age quite distant from ours. The 18th century
poet chose deliberately a late Renaissance-Reformation setting to dram-
atize the 16th century legend. He set up his Faust among the appropriate trappings of a period characterized by the stirring of the modern
scientific spirit within the confines of a mentality addicted to ancient
superstition, to alchemy, astrology, magic. For this was an age when—
according to such authorities as Paracelsus and Luther—spirits, demons,
devils were still in the habit of assuming tangible human or animal
shapes instead of being as finely and widely disseminated and as intangible as they are today. But even if one might be allowed to discount
for a moment the historical setting: What are we here and now to make
of Faust, of this frustrated professor who concludes a pact with the
devil?

There he is: close to retirement age, confined to his cell, to his dark
hole of a study. He has just discovered that he has missed not only the
good things of life—riches, women, worldly power, and honor—but that
he missed equally the very goal that caused him to dedicate his every
moment to the study of all sciences and scholarly and theoretical branch-
es of learning; that he has missed the realization of the vital truth which
animates and pervades this mysterious universe. And if, in order to
transcend the limitations of his condition, he will turn to magic, it is
only to realize that by his own natural endowments, he, the would-be-
superman, cannot hold his own in the company of the universal cosmic
spirit or even in the lowlier company of the ever active, ever creative
spirit of this earth. And now he despairs, and comes close to committing
suicide, again in order to break the insufferable confinement of terrestrial existence. Indeed, he is ready for Mephistopheles, and for the
strange agreement which stipulates that one moment of true satisfaction
will deliver his soul to the devil. If ever Faust will rest content, if ever

he will cease to strive beyond the confines of the moment, of the particular time and place and sphere of action, he will have ceased to live, he will have denied the very essence of his human spirit, and he will thus be the property of the spirit of negation and nothingness incarnate in the amusing guise of Mephistopheles. And now Mephistopheles takes over: he rejuvenates Faust and he seeks to tempt Faust with the realms of the world in order to satisfy or rather: to vitiate and to extirpate, the restless aspirations of his master and victim.

For the devil, as he announced in the Prologue, desires to destroy the pretensions of man's aspirations, that is, of his striving beyond the temporal, of a yearning essentially directed to the infinite and eternal, and consequently to the sphere of divine, of undiminished and unconfined being. He would stop man's impulse to transcend his limitations. He would reduce man's existence to a status in which he would be satisfied to "eat dust." He would have man surrender his attempt to relate himself to the eternity of true being—an attempt that can never be realized in time except symbolically, that is, by way of man's striving beyond any given temporal limitation. The devil would persuade man to become wholly engrossed and consumed in the concern with the dust of temporality, with the nonentity of the moment. And yet it is the paradox of the devil that the power of negation or evil which he represents, must always be productive of the positive or good. For as he attempts to destroy the illusions of man and strives to bring about man's final realization that he is nothing but dust among dust, that he is but temporal nonentity and that all the conditions of temporality add up *sub specie aeternitatis* to precisely nothing, he incites, as an unwilling servant of God, the very opposite tendency in man, namely: man's effort to transcend the insufficiency of all temporal satisfaction, to defeat nonentity, to make still another attempt to relate himself to essential being.

The devil first offers Faust the "small world" (*die kleine Welt*), the private sphere of satisfactions, experiences, vices, sensations available within a subjective and restricted circle represented chiefly by scenes set in a provincial German atmosphere. The prospect of Auerbach's wine cellar, of having his spirit appeased and dampened and reduced to whimpering sentimentality or to animal stupor by indulgence in alcohol, does not attract Faust. Turning procurer, the devil now seems to pin his hope on an affair. However, the pastime of seduction designed to turn Faust into a callous insect, proves the occasion for a drama of erotic passion. Much as Faust proves inferior to the unalloyed power of love, much as Faust (and Mephistopheles via Faust and within Faust) succeeds in perverting the essential purity of Gretchen's erotic self-abandonment, much as Faust is guilty not only of his own crimes but also of Gretchen's crimes, and consequently of turning love into murder and death (of Gretchen's mother, of her brother, of her child, and finally of Gretchen herself), it is nonetheless true that Faust has by no means turned into a dust eater. Nor will the grossly sensual gratifications dramatized in the witches' sabbath on Walpurgisnight appease the appetites of this physical and metaphysical lover.

This is not, of course, to deny that Faust's striving may and does prove itself a destructive force. For it is a "dark", unpurified, even a perverted striving. However, no matter how confused and how conducive to "error" (which in the moral domain is called sin), the human elan, the transmoral spirit of transcendence remains unvanquished.

It would lead too far afield to trace the further evolutions of Faust through the several spheres of the *grand monde,* the wider circles of society and the public domain, the quest for the archetypes of beauty, for an aesthetic ideal, the explorations of the cosmic forces, the pursuit of the active life in statesmanship and the project to subdue the forces of nature in an enterprise designed to serve a future community of man. Yet a central issue in the interpretation of Faust may now be considered.

In the thirties the standard version taught in the schools still claimed Faust as a positive hero developing steadily in the direction of self-improvement and purification. Faust's final project of eternalizing his name by the foundation of a healthy and free nation was to reveal the extent of his progress, e.g., beyond his tragic and destructive involvement with Gretchen. His final insight that man should realize his essence not by the attempt to reach beyond the human condition but by his creative activity *on this earth* was considered to be superior to the exuberant enthusiasm of subjective emotions which characterized his youthful stage. And yet the increasing range of his experience and his increasing concern with vast undertakings do not necessarily argue improvement or purification. For the larger and impersonal enterprises of old age may merely serve to give larger scope to one's essential failure as a human being.

Blind, though undiminished in his zeal, the old Faust pronounces words of wisdom and hope concerning the future of his grand engineering project. But those busy laborers whom he imagines to be at work on this project, are slaving demons shovelling out his own grave. Now he envisions the moment of fulfillment. But clearly he is now, in the very last breath of terrestrial life, as deluded as ever. And at the same time, his striving spirit is now, in the very last breath of life, as undiminished as ever. The fulfillment is not in the eating of dust but in the anticipation of a further *agon* of transcendence, a further illusory vision and further widening of the human circle. Now as ever, this prototype of man is animated by the dynamism of ever unfulfilled aspirations. No, he is not a wiser man but neither has he been vanquished by the devil.

And as for his being a better man, his improvement in moral character . . . Well, there are, for example, two innocent old people, Philemon and Baucis, who annoy the builder Faust, apparently because *they* are content to stay on their ground and to live out their happily restricted lives. He will not tolerate them. He orders Mephistopheles to remove them. Their house is burned down, and they perish in the flames. But while Faust expresses his anger at Mephistopheles' methods, it seems that he wastes no more time on repentance now than he did after the heartrending end of Gretchen. Is he then evil? Yes and no. He is neither simply evil nor simply good much as he was and is both wise and unwise. But if this is so, perhaps this condition reflects Goethe's view of man's essentially hybrid condition.

In view of such considerations, a later school of interpreters felt that Faust was not meant to pass through a positive development. Some even claimed that Goethe had intended the poem to warn of the Faustian character. And some even thought that Faust deteriorated. Was it not easier to sympathize with the tragically involved Faust of the Gretchen-episode than with the relentless entrepreneur of the closing scenes? The truth would seem to be that Faust passes through stages of life, to gain intense and universal experience, to represent the imperfect, erring and striving human being in all phases from youth to old age, from subjective passion to ambitious public enterprise—but that he does not reveal vital or moral progress as far as his essential condition is concerned. The old man would do as little as Gretchen's lover as the lover would do for the engineering project. The removal of Philemon and Baucis is no more considerate and responsible than the killing of Valentine. Faust is a hero only in the sense that he embodies on a titanic scale the emotional, intellectual, vital potential of man (for Goethe's Faust does represent a vast range of human experience), and in that he reveals that this creature, caught between error and truth, darkness and light, devil and God, good and evil, *ens realissimum* and nonentity, can relate himself to a suprahuman order by the very force of dynamic striving, and that he can therefore be redeemed from the condition of nonentity. He does not *deserve* to be redeemed. He has no claim upon grace on the basis of his accomplishments, of goodness or wisdom or good works. But he is redeemable by virtue of his urge to self-transcendence, to go beyond anything that he 'is.' And perhaps it would even be true to say that this urge to self-transcendence *is* man's redemption. Even the purified state of man in the beyond—where Goethe assigns to the ever active and widely experienced spirit of Faust a teaching-position as instructor of the inexperienced souls of infants who died shortly after birth—merely suggests the sublimated continuation of Faustian dynamism. And indeed, the entire heaven of Goethe is in a rapid movement which reflects the transfiguration but not the abolishment of Faustian striving. Heavenly activity, however, is not the theme of Goethe's poem. And while the Lord of the Prologue who claims that he will soon lead Faust up to a higher stage, must have had his heavenly assignment in mind, the play itself which deals with the life of Faust in the years he had bargained for with the devil, hardly shows this ascension to a higher stage.

Moreover, if Faust is as inferior to God as he is superior to the devil; if he is as far from absolute being as he is from mere negation or nonentity, and if his striving is his chief characteristic, it stands to reason that this striving is itself ambiguous—a source of error and the cause for redemption, the very token of man's temporality and the very expression of his yearning for eternal significance, a tendency rendering man incapable of perfection (for yearning implies imperfection) and yet his only approximation to perfection (since he is related to the eternal or perfect only by virtue of his striving). But if man is essentially the striving being, the question would not be whether he should or should not strive but rather what he should make of his striving, how much of it should be expressed and how much of it should be restricted, and what the relationship might be between Goethe's portrayal of the striving Faust and his doctrine of renunciation, resignation, and classical restriction. I shall not consider this question here except insofar as to suggest that it is intimately related to the historical development of the Faust theme and, again, to the varying evaluations and interpertations of Goethe's *Faust*. For Goethe's work does mark the stage at which the Faustian striving has become the ambiguous symbol for a quest that is both man's blessing and man's curse.

II

This is true even though in Goethe's version the wholly affirmative power of divine grace condescends, in the final act, to redeem man from his ambiguous condition so as to transfigure his good-and-evil, his creative-and-destructive dynamism into a positive force and into a symbol of a benevolently active universe. And it is true even though Goethe's poetry manages to transfigure the dubious efforts of man into an aesthetic harmony.

More than ninety years ago, the young Nietzsche claimed that Goethe's Faust represented a turning point in the history of modern man: For in his restless search for knowledge and for its power to improve the human condition, this modern man, Faust, now began to suspect the limitations of the modern intellectual quest, and, finding himself adrift and lost on a desolate ocean of knowledge, he yearned for a safe shore and a harbor. Nietzsche's emphasis on the *intellectual* quest is somewhat misleading. Goethe's Faust is addicted to his search with heart *and* mind, with his emotions and his senses as well as with his intellect. Moreover, Nietzsche may have done violence to Goethe's intent by suppressing the glorification of Faustian striving. For, according to Nietzsche, Goethe's Faust suggests primarily the futility of striving. Nonetheless, this change in perspective is highly significant. For ever since Nietzsche's days the stress has been increasingly on the dubious aspects of Faust's modern Titanism.

The story and theme which Goethe adapted to his own ambiguous purpose have had their ups and downs through the ages. There always was magic—white and black. Ahriman and Ormuzd have been at war for a long time. There always were good men like Job to be tried and tested by God through the agency of his servant, Satan. And there always were men who succumbed and failed the test. Always there were ambitious magi who would enter a pact with evil spirits to assume great power and to be brought down, to be dashed to the ground—as Simon Magus who took wings unto himself and could fly, was brought down by the word of St. Peter. But to cut a long story short—there was quite specifically in the XVIth century a quack, a conceited charlatan— or so it seems—who went by the name of Faust and who soon became the object of legend and the subject of the science fiction of those days as found between retellings of myths, fairytales, fables or fabulous journeys, in cheaply printed and widely-read chap-books. The *Faustbook* of 1587 told of an unholy scholar and magician who in his Titanic arrogance took eagles' wings unto himself and boldly ventured to explore the mercifully hidden heights and depths of God's universe. The pact, the journeys, the magic tricks, Helen, the disciples—the motives for a great drama were there though concealed in the crude composition, or rather in the compositions: for soon there were to be several versions and variants as well as some folksongs on the subject. Inevitably, when the appointed time had run out and the devil returned, Faust came to a terrible end, say, with his presumptuous brain spattered all over the walls of his study, and his rump still twitching on a dungheap while his soul had been delivered to eternal misery. The chapbook reflected two opposite pressures: One—the rise of Humanism, of scientific curiosity, including the desire to rediscover the pagan beauties and the wisdom of Greece. The other: the counterpressure of the Reformation, its religious fervor which soon had turned against the stirrings of the scientific, the scholarly, the Humanistic and the Renaissance spirit, and—in the first round—to defeat it as Luther defeated Erasmus. Hence in the chapbook, the *libido sciendi,* the delight in—pre-scientific—science and in learning is seen from the vantage point and with the jaundiced eye of anti-Humanistic religion—all on a low and popular level, to be sure. And the result is a story about a fascinating kind of villain, a man engaged in the forbidden arts who must, of course, come to grief. In essence, a medieval attitude is restated: namely, the conception of boundless intellectual striving and yearning for power as a sin offending against the God-given limits set to the appointed status, to the nature and to the aspirations of man.

This is not to claim that the Faustian temper and the Faustian aspirations had been entirely foreign to the Middle Ages. However, in keeping with the dominant social framework which was conceived of as static; in keeping with the hierarchies of the Church or of the secular rule, from the Pope down to the laity, from the Emperor down through the degrees of the feudal pyramid instituted *aere perennius,* with every man duty bound to observe his place and station; in keeping with the hierarchic conception of the universe descending from God through the ranks of the angels and heavenly bodies to the spheres of mankind and the animal kingdom,—the intellectual rebels were held in check. Scientific learning and curiosity were subject to close supervision. A man like Gerbert of Aurillac who lived about the year 1000, well versed in the classics and in mathematical science, was easily suspected of being in alliance with the devil even though he had been elected pope. And even when the scholastic science and philosophy began to flourish, a Faustian character such as Pierre Abaillard, the relentless virtuoso of logical dialectic, was quickly apprehended, and the leading spirits of his age—the XIIth century—followed not *his* lead but the guidance of his formidable opponent, St. Bernard of Clairvaux. By the XVIth century, however, the movements of social, political, intellectual and spiritual emancipation from the old order were on the march, and for better and worse the Faustian character was destined to rise to representative status.

To resume our story: In 1588, Marlowe, the protagonist of the true, the Elizabethan Storm and Stress, the overreacher, fatally attracted to titanic, inflated, monstrous and heroic personalities and super-personalities of Renaissance and super-Renaissance dimensions, conceived a great, if unevenly executed, tragedy in which, despite the horror and the anguish attendant upon Faust's final realization of his doom, the consignment to eternal damnation did not detract but rather add to the death and hell-bound greatness, to the dark aura of the hero. English players much beloved by the Germans who had then little theatre of their own, brought Faust back to Germany—more in the form of a spectacle of horrors and in dumb-shows than as regular drama since the language of the comedians was not the language of their audience. And now Faust entered the puppet theatre and flourished at fairs. The legend had long been a favorite of the Germans by the time young Goethe encountered it.

Still, up to Goethe's age, Faust—as a rule—had been condemned. It was Lessing, the founder of modern German literature in criticism, prose, and the drama, who conceived of a redeemed Faust, since the noblest of all impulses, the striving for truth, ought not to lead a man to eternal damnation. In Lessing the intellectual aspect of striving predominated, as it should with a representative of the Enlightenment. Yet his was an intellectualism with a difference. He claimed that he preferred the striving for truth to the possession of truth; for possession merely made men inert and proud while through intellectual striving they would attain ever increasing perfection of their—eternally imperfect and eternally perfectible—nature. He envisaged an unending progress oriented by way of intellectual, rational striving to the fulness of truth possessed by God alone who, being infinite goodness and power and benevolence, was also the guarantor for the rightness of this striving, for its being oriented to truth rather than headed in the opposite direction.

In essence, Goethe was to adopt Lessing's solution; but he translated the intellectual dialectic into existential terms. Lessing's Faust (of which we have but a few fragments and notes) would have sought for rational

insight. When Goethe's Faust speaks of knowledge, he does not exclude
rational insight. But if he does include reason, he does so in order to
go beyond it. Knowledge now means essential awareness, vital—intellectual and emotional—experience. To know the power that shapes and
unifies the universe is to see, to realize, to sense, to live the essence.
Not merely man's dynamic intellect but man's entire dynamic quest
appears now as man's chief distinction. Thus Goethe completes the
reversal of the medieval evaluation of the bold dynamic transgressor
and experimenter. If the Enlightenment reflected increasing optimism
concerning the beneficial potential of man's unhampered *libido sciendi,*
the ultimate version would reflect an optimistic view, a glorification of
man's total dynamism, of his boundless potential in the direction of
Titanic experience and self-realization.

And yet this kind of Promethean optimism—though suggested in
Goethe's early poetry and akin to the pathos of the German Storm and
Stress—was not to be Goethe's final contribution. Much rather, some
aspects of the later Nietzsche would represent, in a rather desperate
and hectic manner, this wholly emancipated vision of the self-reliant
self-creator and self-destroyer, of Titanic man and superman.

As indicated above, Goethe's *Faust* remains ambiguous. Goethe sees,
he sympathizes with, the Titanic quest. He represents its spirit in the
grandiose though questionable image of Faust. But this poetic portrayal
retains, as far as the evaluation of the Faustian urge is concerned, a
curious neutrality, a lack of partisanship—in marked contrast, incidentally, to other major works of the mature Goethe in which he quite
definitely takes sides and pronounces a message; but it is a message
of self-containment and self-mastery, of renunciation of the Titanic aspirations and yearnings of his own youth. Still and all, in Goethe's poetry,
the image of Faust's turbulent journey through life and, in particular,
of Faust's error-and-truth-bound striving is still seen to reflect the eternal law in the dim and distorting mirror of the limited temporal human
universe. The temporal quest and journey and failure of the would-be-
Titan is still a symbol—only a symbol but still a symbol—of the eternal,
imperishable and divine order of the macrocosm. Faust's reach ever
exceeds his grasp; his erratic career on earth is pronounced a tragedy;
but this tragedy of man's error and insufficiency does reflect somehow
the *divina commedia* of God's universe.

Not so the later versions of Faust which come to mind: e.g., Lenau's
late Romantic poem or Thomas Mann's novel *Doctor Faustus,* the allegorical commentary on the life of Nietzsche, on the corruption and

collapse of Germany, on the hellbound despair of the artistic, the creative—one is tempted to say: of the European psyche. These late elabora-
tions of the myth return to the older version, to the condemnation of
Faust, to a tragic conclusion unmitigated by a metaphysical happy end.
For between the age of Enlightenment and the XXth century, the literary
mind at least, had grown skeptical of the Titanism of man's wholly
emancipated quest and striving. And indeed, this skepticism is akin to
the attitude expressed in contemporary ruminations on the subject of
science and notably on the Titanic applications of science in technology
and to warfare, akin to the note of justified concern, fear and anxiety
that this dynamism might be headed for self-destruction rather than,
as Lessing had said with respect to the intellectual exercise, toward
increasing self-perfection on the road of eternal progress. And it is this
contemporary sense of the crisis of modern, of Western man which, in
turn, has affected, slanted, reoriented the interpretations of the janus-
faced poem of Goethe.

III

The preceding observations on the nature of Goethe's theme bear
directly upon the crucial question concerning the external and the
inner form of a work that appears to defy some standard categories of
literary criticism. Goethe's dramatic pageant or poetic masque of humanity makes use of lyrical, dramatic and epic forms. The opening is
essentially a lyrical soliloquy. The Gretchen tragedy is intensely dramatic.
The fact that the major episodes are quite self-contained rather than
ancillary to the development of a unified action; the relish for the
panoramic view or for well-rounded and detailed portrayal, the host
of minor characters and events, suggest qualities usually associated with
epic poetry or with the accommodating scope of the novel. And indeed,
the work does not owe its fame or popularity to the theatre. Some parts
were, apparently, never intended for live performance; and to judge
Faust as a play that ought to come to life on the stage in order to prove
its effectiveness, is to apply an irrelevant criterion. Even so, stage versions, frequently restricted to the First Part, constitute regular and
successful items in the standard repertory of German theatre though
the work has also served as a kind of lyrical anthology and as a collection of aphorisms, as an inexhaustible breviary of a philosophy of life
and of worldly wisdom, as a book to be read in even at random, or
as a secular bible. Yet to claim that Goethe's *Faust* transcends all genres,
is to evade rather than to answer the question as to the essential form—
or formlessness—of the work.

Certainly, on first sight, *Faust* appears to be remarkable for its variety and breadth rather than for its singlemindedness or strict consistency. Literary histories are wont to inform their readers that the work ranges over three thousand years of human history; and in point of mythical and terrestrial geography it certainly does range from heaven to hell, and far and wide over the lands and landscapes of Europe. Indeed, the variety of this fabulous poem is so very great that generations of Goethe scholars amused themslves by taking apart what Goethe put together, by showing that this poetic summary contained all the fragments of Goethe's great confession, that parts of it, e.g., the Gretchen-tragedy, were pure Storm and Stress, and other parts, for example, the Helena episode, were models of classicism while still others, e.g., the Catholic imagery of the conclusion, pointed to Germany Romanticism. And as for verse—there are German *Knittelverse, Freie Rhythmen*, alexandrines, all sorts of classical metres, *terza rima, ottava rima* . . . and there are ancient Greeks and witches from the Harz mountains, 18th century caricatures and medieval saints, pure allegories and realistic character portrayals . . .

Yet this is an odd sort of compliment to pay to a work of art. For, surely, an aesthetic whole should reveal some sort of unity rather than the lack of unity and thus: the lack of form. Is Goethe's *Faust* to be commended for offering a hodgepodge of protagonists, plots, styles and subject matter? This "tragedy" with a happy ending may not be obliged to conform to the rules of neo-classicism. Let it defy the unities of time and place. But what of the far more relevant unity of action? The work is unified to some extent by the character of Faust. And yet this character constantly changes: from old age to youth, from youth to maturity, from maturity to old age. And even Mephistopheles reveals a spectrum of varied aspects as he changes from a tempter to a seeming servant, and from an active mastermind to a subordinate of Faust's designs. The character of Faust and of his dramatic biography is unified by the theme of striving. But other than that, the work does, indeed, consist of a series of episodes.

These objections are familiar. For various modern critics, who are boundlessly tolerant of experiments in the novel as well as in poetry, have turned pedants when confronted with the experimental narrative and poem which Goethe conceived in the form of a dramatic spectacle. And yet, some reflection on the theme of Goethe's *Faust* should suggest the fact that no conscientious artist could have possibly represented this theme in the form of a neat dramatic construction. Goethe evidently did not believe that the essential image of the life of modern man could or should assume such a form. The temporal phase of man's life was to him much rather an epic, dramatic, and lyrical journey through widening circles of experience.

"The imitation of the content in the form," says Kierkegaard, "is essential to all artistry." What else could Goethe have chosen but the open form of circle upon circle—to show the incessant flow and metamorphoses of the heedless Faustian energy that fills each containing reservoir to overflow and to fill and to overflow a new container? What else could he have done but to imitate in the very form of his work its theme: the dynamic striving which transcends and destroys any given limitation to energize, create and destroy and transcend a further circumscribed sphere? And indeed, it is this organic dialectic of self-creative and self-destructive growth, death, rebirth; it is this movement of metamorphosis which determines the form of the poem—from Goethe's conception of heaven and hell, of God and devil, of Faust and Mephistopheles, from his scheme of the passage through the orbits of the small and the great world down to the single episode and the linguistic detail of poetic style.

A few illustrations may serve to suggest what would needs be the burden of a more elaborate analysis and interpretation: The devil of the Prologue speaks of the vital and spiritual elan of the human being by describing man as a grasshopper who would ever leap and fly but to squat again in the grass or to thrust his nose into a heap of dung. As the play will demonstrate, he is quite right after his own fashion. Yet seen from on high, these ineffectual efforts of man to leap and soar above the restraints imposed upon the animal that he is, appear as preliminary exercises, obscure and frequently misguided, yet necessary for the attainment of a higher form of being. And this polarity, which is, of course, inherent in the dialectic of striving, is reasserted and dramatized in countless details throughout the poem. Thus Faust's opening lines state his dissatisfaction with finite human learning and with the conditions of his merely terrestrial existence in order to announce his decision to transcend those boundaries through magic (11. 354-385). The following stanza ("O, sähst du, voller Mondenschein") contains a dream of emancipation from all human limitations and of communion with the spirits (11. 386-397). The grasshopper is borne aloft. Yet this ascent is succeeded, in turn, by a rude awakening, a descent of the mind, that is, by a bitter indictment of the narrow terrestrial cell that still imprisons Faust (11. 398-409). And consequently the next group

of verse will start out once more from this lowly plane by blaming
Faust's suffering upon his unnatural confinement (11. 410-417) while
a further stanza ("Flieh! auf!") will describe again the upward movement of his mind toward spiritual communion (11. 418-429).[1] Indeed,
the rhythms of elevation-and-descent (and of descent-and-elevation) per-
vade the work throughout. Thus Faust "descends" or "rises" to the
sphere of the Mothers; the *Pater Ecstaticus* is discovered in constant
upward and downward motion; and when Lynkeus sings his praise of
the eternal beauty ("ewige Zier") of the world, it is but to be shattered
in his sense of sublimity by the sight of the horror perpetrated in order
to consign the two "good old people" to the flames that envelop their
idyllic abode.

Analogously, the larger units, such as the scenes and the nexus between them, are dominated by larger curves and undulations inherent
in the fluctuating movement of ever frustrated and ever undiminished
striving. As we have seen, the opening scene dramatizes Faust's insistent
and recurrent desire to transcend the limits imposed upon the human
quest for knowledge. Yet as his efforts to soar beyond his condition
and to unite with the cosmic spirit result in failure, he is sent back to
the spirit of the earth but to descend further: to the involuntary communion with the academic pedantry of Wagner, and thence, finally, to
the thought of suicide. And while, in the subsequent scene ("Vor dem
Tor"), Faust is moved in a direction that runs counter to the initial
upward surge: to seek reconciliation with terrestrial life and with the
colorful spectrum of human and all-too-human gratifications that are
unimpaired by intimations of the sublime, he will be seized again by
the yearning to leave the lowly planes and to rise "zu den Gefilden
hoher Ahnen," to the transcendent realms of man's divine origins, a
desire which, ironically enough and in keeping with the status of the
human grasshopper, merely results in attracting the spirit of Mephistopheles in the guise of a black poodle. Nor will the oscillation between
polar extremes relent when we meet Faust again in his study. For though
he is now engrossed in sublime speculation, he will be disturbed, tempted, and, finally, fooled by the low spirit of Mephistopheles who, even
as he puts Faust to sleep with a deceptive dream of pleasurable escape

---

[1]The units to which this interpretation refers, are marked as separate stanzas
(in a loose sense of the term) in the original text. For a paradigmatic statement
of the entire circular motion which leads from heaven to earth and from earth to
heaven, cf. also Goethe's poem "Gesang der Geister über den Wassern."

from all terrestrial limitations, effects his own escape with the help of vermin.

Each attempt at elevation will be attended by failure and by a descent into the nether region much as each immersion in the nether region will give rise to a further attempt at elevation. As indicated above, the attempt to ensnare Faust in mere or pure erotic adventure gives rise to a passionate transfiguration which, in turn, issues in tragic failure and in a violent descent into the depths of dissipation, crime, guilt, and anguish; and even the last scene reveals Faust engaged in a dream that transfigures terrestrial achievement into a transcendence of temporal failure while, in truth, the lemurs are merely preparing the ground which is to receive his lifeless body destained to turn into earth. And yet again, this final failure prepares a new ascent.

Moreover, as Faust lives through, and breaks out of, each containing circle of experience, he describes a movement which entails both the attempt at the transcendence of each given orbit and a failure to do justice to its specific demands. He does not fulfil the requirements which the learned Wagner patiently strives to satisfy. For he is more and less than a scholar. He does not fulfil the circle that is Gretchen's. Much rather he destroys her sphere. He is more and less than a true lover. He does not satisfy even the conditions of a proper magician. Incontinently, madly, and yet with a passion not unworthy of genius in pursuit of perfection, he falls in love with the spirit of Helen that he has conjured up. He does not, it seems, succeed as engineer of a future community. And it is questionable throughout whether he is too great or too inadequate to succeed in any limited venture. He is impelled to wander through all spheres of experience in order to demonstrate both the inadequacy of all human experience and the irrepressible striving for a higher form of existence. He must reveal that the quest which animates him, is both unrelenting and inconclusive, both tragic and glorious, both pathetic and sublime; and that this quest is nonetheless a—temporal and inadequate—analogue of eternal perfection.

Suggestions for Further Reading

Atkins, Stuart. *Goethe's "Faust."* Cambridge, Mass., 1958.
Bergstraesser, Arnold, ed. *Goethe and the Modern Age.* New York, 1949.
Cassirer, Ernst. *Rousseau, Kant and Goethe.* New York, 1963.
Eliot, T. S. "Goethe," *On Poetry and Poets.* New York, 1957.
Fairley, Barker. *A Study of Goethe.* Oxford, 1947.

Hatfield, Henry. *Goethe: A Critical Introduction*. New York, 1963.

Knight, G. Wilson. *The Christian Renaissance: With Interpretations of Dante, Shakespeare and Goethe*. . . . New York, 1962.

Mann, Thomas. *Essays of Three Decades*. New York, 1947.

Santayana, George. *Three Philosophical Poets*. New York, 1953.

Vietor, K. *Goethe the Poet*. Cambridge, 1949.

————. *Goethe the Thinker*. Cambridge, 1950.

Richard Haven

Wordsworth and
the Language of Poetry

⌖⌖⌖

Anyone who has been exposed even briefly to the study of English Romanticism knows of Wordsworth's concern, theoretical as well as practical, with problems of poetic language. When, in his prefatory "Advertisement," he introduced the first edition of *Lyrical Ballads* as an experiment, it was the language of the poems in particular to which he called attention. They were, he said, "written chiefly with a view to ascertain how far the language of conversation in the middle and lower classes of society is adapted to the purposes of poetic pleasure. Readers accustomed to the gaudiness and inane phraseology of many modern writers . . . will perhaps frequently have to struggle with feelings of strangeness and aukwardness [sic]." In the famous Preface to the second edition of *Lyrical Ballads* in 1800, again in the Appendix to that preface added in 1802, and finally in the "Supplementary Essay" published with his *Collected Poems* in 1815,[1] he devoted much of his efforts to the explanation and justification of this principle.

The general tenor of all these remarks seems simple enough. Wordsworth objected to the stylization, to the conventionalized 'poetic' diction and imagery, especially in pastoral poetry, which seemed to him to have been characteristic of the eighteenth century. He insisted that the language of poetry should be that "really used by men," and that, except for meter and perhaps rhyme, it should "in no respect differ from that of good prose." "The poet," he wrote, "thinks and feels in the spirit of human passions. How, then, can his language differ in any material degree from that of all other men who feel vividly and see clearly?"

---

[1]In the following pages, all prose quotations are from these sources.

His own language in *Lyrical Ballads,* he adds, is not only that "really used by men" but is that of "humble and rustic life . . . (purified indeed from what appear to be its real defects, from all lasting and rational causes of dislike and disgust)."

To anyone who has read a little eighteenth century poetry, the point seems clear. As he rejects the lovesick swains and hard-hearted nymphs drawn from the never-never land of pastoral tradition, so Wordsworth rejects a poetic language which speaks of "plumy people" and "the finny race" instead of birds and fish. He will "choose incidents and situations from common life" will "look steadily at [his] subject," and avoid "falsehood of description." And he will use the language in which ordinary men express what they think and feel. He will turn from the artificial and conventional to the 'natural' and the 'real'.

When, however, we read the Preface more carefully and when we read Wordsworth's poetry as well, we discover some difficulties. The image suggested by the Preface of a poet of careful observation, realistic description, and colloquial utterance is perhaps not wholly false, but it is certainly inadequate. The poems present us not so much with the characters and scenes of rural life as with Wordsworth's brooding consciousness of them. And if he does not shun colloquial words and phrases, neither does he by any means confine himself to words which might be spoken by a Cumberland shepherd, and still less to his patterns of speech. Is his language, we may well ask, any more accurately described as a "selection" from the language of rustic life than it is as a selection from the language of sophisticated life? Has he not perhaps been carried away on a theoretical tangent by means of which he tries to justify his deviation from some current conventions but which really has little to do with his actual practice?

Such conclusions find some support certainly in the fact that Wordsworth's views on rustic life and language were partly theoretical in origin. The notion that the essential truth of human nature was found in primitive or simple man, in the 'noble savage', undisguised and undistorted by artificial customs and institutions was current during the eighteenth century and unquestionably influenced Wordsworth. Believing that it is not the sophisticate or the intellectual who is most in touch with reality but the primitive, the peasant, and the child; that it is they whose lives reveal the universal and permanent in human experience, it was, we may say, natural for him to imagine that he could find in rustic life the most suitable subjects and in rustic language the most direct expression for poetry whose "object is truth, not individual and local, but general and operative; not standing upon external testimony, but carried alive into the heart by passion."

But while it is helpful and informative to consider Wordsworth's Preface in this way, it is not enough. Wordsworth was primarily a poet and not a theoretician. His object in the various prefatory and supplementary essays was the defense of his own poetic practice. If there appears to be a discrepancy between the theory and the practice, then we need to examine the language of actual poems to see what Wordsworth was trying to defend and the reasons why this particular defense seemed to him satisfactory.

Let us consider first the kind of poetry which Wordsworth rejects. In addition to mentioning various names, he gives three examples: one in the Preface of 1800 and two in the Appendix of 1802. The first is a sonnet by Gray, who, he says "was more than any other man curiously elaborate in the structure of his poetic diction"; the second is Dr. Johnson's metrical paraphrase of Proverbs vi: 6-11; and the third is an extract from Cowper. Now one remarkable thing about all three examples is the fact that they seem relatively free from the kind of diction which we should expect to find in them. If Wordsworth was complaining about words used only by poets, about the kind of thing illustrated by the periphrases we noted earlier ("plumy people" and "finny tribe") then he was familiar with many far more striking examples than these. Apart from the use of the name *Phoebus* for the sun and possibly the phrase "amorous descant" to describe the song of birds, Gray's language seems unremarkable (there are several inversions of normal word order, but two of these are in lines exempted from stricture and Wordsworth was much given to inversion himself). Johnson's paraphrase is in regular heroic couplets and is somewhat longer than the original (114 words instead of 78) but it introduces no very unusual words or expressions. And while Cowper's lines are undistinguished as poetry, their language seems merely trite rather than artificially 'poetic.'

In the first two cases Wordsworth makes little attempt to point out just where his objection lies. Of Gray, he says that "it will easily be perceived that the only part of this sonnet which is of any value" is the five lines which he prints in italics. Johnson's paraphrase he calls a "hubbub of words" and he quotes the original biblical passage for contrast. But concerning Cowper, he is a little more explicit. Here are the lines in question, supposedly uttered by a shipwrecked sailor:

> Religion! what treasure untold
> Resides in that heavenly word!

> More precious than silver and gold,
> Or all that this earth can afford.
> But the sound of the church-going bell
> These valleys and rocks never heard,
> Ne'er sighed at the sound of a knell,
> Or smiled when a sabbath appeared.

The first four lines Wordsworth dismisses with some justice as merely "poorly expressed." But the phrase "church-going bell" he describes as "an instance of the strange abuses which Poets have introduced into their language, till they and their Readers take them as matters of course, if they do not single them out expressly as objects of admiration." And the last two lines he condemns as "an instance of the language of passion wrested from its proper use, and . . . applied upon an occasion what does not justify such violent expressions; and I should condemn the passage . . . as vicious poetic diction."

In both instances, Wordsworth, presumably unaware that the employment of *church-going* as an adjective was in fact a colloquial usage, is objecting to figurative language. And he objects because, he feels, such figurative language is not justified by the circumstances of the poem and therefore calls attention to itself. Figurative language, he says, is properly "the language of passion." While intellectually we know that valleys and rocks neither smile nor sigh, we often feel that our subjective human emotions find a response in the external world. To the joyful man, nature may seem to 'smile' in sympathy; to the grieving man, it may seem to sigh. In such circumstances figurative language is proper because it embodies a relationship which the speaker feels to exist. But in Cowper's lines, Wordsworth thinks, the relationships are not ones which we believe the speaker feels to exist, and they therefore have no valid basis outside the statement. They are ones which the poet has contrived to give his lines a specious air of poeticality.

In a poem such as this, where the lines are ostensibly spoken by a dramatic character, Wordsworth's point may seem obvious. But he applies the same principle to all poetic language. This is the way he puts it in the Preface:

> What has been thus far said applies to poetry in general, but especially to those parts of composition where the poet speaks through the mouths of his characters; and upon this point it appears to authorize the conclusion that there are few persons of good sense who would not allow that the dramatic parts of composition are defective in proportion as they deviate from the

real language of nature and are colored by a diction of the poet's own, either peculiar to him as an individual or belonging simply to poets in general. . . . It is not, then, in the dramatic parts of composition that we look for this distinction of language; but still it may be proper and necessary when the poet speaks to us in his own character. To this I answer by referring the reader to the description before given of a poet. Among the qualities there enumerated . . . is implied nothing differing in kind from other men, but only in degree. . . . The poet is chiefly distinguished from other men by a greater promptness to think and feel without immediate external excitement, and a greater power in expressing such thoughts and feelings as are produced in him in that manner. But these passions and thoughts and feelings are the general passions and thoughts and feelings of men. And with what are they connected? Undoubtedly with our moral sentiments and animal sensations, and with the causes which excite these; with the operations of the elements, and the appearances of the visible universe; with storm and sunshine, with the revolutions of the seasons, with cold and heat, with the loss of friends and kindred, with injuries and resentments, gratitude and hope, with fear and sorrow. . . . The poet thinks and feels in the spirit of human passions. How, then, can his language differ in any material degree from that of all other men who feel vividly and see clearly? It might be *proved* that it is impossible.

Wordsworth says, in effect, that poetic language is always dramatic. The poet identifies himself, if only in imagination, with the situation the poem presents, and his response is that of a sensitive but still typical human being. The poem is the "spontaneous overflow of [his] powerful feelings" into words. Furthermore, Wordsworth suggests that the language of poetry thus derives immediately from a level of experience that is essentially non-verbal. The verbal utterance, that is, expresses and is determined by elemental human feelings and sensations which can be known without being named. The words of such language, he says, are "*emanations*" of "reality and truth" and are superior to anything which the poet's "fancy or imagination can suggest."

This, then, is the basis for Wordsworth's rejection of what he calls 'poetic diction.' Poetic diction to him means the replacement of 'genuine' expression by the conscious verbal fancy of the poet who stands outside his subject and meets it not on the intuitive level of sensation and passion but on the intellectual level of conceptions and words. Cowper, as we have seen, does not connect "smiled" and "sighed" with valleys and rocks because the speaker in such a situation would have felt such a connection but because *smiled* goes with *sabbath* and *sighed* goes with *knell.* From Wordsworth's point of view, this is not a significant expression but a mere playing with words. And his objection to his other examples is obviously similar. Johnson's elaboration of the biblical passage is entirely verbal and seems to serve no purpose other than to enable him to cast the whole in artfully balanced couplets. That part of Gray's sonnet which Wordsworth considers of no value is a description of the morning employing figurative language which, like Cowper's, has no basis in the anguish of the bereaved speaker.

As a general critical principle, this is obviously open to serious objection, and it leads Wordsworth to reject a great deal of good poetry including Gray's by no means negligible sonnet. But what Wordsworth is condemning is not in fact bad writing but a kind of language which does not suit his own poetic purposes. Wordsworth, as we have said, finds significance not in the conceptual patterns of the intellect but in the immediate intuitions of experience, when, he felt, man touches reality without the intervention of words. What he therefore required of language was that it be so to speak transparent, so as to convey the impressions and feelings of a moment of significant awareness without the distortion introduced by the "meddling intellect" which "murders to dissect." The eighteenth century language of artful and sophisticated intelligence, with its literary echoes and allusions, and, as he felt, severed from experience, did not meet such a requirement.

Let us turn then to an example of Wordsworth's own use of language. Consider the following poem:

> Strange fits of passion have I known:
> And I will dare to tell
> But in the Lover's ear alone
> What once to me befell.
>
> When she I loved looked every day
> Fresh as a rose in June,
> I to her cottage bent my way,
> Beneath an evening-moon.
>
> Upon the moon I fixed my eye,
> All over the wide lea;
> With quickening pace my horse drew nigh
> Those paths so dear to me.
>
> And now we reached the orchard-plot;
> And, as we climbed the hill,
> The sinking moon to Lucy's cot
> Came near, and nearer still.

> In one of those sweet dreams I slept,
> Kind Nature's gentlest boon!
> And all the while my eyes I kept
> On the descending moon.
>
> My horse moved on, hoof after hoof
> He raised, and never stopped:
> When down behind the cottage roof
> At once, the bright moon dropped.
>
> What fond and wayward thoughts will slide
> Into a Lover's head!
> "O mercy!" to myself I cried,
> "If Lucy should be dead!"

What distinguishes the language of this poem from that of the examples we have considered is not the words themselves but the purpose for which they are used. The vocabulary and word-order are no more and no less close to those of ordinary speech than those of Cowper. But the language here is used not to make a 'poetic' statement but to convey the impressions and feelings which constitute the lover's intrinsically poetic experience. We do not have an analogy established by the conscious articulate mind of the poet between the idea of the setting of the moon and the idea of human mortality, something like "Our fate the moving moon writes in the sky/ For she must set and all of us must die." Wordsworth is concerned not with an intellectual formulation but with an intuitive awareness produced by a certain conjunction of impressions on a particular state of mind; with, we might say, a figure of experience rather than a figure of speech.

The difference is apparent when we examine the relation between the poem and the events which it describes. The speaker in the poem, the lover, is not really thinking at all. As he rides along, he is lulled into a kind of stupor much like that which Wordsworth elsewhere describes in the lines "A slumber did my spirit seal;/ I had no human fears." He is aware of the measured movement of his horse, the slow movement of the moon, but he is not *thinking* about them. And the sudden disappearance of the moon does not lead him to *think about* human mortality. Unexpected though inevitable, the setting of the moon produces not an intellectual response but an emotional shock, a sudden fear which tears from him, without his understanding why, the words "O mercy, if Lucy should be dead." We can, certainly, construct a series of conceptual steps to lead from the perception of the setting moon to the thought of Lucy's death. But the lover does not do this. The connection takes place below the level of consciousness. For him, it is an impulsive and spontaneous association, an example of "fond and way-ward thoughts."

The purpose of the language of the poem, then, is not to define verbal and intellectual relationships which are not part of the lover's consciousness but so to involve us in the situation that we share the lover's awareness as we might if we found ourselves in fact in the same state of mind and in the same circumstances. We are not given the poet's description of a lover who sees and feels but are led in imagina-tion to see and feel as he does. The sequence of images is the sequence of the lover's impressions and the words—*moon, lea, orchard, hill*—introduce no extraneous associations. The rhythm of the poem conveys the almost hypnotic effect of the slow, jogging movement of the horse:

> My horse moved on; hoof after hoof
> He raised, and never stopped:
> When down behind the cottage roof,
> At once, the bright moon dropped.

And with the heavy syllable *dropped,* this rhythm is broken as the disappearance of the moon breaks the lover's dreamy trance. All this prepares us for the lover's final words by producing in us a sympathetic identification with him.

The difference in the function of the language here from what we have considered earlier may be clearer if we think how little of Words-worth's poem would be lost if the same situation and images were pre-sented in a film, silent except for the lover's final words. Cowper's lines obviously could not be so presented. Or take the following couplet from a lover's complaint in one of Pope's pastorals:

> The bleating sheep with my complaint agree,
> They parched with heat; and I inflamed by thee.

A *picture* of a passionate lover bewailing his condition surrounded by thirsty bleating sheep would be either ludicrous or pointless. The com-parison works only when it is put into these words: we have to think of *heat* on the one hand and *inflamed* on the other. With Wordsworth, we have to *see* the moon and *feel* the shock of its disappearance.

These characteristics of "Strange Fits of Passion" may bring us back for a moment to the question of the language of "conversation" and of "humble and rustic life." In the first place, we may now observe that the language of ordinary conversation does not differ from that of eighteenth century poetry only in vocabulary. We have said that the eighteenth century poetic world was verbal and conceptual. And the poet assumes as the basis of communication that his reader will share the same intellectual and literary background, will have the same conceptual and literary associations. In conversation, while we of course assume that our listener will attach more or less the same definitions to words that we do, we also depend a great deal on the assumption of a common humanity, of common experience or potential for experience. We expect our listener to know more than we can say. This is why we so often use expressions such as "you understand me" or "you can imagine how I feel." Wordsworth's language is conversational in this sense. His words are more frequently suggestive than definitive. Pope's lines assume that we are familiar with the ideas which his words denote and perhaps with the literary tradition from which they derive. They do not require that we have any actual experience of shepherds or sheep, of grief or love. Wordsworth's lines however do depend upon remembered experience, upon the reader's ability in imagination to ride a plodding horse under an evening moon, and upon his having felt or being capable of feeling as a lover. Pope's lines are addressed to the literate and sophisticated reader; Wordsworth's are but for "the lover's ear alone," since only he will understand how I feel. If the reader is unable to be a lover while he reads the poem, a part of the basis of communication is lost and the poem fails.

Such explicit indication of the role which the reader must assume is common in Wordsworth, and where it is not explicit it is nevertheless implicit. And where he appears to have failed, when a poem seems trivial or silly, the cause is often the reader's inability to make the necessary sympathetic identification. This is a difficulty of which Wordsworth was aware. "I am sensible," he wrote in the Preface, "that my associations must have sometimes been particular instead of general [and] . . . that my language may frequently have suffered from those arbitrary connections of feelings and ideas with particular words and phrases from which no man can altogether protect himself. Hence I have no doubt that, in some instances, feelings, even of the ludicrous, may be given to my Readers by expressions which appeared to me tender and pathetic." But his intention is to assume "this knowledge which all men carry about with them" simply by being human, and "these sympathies in which, without any other discipline than that of our daily life, we are fitted to take delight."

We are now in a better position to understand Wordsworth's concern with the situations and language of "humble and rustic life." In humble life, Wordsworth believes, we find most clearly, unobscured and undistorted, the essentials, the universals, of human experience in which all men share. "In that condition the essential passions of the heart find a better soil . . . our elementary feelings co-exist in a state of greater simplicity, and, consequently, may be more accurately contemplated, and more forcibly communicated." And the language of humble life is the universally intelligible expression of the essentials of human experience:

> They convey their feelings and notions in simple and unelaborated expressions. Accordingly, such a language, arising out of repeated experience and regular feelings, is a more permanent, and a far more philosophical language, than that which is frequently substituted for it by Poets, who think that they are conferring honor upon themselves and their art in proportion as they separate themselves from the sympathies of men, and indulge in arbitrary and capricious habits of expression, in order to furnish food for fickle tastes and fickle appetites of their own creation.

It is apparent that Wordsworth's concern is not with simple verbal fidelity but with function, with the fact, as he believes, that it is essentially a pure and immediate expression of what all human beings think and feel.

"Strange Fits of Passion" is a particularly simple and obvious illustration of the characteristics which we have been discussing. But the relevance of what we have said is not confined to this and similar poems. It also helps us to understand what is involved in cases where Wordsworth seems to depart much more drastically from what we would at first have thought of as simple and colloquial. As a final example, let us consider "Nutting." This is a slightly longer poem, but I shall quote it entire as otherwise its character would be obscured.

It seems a day
(I speak of one from many singled out)
One of those heavenly days that cannot die;
When, in the eagerness of boyish hope,
I left our cottage-threshold, sallying forth
With a huge wallet o'er my shoulder slung,
A nutting-crook in hand; and turned my steps
Tow'rd some far-distant wood, a Figure quaint,

Tricked out in proud disguise of cast-off weeds
Which for that service had been husbanded,
By exhortation of my frugal Dame—
Motley accoutrement, of power to smile
At thorns, and brakes, and brambles—and, in truth,
More ragged than need was! O'er pathless rocks,
Through beds of matted fern, and tangled thickets,
Forcing my way, I came to one dear nook
Unvisited, where not a broken bough
Dropped with its withered leaves, ungracious sigh
Of devastation; but the hazels rose
Tall and erect, with tempting clusters hung,
A virgin scene!—A little while I stood,
Breathing with such suppression of the heart
As joy delights in; and, with wise restraint,
Voluptuous, fearless of a rival, eyed
The banquet;—or beneath the trees I sate
Among the flowers, and with the flowers I played;
A temper known to those, who, after long
And weary expectation, have been blest
With sudden happiness beyond all hope.
Perhaps it was a bower beneath whose leaves
The violets of five seasons re-appear
And fade, unseen by any human eye;
Where fairy water-breaks do murmur on
For ever; and I saw the sparkling foam,
And—with my cheek on one of those green stones
That, fleeced with moss, under the shady trees,
Lay round me, scattered like a flock of sheep—
I heard the murmur and the murmuring sound,
In that sweet mood when pleasure loves to pay
Tribute to ease; and, of its joy secure,
The heart luxuriates with indifferent things,
Wasting its kindliness on stocks and stones,
And on the vacant air. Then up I rose,
And dragged to earth both branch and bough, with crash
And merciless ravage; and the shady nook
Of hazels, and the green and mossy bower,
Deformed and sullied, patiently gave up
Their quiet being; and unless I now
Confound my present feelings with the past;
Ere from the mutilated bower I turned
Exulting, rich beyond the wealth of kings,
I felt a sense of pain when I beheld
The silent trees, and saw the intruding sky—
Then, dearest Maiden, move along these shades
In gentleness of heart; with gentle hand
Touch—for there is a spirit in the woods.

As was the case in "Strange Fits of Passion," this poem centers on a moment of sudden awareness which involves a relation between the perception of natural phenomena and a particular state of mind. But in this case the language seems much more complicated and much less colloquial. Some of it, as in the other poem, is purely and vividly descriptive. But near the beginning we find

> a Figure quaint,
> Tricked out in proud disguise of cast-off weeds
> Which for that service had been husbanded,
> By exhortation of my frugal Dame—
> Motley accoutrement, . . .

lines which by no stretch of definition could be called conversational or rustic language. And from the phrase "a virgin scene" onwards we are increasingly aware of a figurative use of language which makes us see the literal action of the poem as a rape: *virgin scene, voluptuous, merciless ravage, deformed and sullied, mutilated.* Both of these would seem to be departures from the language of "Strange Fits of Passion," and in both cases we need to consider the function which this language serves in this poem.

This figurative language, then, however much it may differ from sort that Wordsworth considered the real "language of passion" and therefore proper to poetry. It is not the writer who sees and states an analogy between the boy's actions and a rape. The analogy is implicit in the experience and remains implicit in the language. There is in the boy's consciousness an extra level of awareness, a sense that nature is not merely something to be used, that there is "a spirit in the woods." And it is this which makes the experience significant. The boy does not draw the analogy any more than does the lover; he does not say "I felt as if I had committed a rape." There is only "a sense of pain." But that sense of pain derives from the fact that the grove *seemed* to him not merely tempting or beautiful but *virginal* and aroused in him a kind of lust, a *voluptuous* desire. He feels as if nature were a living woman as lover-like he fondles the flowers, feasts his sight on violets "unseen by any human eye," nestles his cheek on a mossy stone. And it is these feelings that make his action an assault, a "merciless ravage" and that produce, mixed with his sensual satisfaction, a sense of regret, of "pain."

This figurative language, then ,however much it may differ from that of ordinary or rustic speech, performs the function which Wordsworth attributed to such speech. The same cannot, however, be said of the lines earlier in the poem which describe the boy setting out dressed in an assortment of worn-out clothes. The language here seems, in Wordsworth's phrase, to involve the writer's attempt to "trick out or elevate nature." It does not serve to render more exactly the impressions and feelings of the boy but if anything obscures them. We are more conscious of the rhetoric than of the image. But the point is that in this case there *are* no significant impressions or feelings; there is nothing that forms part of the pattern of experience which is the heart and focus of the poem. The image is in itself uninteresting, neutral. And Wordsworth appears to have resorted to purely verbal elaboration in order to make this image *seem* "poetic," *seem* in keeping with the whole poem. This is not the "language of nature" but is much closer to the kind of thing which Wordsworth so vigorously and frequently condemns.

"Nutting" moves, we may say, from a purely ordinary world to a world of heightened awareness and significance, from a world of objects and events which we need only recognize to a world in which there is a more intense and more complex interaction between nature and human consciousness. And as we move from one world to the other, the language changes from one which lends a 'poetic' coloring to objects and events to one which embodies a poetic experience, to, that is, the "language of nature."

Such a situation, such a movement, is common in Wordsworth and reveals, I think, the role that the "language of nature" actually plays. For him, moments of sudden intuition, "spots of time," "gleams like the flashing of a shield" were the focal points of experience, the source of truth and wisdom. It was for the expression of such moments that the poetic language of his day seemed inadequate, and it is in his expression of such moments that we find the "language of nature" most clearly exemplified and most amply justified. But as even for him such moments did not constitute all of experience, so we do not find him always writing in the language of nature.

Not all experience is of such intensity as to seem to dominate language, to demand and determine its own form. It is this which leads Wordsworth to look elsewhere for support. Sometimes he employs an ornate diction like that in "Nutting" or in these lines from *The Prelude*:

> Our daily meals were frugal, Sabine fare!
> More than we wished we knew the blessing then
> Of vigorous hunger—hence corporeal strength
> Unsapped by delicate viands; . . .

More often he turns to an elaborate rhetoric as in this passage, again from *The Prelude*:

> More frequently from the same source I drew
> A pleasure quiet and profound, a sense
> Of permanent and universal sway,
> And paramount belief; there, recognized
> A type, for finite natures, of the one
> Supreme Existence, the surpassing life
> Which—to the boundaries of space and time,
> Of melancholy space and doleful time,
> Superior and incapable of change,
> Nor touched by welterings of passion—is,
> And hath the name of, God. Transcendent peace
> And silence did await upon these thoughts
> That were a frequent comfort to my youth.

In Wordsworth's later and generally inferior work, such language becomes more and more frequent, the "language of nature" more and more rare. But in the earlier Wordsworth and the best, we can trace the ebb and flow of his visionary passion in the ebb and flow of a language which if sometimes turgid or ornate repeatedly thins away to a pure transparency through which we are confronted with elemental forms of terror and delight in which, for Wordsworth, lay man's closest approach to reality and truth.

Leon Barron

Wordsworth's <u>Michael</u>
as Transposed Epic

In suffusing the commonplace with mystery, perhaps no other poem in the Wordsworth canon satisfies the demands of The Preface to *Lyrical Ballads* so well as "Michael." Except for the rather startling remark that Luke "carried in his cheek/ Two steady roses that were five years old," the poem is strikingly bare of metaphor, poetic diction, and other traditional ornaments. It contains little of the elevation that distinguishes "Tintern Abbey" and the "Ode on Intimations." With almost complete prosiness, it tells the history of the industrious old couple who lose their only child to the wickedness of the city. The line of blank verse is rarely respected as a unit of sense or rhythm; the usual pattern is a run-on so flat as to be comic when considered in isolation: "Distressful tidings. Long before the time." Although subtitled "A Pastoral Poem," and set in the country, "Michael" is apparently without the arguments, the ritualized deaths and mournings, the celebrations, courtships or rebirths that are found in conventional expressions of that genre. Nature, to be sure, informs the work, but it neither fades nor blooms in reflection of the adversity or well-being of the central character. Instead of a formalized request to weep for Michael or Luke or even Isabel, we find only the slow accumulation of detail and the casual tone of a speaker who claims little for the history except that it "was the first/ Of those domestic tales that spake to me/ Of shepherds, dwellers in the valleys, men/ Whom I already loved" (11. 21-24), that it is "not unfit, I deem, for the fireside,/ Or for the summer shade," and that it is related "For the delight of a few natural hearts" and "for the sake/ Of youthful poets" (11. 36-38). Despite all this, "Michael" is one of Wordsworth's most moving poems. It is successful, I believe, because we sense that the apparent artlessness

123

is informed by patterns and devices usually found in more traditional works. These devices are treated so organically, attuned so precisely to the key of Wordsworth's song, that, instead of being glaringly obvious they act as subtle intensifiers of the deceptively simple tale.

Some of these devices are to be found in the method of elevating the figure of the shepherd, making him large enough to convey the cluster of important themes transmitted by the poem. First of all—and here is the great paradox behind this simple story of a dweller in the valley—Wordsworth used conventions usually associated with the epic, transforming or "transposing" them by understatement to satisfy the demands of the tone and subject matter of his "pastoral." Some of these conventions—the massing of detail, the scope of time, the mood of nostalgic retrospection, the episodic quality, the beginning, if you will, *in medias res*—seem at first glance rather fortuitous, but, supported by others, argue an intentional enlargement of the picture of a man whose homely shepherd's task is interpreted as having proportions of grandeur. In this respect, we note the metamorphosis of Michael from domesticated rustic into hero. Physically and mentally, he is given some of the extraordinary attributes of a Ulysses or a Moses. "His bodily frame had been from youth to age/ Of an unusual strength" (11. 43-44), the speaker tells us twice; once before getting into the story proper, and once again after the catastrophe (11. 460-61). At sixty-seven he sired a child; at eighty-four he resumed tasks that would have been almost impossible for an ordinary man. Up to his death at ninety-one, he was able to go among the rocks, tend his sheep, work at his fold. Mentally, too, Michael was superior, suggestive even of the quick-witted Ulysses:

> His mind was keen,
> Intense and frugal, apt for all affairs,
> And in his shepherd's calling he was prompt
> And watchful more than ordinary men.
> (11. 43-47)

His mental and physical excellence had prepared him for a communion with nature that parallels an epic hero's conversation with the gods, or even Moses' receiving the Commandments:

> Hence had he learned the meaning of all winds,
> Of blasts of every tone; and, oftentimes,
> When others heeded not, he heard the south
> Make subterraneous music, like the noise
> Of bagpipers on distant Highland hills.

> The shepherd, at such warning, of his flock
> Bethought him, and he to himself would say,
> "The winds are now devising work for me!"
> And, truly, at all times, the storm—that drives
> The traveller to a shelter—summoned him
> Up to the mountains: he had been alone
> Amid the heart of many thousand mists,
> That came to him and left him on the heights.
> (11. 48-60)

It was, of course, by means of such communion that Michael's relationship with Nature, strengthened in accordance with the Romantic doctrine of association, became "A pleasurable feeling of blind love" (1. 78), composed of moral virtues such as courage, cheerfulness, kindness, and even "the certainty of honorable gain."

Just as this aptness of mind suggests that of the Greek hero, and the communions on the mountain resemble those of Moses, so the occasion for the catastrophe recalls another traditional motif, toned down, to be sure. Like King Arthur betrayed by his nephew, or King Mark duped by Tristam, Michael comes to difficulty because he had been "bound/ In surety for his brother's son" (11. 216-17). He forgives his nephew, but not before expressing more than a note of dissatisfaction:

> An evil man
> That was, and made an evil choice, if he
> Were false to us; and if he wrote not false,
> There are ten thousand to whom loss like this
> Had been no sorrow. I forgive him—but
> 'Twere better to be dumb than to talk thus.
> (11. 242-47)

But more immediately apparent than the uncle-nephew relationship is the theme of dynastic succession, characteristic of great epics whether literary or traditional. The difficulties of continuing a line, or reinstating a family, are to be found in Michael as surely as they are in the *Aeneid* or the *Odyssey*. Hence the stress, during Michael's last scene with Luke, upon the past and the labor of clearing the title to the original inheritance so that it can be passed on intact:

> Even to the utmost I have been to thee
> A kind and good father: and herein
> I but repay a gift which I myself
> Received at others' hands; for though now old
> Beyond the common life of man, I still

126

WORDSWORTH'S MICHAEL AS TRANSPOSED EPIC

Remember them who loved me in my youth.
Both of them sleep together: here they lived
As all their forefathers had done; and when
At length their time was come, they were not loath
To give their bodies to the family mould.
. . . .
These fields were burdened when they came to me;
Till I was forty years of age, not more
Than half of my inheritance was mine.
I toiled and toiled; God blessed me in my work,
And till these last three weeks past the land was free.

(ll. 367-84)

or again:

amid all
And all temptation, Luke, I pray that thou
Mayst bear in mind the life thy fathers lived,
Who being innocent, did for that cause
Bestir them in good deeds.

(ll. 414-18)

The relationship between father and son is even closer than in most epics, for Michael is also the Chiron to his Achilles, instructing him in the lessons of his life and trade, and fulfilling the role of playmate as well as that of mentor. In connection with this role of instructor, we note that the staff which Michael gives to his son is described as if it were the epic making of an heroic weapon:

Then Michael from a winter coppice cut
With his own hand a sapling, which he hooped
With iron, making it throughout in all
Due requisites a perfect shepherd's staff,
And gave it to the boy. . . .

(ll. 186-90)

To illustrate further the uncommon ordinariness of his hero, Woodsworth uses another technique often found in the epics, in which the central figure not only dwarfs the other human characters but is constantly the object of their vigilance as the possible source of their hope or despair, as Ulysses and Achilles were to the suitors of Ithaca and the armies of Troy. Although there is no overt statement that Michael's actions could have effect upon his neighbors, we are shown throughout the poem that he is constantly watched, and that when he is dead

his story continues as legend, ready to be retold for the edification of
the curious. Michael's family, we are told, "were as a proverb in the
vale/ For endless industry" (ll. 96-97). The very light from their cot-
tage was constantly observed:

> This light was famous in its neighbourhood,
> And was a public symbol of the life
> The thrifty pair had lived. . . .
> And from this constant light, so regular
> And so far seen, the house itself by all
> Who dwelt within the limits of the vale,
> Both old and young, was named The Evening Star.
>   (ll. 136-46)

Similarly, Michael and Luke were observed by circles of neighbors as
they sat in the shade of "The Clipping Tree, a name which yet it bears"
(l. 175). And after Luke's transportation, the observation continued:

> I have conversed with more than one who well
> Remember the old man and what he was
> Years after he had heard this heavy news.
>   (ll. 457-59)

In addition to enhancing his subject by means of epic conventions,
Wordsworth employs patterns originating in works more purely religious,
such as the story of Moses already mentioned, a borrowing not startling
in view of the theme of natural piety that informs the poem. Perhaps
his Biblical readings, especially the story of Samson and Manoa, were
in his mind as he had Michael inform Luke:

> with full heart
> I look upon thee, for thou art the same
> That wert a promise to me ere thy birth. . . .
>   (ll. 388-40)

We notice, too, the father's reference to the unbuilt sheepfold as a
covenant, a promise of his permanent love for Luke, a nomination and a
purpose reminiscent of the epilogue to the story of The Flood.

Supported and enhanced by heroic devices, Michael is visualized
not as an ordinary shepherd but as a man apart, whose actions and
affairs are capable of conveying meanings of almost transcendental co-

gency. What could have been mere sentimentality or pathos, had the shepherd not been so heroically set, now becomes tragedy. Like many a tragic hero, Michael in attempting to live up to his own principles is the means of his own catastrophe. Having struggled to obtain a clear title to his land, he is loath to leave it encumbered. Although he suspects the city and is disquieted by the thought of submitting Luke to its evil influences, he sends his son off, believing that only in this way can he leave the boy his rightful inheritance and justify his lifetime of industry. One verse paragraph is enough to indicate the boy's moral collapse and his transportation; no details are necessary about urban life because Michael's is the action we are to study; his response will be the measure of his strength. That he can live an additional seven years, tending his sheep and even working occasionally on the sheepfold is the signature of his greatness. Habits of diligence have so framed his mind that the depth of his grief can be gauged only by a rumor:

> And 'tis believed by all
> That many and many a day he thither went,
> And never lifted up a single stone.
>   (11. 470-72)

Given a man whose industry had been raised to heroic proportions, the failure to act becomes the symbol of the destruction of the habits of a lifetime, the blasted hope.

Most of the themes of "Michael" are thus conveyed by a central character whose treatment is epical: the personalization of the natural is opposed to the anonymity of the city; the world of pious industry is opposed to the world of trade; progress, that unfeeling plow of enclosure which has been through Michael's small holding, has dismantled all but the evidences of the sheepfold and his other personal symbol, the old oak tree. Michael, the hero of a former, more noble, more independent way of life, has gone. A golden age has passed; Ulysses will never again see Telemachus.

But still more is said about Michael by means of the speaker of the poem, the voice which celebrates the hero and the earlier way of life. Upon initial consideration, this speaker is handled rather erratically, intruding autobiographically at the beginning of the poem, again emerging at line 216 to explain the antecedent circumstances which force Michael to jeopardize Luke's future, and reappearing again only in the penultimate verse paragraph to indicate the history of the shepherd's last years. One has the feeling, however, that the speaker's appearance do not in any way detract from the total structure and intention but somehow fortify them. What one senses here, as in the narrative proper, is an organic mingling of epic devices with those characteristic of the pastoral elegy.

In this respect, the opening verse paragraph may be seen as an equivalent to the prefatory argument of ancient epics. In this argument, however, it is not "arms and the man" but "nature and the man" that we are told about, and there is an unaccustomed intimacy in the voice of the bard, a note of personal implication quite foreign to the music of an epic singer. Here, I believe, conventional aspects of the pastoral elegy must be considered.

Since "Michael" is, in short, a celebration of the dead, a mourning, though unconventionally expressed, Wordsworth, like Milton before him, must establish a personal relationship with the object of his tribute, showing that his praise is based upon first-hand knowledge. He had not, in any strict sense, gone to school with Michael, nor had he driven flocks afield with him, but he had, he informs us, responded similarly to the same natural settings and stimuli. Like the shepherd, the speaker had been instructed and formed by his contact with nature. We are told how the book of Michael's being was written:

> Fields where with cheerful spirits he had breathed
> The common air; the hills, which he so oft
> Had climbed with vigorous steps; which had impressed
> So many incidents upon his mind
> Of hardship, skill or courage, joy or fear;
> Which like a book preserved the memory
> Of the dumb animals, whom he had saved,
> Had fed or sheltered, linking to such acts,
> So grateful in themselves, the certainty
> Of honourable gain, these fields, these hills,
> Which were his living being, even more
> Than his own blood—what could they less? had laid
> Strong hold on his affections, were to him
> A pleasurable feeling of blind love,
> The pleasure which there is in life itself.
>
> (11. 65-79)

The speaker, too, in giving his credentials, reveals his membership in this spiritual university. Of the story of Michael, he says:

> It was the first
> Of those domestic tales that spake to me
> Of shepherds, dwellers in the valleys, men

Whom I already loved;—not verily
For their own sakes, but for the fields and hills
Where was their occupation and abode.
And hence this tale, while I was yet a boy
Careless of books, yet having felt the power
Of nature, by the gentle agency
Of natural objects led me on to feel
For passions that were not my own, and think
(At random and imperfectly indeed)
On man, the heart of man, and human life.

(11. 21-33)

Because, then, he had been prepared by an intercourse with nature similar to that which Michael had experienced, he was able to understand and to be morally strengthened by the shepherd's story. In other words, to one who has the proper faith, Michael, like Lycidas, has become "a Genius of the shore/ For all who wonder on the perilous flood." Having fulfilled himself, he is not to be mourned but praised.

Milton wrote "Lycidas" compelled by a "sad occasion drear" which he had to objectify in order to understand. In the early sections of the poem, he announces that one of his hopes is to establish a connection with those who come after him, especially with the poet who might "in passing turn,/ And bid fair peace be to my sable urn." Wordsworth, too, hopes to exercise an influence upon posterity. In his reshaping of this convention, he states that his tale is intended:

For the delight of a few natural hearts;
And, with yet fonder feelings, for the sake
Of youthful poets, who among these hills
Will be my second self when I am gone.
(11. 36-39)

But we note something more here. Wordsworth wants to do what Milton had done, but he also wants to fulfill Michael's desire: to leave clear title to a spiritual inheritance. Like Milton's shepherd, who in understanding the meaning of King's death and rebirth is reborn himself, emerging from the depths of self-consciousness and fear to "green pastures new," Wordsworth's speaker has identified himself with Michael. He has gone through the same sort of experience, becoming him, not in Christ perhaps, but in natural religion. Understanding Michael has meant understanding himself and the general problems of man, and he wishes to bequeath this understanding to others who will become his "second self."

It is perhaps because of his identification with Michael that the speaker, as an individual, vanishes in the last verse paragraph. We have a picture of the old shepherd as he was last seen, sitting by the sheepfold with his faithful dog, a rapid statment about the deaths of Michael and his wife, and a curt reminder about the "great changes" which have been wrought by the new era. Then the poem concludes in understatement, a brief but slow-cadenced reminder of the things that have resisted change:

> yet the oak
> That grew beside their door; and the remains
> Of the unfinished sheep-fold may be seen
> Beside the boisterous brook of Green-head Ghyll.

Permanence is thus pitted against change and is triumphant. The three surviving symbols—the oak, the sheepfold, and the brook—exist as memorial to the life lived close to nature. Enhanced by conventions common to the pastoral elegy and the epic, Michael's unassuming life was shown to be heroic, a fit and inspirational lesson for future generations.

Arnold Silver

The
Wordsworthian Dialetic

In considering the work of a great poet of Nature, it is fitting to begin with a generalization about earthly life. Animals and plants, as we know, require for their survival some sort of cooperation between opposing forces. Destruction and construction, for example, must both be at work within us if we are to stay alive: the food we pulverize gives birth to energy, skin tissue dies so as to allow for needed replacement, leaves must fall before the new life of the tree can emerge. Again, contrary motions must exist in balance: the downthrust of a tree's roots sustains the upthrust of its stem, the movement of the blood towards the heart is counterpoised by a movement away from the heart. If either force is deprived of its opposite, the organism dies.

Similarly in art, opposing forces must be present, and a perpetually threatened equilibrium must be maintained. If either force gets the upper hand, the art work dies. Variety and regularity, for example, must both contribute to the rhythmic life of a poem, a symphony or a dance. Relentless variation of rhythm creates chaos, relentless regularity produces the dead monotony of a clock. This presence and competition of opposing forces in a work of art is called its dialectic, though a proviso should at once be added that the competition is somehow made invisible by the artist. For one of the mysteries of art is the fusion of opposing forces into a new force greater than the sum of its components. Such a fusion, or synthesis—which Coleridge termed the essential achievement of the creative imagination—aims to have a unified and harmonious effect on the reader. But for purposes of appreciating the artist's accomplishment, we may sometimes take his fusion and reduce it to its separate components, dissecting by analysis the living seamless tissue of the poem.

Let us contemplate a much-loved sonnet by Wordsworth in terms of its dialectic. It is entitled "Composed Upon Westminster Bridge," and in it Wordsworth describes the view of London in early morning:

> Earth has not anything to show more fair:
> Dull would he be of soul who could pass by
> A sight so touching in its majesty:
> This City now doth, like a garment, wear
> The beauty of the morning; silent, bare,
> Ships, towers, domes, theatres, and temples lie
> Open unto the fields, and to the sky;
> All bright and glittering in the smokeless air.
> Never did sun more beautifully steep
> In his first splendour, valley, rock, or hill;
> Ne'er saw I, never felt, a calm so deep!
> The river glideth at his own sweet will:
> Dear God! the very houses seem asleep;
> And all that mighty heart is lying still!

Now one set of opposing forces in this lovely poem clearly relates to action. The city is caught at a moment of nearly total immobility, the very houses seem asleep. Yet that there is action in the poem is indicated by the glittering of the buildings, the gliding of the waters, the sun's saturating the scene with its rays. The last line, "And all that mighty heart is lying still," wonderfully fuses action and inaction, for the mighty heart suggests a ceaseless pulsation of energy which we cannot completely banish from our minds even though we are told that momentarily the heart is lying still. In addition, the poem strengthens its thematic harmonies by fusing the traditional discord between city and country. The city's towers, domes and theatres lie open unto the country's fields, unto a sky which overarches both city and country, and unto a sun which shines on both with equal beauty. The sky-directed towers, spires and masts are akin to the sky-directed mountains and hills of the country. That which is man-made is usually opposed to that which is made by nature, yet in this poem the man-made is felt to be a part of nature: mother earth has not anything to show more fair than this city at this moment. Again, we customarily associate a city with power, and at the close of the poem we have the reference to the city's mighty heart. But Wordsworth plays off against this a daring opposite notion, for he makes us feel a degree of tenderness towards this powerful organism. He has it lying open and vulnerable to the fields and sky, accepting without resistance the sun's steeping beams. The city is given the vulnerability of a sleeping child. True, it has majesty, but it is a "touching" majesty, the very adjective we often use in conjunction with the childlike or the pathetic.

The most pervasive opposition in the poem, however, is between explicit praise of the city and implicit criticism. The praise is there in almost every line, visible criticism is entirely missing. Yet in a remarkable fusion of opposites, the criticism is really contained in the praise, or rather in the type of praise. The city is beautiful because it is nearly dead as a city. Its characteristic noise, smoke, swirling activity and swarming life are absent. It has none of the din, the joyless daylight, the fretful stir and feverishness that Wordsworth identified with the city in "Tintern Abbey." Though admiring the city at dawn, Wordsworth selects items for praise which indicate that he would not celebrate the city when it is most typically itself. One might almost say that he is praising death, at the birth of a new day.

Here, then, we have an amalgam of opposite forces that gives the poem its quiet tensile strength. It alloys inaction with action, city with country, power with touching weakness, explicit praise with implicit condemnation, birth with death.

Now this way of approaching a poem is of course only one among several useful approaches, and it can be applied not only to the dialectic within the subject matter but also to the dialectic between language and subject, rhythm and imagery, facts and ideas. The method differs somewhat from the valuable one advocated by Professor Cleanth Brooks, who argues in his influential book *The Well Wrought Urn* that poems can best be examined as successful paradoxes, paradoxes which are carefully excluded from the world of science. The presence of paradoxes in the sonnet we have just examined lends support to Professor Brooks' contention, but I believe that if we use the Coleridgean technique of seeing works of art as a fusion of opposites, the yield from analysis will be greater; and we may also see, as Coleridge saw, that poetry possesses what all other vital entities and living organisms in the universe possess, and that therefore the literary critic and the scientific analyst are often engaged in a similar enterprise. The physicist may seek to identify the opposing forces of attraction and repulsion in an atom and to disclose the ways in which these forces are interdependent. The biologist may study the life of a single self-absorbed cell and then turn to the dynamic equilibrium it establishes with all other cells in a complex living organism.

In Wordsworth the fusion of opposites can be noticed in varying degrees in every one of his poems although it is not always in the subject matter itself. Consider the delicate lyric "She Was a Phantom of Delight," with its description of a woman happily engrossed in earthly tasks while being simultaneously a lovely apparition, a spirit "bright with something of angelic light." Consider the sonnet called "Nuns Fret not at Their Convent's Narrow Room," which explores as well as exemplifies the union of bondage with freedom. Observe that the sonnet to Milton ("London, 1802") honors the great poet for himself combining in the course of his life the opposing demands of living humbly in the world and yet living majestically apart from the world. Take the last of the Lucy poems, "A Slumber Did My Spirit Seal," which fuses, with marvellous simplicity of utterance, the polar opposites of life and death.

But let us look with a little closer regard at another beautiful Wordsworth poem, "I Wandered Lonely as a Cloud," for indeed this one might seem at first glance to lack any dynamic oppositions.

> I wandered lonely as a cloud
> That floats on high o'er vales and hills,
> When all at once I saw a crowd,
> A host, of golden daffodils;
> Beside the lake, beneath the trees,
> Fluttering and dancing in the breeze.
>
> Continuous as the stars that shine
> And twinkle on the milky way,
> They stretched in never-ending line
> Along the margin of a bay:
> Ten thousand saw I at a glance,
> Tossing their heads in sprightly dance.
>
> The waves beside them danced; but they
> Out-did the sparkling waves in glee:
> A poet could not but be gay,
> In such a jocund company:
> I gazed—and gazed—but little thought
> What wealth the show to me had brought:
>
> For oft, when on my couch I lie
> In vacant or in pensive mood,
> They flash upon that inward eye
> Which is the bliss of solitude;
> And then my heart with pleasure fills,
> And dances with the daffodils.

Surely here, we incline to say, is a simple and innocently lyrical celebration of a beautiful natural scene, yet scrutiny reveals that the poet
achieves this simplicity by artfully mastering (not banishing) complex-
ities, by successfully fusing (not eliminating) opposites. The goldenness
of the daffodils remains bright in our minds partly because Wordsworth
has hinted at the blackness of night. And their gaiety is made more
memorable by having been quietly contrasted with the poet's loneliness
—quietly because the poem is combining its opposites rather than calling attention to them. Then again, we have Wordsworth's wonted per-
sonification of nature as he describes the daffodils in terms of human
activities: dancing, tossing their heads, expressing glee. The opposite at
this point is, ironically, the poet himself, whose passivity is almost veg-
etable like. At the opening of the poem he is without will or inner
direction, moving with the passivity of a cloud floating on wind currents; in the last stanza he is lying on a couch in a vacant mood or
letting his mind wander dreamily.

But the most noteworthy fusion of opposites is that between the self
and the many, the lonely poet and the crowd of flowers. The contrast
between these two is not at all a quiet one throughout most of the poem.
In fact, until the last stanza it is emphasized, and the poet is happy to
replace his loneliness by remembering the jocund company of dancing
flowers. Yet the equilibrium between the one and the many is restored
in the final stanza, for there Wordsworth does not say that when he
feels lonely and depressed he thinks happily of the daffodils. No, he
speaks of lying pensively on a couch, in solitude rather than loneliness,
quite enjoying a time of inwardness and dreamy meditation, the bliss
of inwardness provided by the solitude. Recollecting the daffodils, he
finds his heart filled with pleasure and dancing with them. In short,
he enjoys simultaneously the pleasures of being alone and of being in
company, of being pensive and of being merry. His pleasure is a compound one, a compound of opposites.

II

Were we to analyze attentively a number of a poet's poems, we
would begin to see not only a union of opposites but a union of particular sets of opposites. And in discovering these, we would come
close to the center of a poet's distinctive concerns, the particular dilemmas, or contradictory demands, that he tries to reconcile through the
power of his art and that give living tension to his art. They may be
personal, emotional dilemmas, or deeply felt intellectual dilemmas; they
may be the dilemmas of his age, to which he responds with eager

sensitivity, and internalizes. They may be all of these combined, with a consequent heightening of the pressures the poet brings to his work.

For Wordsworth there are I believe four intertwining dilemmas which regularly appear in his poems and comprise their total dialectic. One relates to his intense awareness of the manifold life of nature, "of all that we behold/ From this green earth, of all the mighty world/ Of eye and ear." But along with this went an unusually strong sense of an invisible power within or behind the world of phenomena,

> Of something far more deeply interfused,
> Whose dwelling is the light of setting suns,
> And the round ocean and the living air,
> And the blue sky, and in the mind of man:
> A motion and a spirit, that impels
> All thinking things, all objects of all thought,
> And rolls through all things.

And when feeling this, he finds that the welter of visible phenomena is penetrated and its inner life revealed. He calls it "that blessed mood":

> In which the burthen of the mystery,
> In which the heavy and the weary weight
> Of all this unintelligible world,
> Is lightened:—That serene and blessed mood,
> In which the affections gently lead us on,—
> Until, the breath of this corporeal frame
> And even the motion of our human blood
> Almost suspended, we are laid asleep
> In body, and become a living soul:
> While with an eye made quiet by the power
> Of harmony, and the deep power of joy,
> We see into the life of things.

Since the eye that sees into the life of things is not the physical eye, we can term this conflict one between the seen and the unseen world, between Wordsworth's attachment to the separate physical beauties of the world, and Wordsworth's sensing a unified spiritual realm beyond and greater than the material world. The poems "Nutting," "To the Cuckoo" and "She Was a Phantom of Delight" are typical explorations of this theme.

A second dilemma in Wordsworth, overlapping the first one but distinguishable from it, is that between the pleasures of childhood and those of adulthood. He longs to recapture the joys of his early years but he also desires the philosophic mind of adult life, the ability to "look on nature, not as in the hour/ Of thoughtless youth" for then she cannot "feed with lofty thoughts" our meditative moments. The satisfactions of childhood and of adult life seem mutually irreconcilable to Wordsworth, except in the reconciliation effected in his poetry. Since much of *The Prelude* and all of the "Immortality Ode" deal with this set of opposites, we shall return to it at a later point.

The third dilemma, often merging with the second, can be termed the conflict between freedom and necessity. Men, we readily admit, always seek some large justification for their actions: they legitimatize their behavior and desires by referring to God's will, or to society's ways, or to human nature, or to mother nature. Wordsworth used the last of these, and he read into nature, or took from her, principles that sanctioned his needs. And since these needs were often as conflicting for Wordsworth as for most of humanity, he often drew from nature opposite principles. In his earlier and generally greater poetry, until about 1804, he celebrates the unbounded freedom of natural forces. In his sonnet to Toussaint L'Ouverture, who was languishing in prison because of his attempt to free Haiti from French rule, Wordsworth says that Nature is on the side of liberty: "Thou hast left behind," he declares, "Powers that will work for thee; air, earth, and skies;/ There's not a breathing of the common wind/ That will forget thee." But alongside of this praise of liberty, and with increasing persistence after 1804, Wordsworth indicates the burdensomeness of liberty, the confusions and dangers it creates for its disciples. He is drawn to those of nature's children who patiently and predictably do what is expected of them, even though they be humble and obscure—daisies, celandines, daffodils, an isolated thorn tree. The *rootedness* of flowers and trees appeals to him, as do also such fixed and enduring things as rocks and mountains. (Shelley, by contrast, preferred birds and oceans, the restless and the free.) In the course of Wordsworth's development, Toussaint L'Ouverture is replaced by The Happy Warrior, who is able to endure, whose law is reason rather than feeling, who prefers domesticity to the wild delights of nature. The *Ode to Duty* (1805) most sharply expresses this dilemma, and opposites combine when the poet addresses duty as the "Stern Daughter of the Voice of God," "the Stern Lawgiver" upon whose countenance, nevertheless, there appears the fairest of smiles. "Me," the poet asserts:

> Me this unchartered freedom tires;
> I feel the weight of chance-desires:
> My hopes no more must change their name,
> I long for a repose that ever is the same.

Wordsworth probably found the sonnet form exceptionally congenial because, with its bounded freedom, it reconciled some opposing demands of his nature; and one may wonder whether his early liking for the form does not in itself emotionally prefigure the changes that later developed in his philosophy.

Finally we have the conflict between the self and society, or the one and the many. Wordsworth was a notably self-sufficient man, of strong character and highly developed ego. He much enjoyed being apart from other men, of being alone with nature, and he sympathetically identified with solitary men of the mountains—recluses, hermits, lonely wandering soldiers, isolated leech-gatherers, unattached beggars. Yet he strove to curb the misanthropic streak in his temperament, a streak made powerful by his precocious self-reliance and his vividly experienced companionship with natural objects. He strove to school himself to love other men and to concern himself with their tribulations. That usually the tribulations—as of Michael, or Alice Fell, or the leech-gatherer—had to be extreme before they could elicit Wordsworth's sympathies attests to the depth of his love of solitude; he had to use extreme instances in order to join his heart to the common pulse beat of humanity.

These major Wordsworthian dilemmas I have mentioned are not, of course, unknown in some measure to most human beings, and thus we are affected when this great poet honestly expresses them and grapples with them.

III

Turning now to Wordsworth's celebrated Preface to the second edition of the *Lyrical Ballads*, we may briefly summarize its main contentions in the light of the probability that they too will embody a dialectic, for any artist's theoretical formulations are born of his own special problems as an artist and are validated in the first instance by his own practices. Let us begin then with Wordsworth's famous definition of poetry:

> Poetry is the spontaneous overflow of powerful feelings; it takes its origin from emotion recollected in tranquillity: the emotion is contemplated till, by a species of reaction, the tranquillity gradually disappears, and an emotion, kindred to that which was before the subject of contemplation, is gradually produced, and does itself actually exist in the mind. In this mood successful composition generally begins, and in a mood similar to this it is carried on. . . .

Now a great deal has been written about this definition, and it certainly is in need of some qualification. Not all poetry takes its origin from emotion recollected in tranquillity, not even all of Wordsworth's poetry, as is indicated by the very title of the sonnet we discussed earlier: "Composed Upon Westminster Bridge." Yet surely Wordsworth's definition can apply to most poetry and to nearly all of his poetry, for when any human being is experiencing powerful feelings he is too involved in those feelings to take up pen and paper and describe his emotional state. To do so would, at the very least, dilute the feelings, and probably would destroy them. That other poem we considered a few pages back, "I Wandered Lonely as a Cloud," more typically represents the usual manner of poetic creation; one fancies that Wordsworth's heart was filled with pleasure at recollecting the dance of the daffodils and that he rose from his couch and began writing the poem. But as the poem itself amalgamates opposites, so too does Wordsworth's definition, for tranquillity precedes the powerful feelings, the bodily emotion is created by the mind's contemplation, premeditation results in spontaneity, and the past returns to present life.

Of his subject matter, Wordsworth says that he chose "incidents and situations from common life," and more specifically, from "humble and rustic life." We know exactly what he means if we recall the subjects of such poems as "The Old Cumberland Beggar," "The Solitary Reaper," "Resolution and Independence," "Peter Bell" and "Michael." He feels that too much eighteenth-century poetry has either omitted these country subjects or else sentimentally idealized them: Wordsworth's beggar from Cumberland will be a man with withered face and infirm mind scarcely able, when eating, to carry any scraps of food to his mouth because of the twitchings of his palsied hand. Wordsworth's own poetry would be dedicated to fulfilling this principle of realism, to dealing with the ordinary events of village and country life. The continuing vitality of poetry, he believes, required an emphasis on such subjects, as a counter-force to the poetry dealing with city and court, or with abstract ideas, or with idyllic shepherds, or with sensational happenings. But it is important to recognize that Wordsworth's impulse towards realism is prompted by something more than a desire to extend the range of poetry's subjects and by something very different from the tough-minded intention of most latter-day realists to open our eyes to the sordid truths of rural existence. On the contrary, Wordsworth believes that rural life is basically nobler than city life, that people in the country have less of their fundamental humanity corrupted than do their city cousins. In the country "the essential passions of the heart find a better soil in which they can attain their maturity. . . ." It is above all this conviction that prompts Wordsworth's realism and that also governs his strictures on poetic language.

For Wordsworth holds that the diction of poetry, to do justice to its subject matter, should also aim at realism, should incorporate the language really spoken by ordinary country people:

> Because such men hourly communicate with the best objects from which the best part of language is originally derived; and because, from their rank in society and the sameness and narrow circle of their intercourse, being less under the influence of social vanity, they convey their feelings and notions in simple and unelaborated expressions. Accordingly, such a language, arising out of repeated experience and regular feelings, is a more permanent and a far more philosophical language than that which is frequently substituted for it by Poets, who think that they are conferring honor upon themselves and their art, in proportion as they separate themselves from the sympathies of men, and indulge in arbitrary and capricious habits of expression, in order to furnish food for fickle tastes, and fickle appetites, of their own creation.

Now language usage oscillates between the poles of decoration and functionalism, between being an end in itself and being a means to an end. A man skilled in the use of words is tempted to form them into something deserving appreciation in itself; he makes, as it were, a verbal stained glass window. Carried too far, this use of language destroys its communicative function and darkens the vital relationship between art and life. Countering this tendency, Wordsworth calls for a language of utter transparency, one that will not add foreign splendors of diction to the passions and activities of the people being described. He tells us that he himself tried to avoid poetic diction, arbitrary and capricious habits of expression, and to use instead the plain and emphatic language of plain people. Since ornamental language, by calling attention to itself calls attention to the one who so cunningly fashioned it, Wordsworth goes on to say that the poet must subordinate himself to his material, endeavoring at all times to look steadily at the subject.

If we examine Wordsworth's assertions attentively, we will undoubtedly be able to see ways in which he overstates his position and universalizes his preferences. And we may fairly test our critical sharpness by measuring our conclusions against those of Wordsworth's friend and collaborator, Samuel Taylor Coleridge, whose *Biographia Literaria* (chapters fourteen through twenty) contains an acute and just account of the precise limitations of Wordsworth's theories. Yet with all the necessary modifications, it is still true that by insisting on a return to life and a return to the real language of men, and by showing in dozens of good poems and a few great ones how this might be done, Wordsworth impressively helped to revitalize English poetry at a time when it had grown enfeebled.

There is, however, one final aspect of the Preface that merits close attention since it bears directly upon Wordsworth's practice as a poet. I have implied earlier that in his argument against the poetry of his eighteenth-century predecessors, he upheld the overriding importance of subject matter rather than of language, that he wanted the subject matter almost to dictate the language. But if one wants a return to the prosaic realities of life, there is danger that the language will become prosaic; and if one uses the real language of men, one's poems will contain much that is vulgar and dull. And if the poet subordinates himself to his subject, the poem may become merely reportorial and thus be deprived of the poet's distinguishing voice and vision. Wordsworth's principles, if strictly followed, might indeed return us to life and the language used by men, but the poetry would be as monotonous and trivial as life itself can often be.

Wordsworth of course realized all this, and he tries to deal with these difficulties by introducing in the Preface various qualifications to his forceful assertions. He speaks of using "a selection of language really used by men," and of throwing "a certain coloring of imagination" over the incidents of common life. He speaks further of including a worthy purpose in each poem rather than merely giving reportorial realism, and of offering the reader immediate pleasure as well as moral improvement. We can, I am sure, perceive that some of these demands seem to oppose each other. The *selection* of language depends on the one who does the selecting and we are not told what principles determine the selection except, in effect, good taste; yet good taste shifts with the generations, and Wordsworth is himself busily arguing for a new standard of taste in subject matter and language. Again, imaginative coloring intrudes the poet on his subject matter, which presumably should be allowed to stand on its own; the coloring, moreover, is obviously secured by imaginative words among other means. Still again, both imagination and moral purpose depend upon the quality and character of the poet's own imagination and moral views. Wordsworth's modifications of his theories, in short, drive us back towards some of the very practices and principles he rejected, back towards poetic diction, and imaginative reshaping of chaotic reality, and the poet as a man apart from other men, "a man pleased with his own passions and volition, and who rejoices more than other men in the spirit of life that is in him." For all of Wordsworth's insistence that the poet should subordinate himself to his subject, his own poems bear unmistakably the stamp of his own personality, his outlook, and especially his diction. This is part of the seeming paradox of his impersonal theory of poetic composition. But it does not at all follow (as some have argued) that he is most successful as a poet when he most ignores and violates his poetic theories. Rather, he is most successful when he resolves or holds in equipoise their contradictions. When his poetry falters, it is because one or the other opposing demand gets the upper hand; the dialectic of his theory, and the dialectic between his theory and his practice, fail to have their opposing demands mutually satisfied and synthesized by the fusing power of his imagination.

IV

Having now identified in a very rapid fashion the main strands of the Wordsworthian dialectic, we may fittingly conclude our discussion by noticing, again rapidly, the manner in which the dialectic appears in two of Wordsworth's greatest poems, "Tintern Abbey" and the "Immortality Ode."

In the former poem, we see that soon after the lovely descriptive opening Wordsworth speaks in line 60 of a "sad perplexity." It is a phrase strangely unclarified in any explicit way although the rest of the poem implicitly supplies the needed clarification. Explicitly, Wordsworth recounts his former delights among these hills he now revisits:

> when like a roe
> I bounded o'er the mountains, by the sides
> Of the deep rivers, and the lonely streams,
> Wherever nature led: more like a man
> Flying from something that he dreads than one
> Who sought the thing he loved. For nature then
> (The coarser pleasures of my boyish days,
> And their glad animal movements all gone by)
> To me was all in all.—I cannot paint
> What then I was. The sounding cataract
> Haunted me like a passion: the tall rock,
> The mountain, and the deep and gloomy wood,
> Their colours and their forms, were then to me

An appetite; a feeling and a love,
That had no need for a remoter charm,
By thought supplied, nor any interest
Unborrowed from the eye.—That time is past. . . .

That time is past. But since adult satisfactions provided by nature have
replaced his boyhood pleasures, there is no cause for complaint. The
compensation is abundant:

For I have learned
To look on nature, not as in the hour
Of thoughtless youth; but hearing oftentimes
The still, sad music of humanity,
Nor harsh nor grating, though of ample power
To chasten and subdue. And I have felt
A presence that disturbs me with the joy
Of elevated thoughts. . . .

The pleasures of youth were intense but thoughtless, those of age are
(we are later told) the "sober pleasures" of loftly thought. Something
has been lost, something gained—and there is a kind of equivalence in
the exchange.

But the poem provides enough hints that this equivalence, this
abundant recompense, is not really convincing to Wordsworth himself.
And therein lies the sad perplexity that gives the poem both the tension
of the dilemma and the slightly wistful undercurrent which balances
the positive assurances on the surface. "That time is past," he tells us:

And all its aching joys are now no more,
And all its dizzy raptures. Not for this
Faint I, nor mourn nor murmur; other gifts
Have followed; for such loss, I would believe,
Abundant recompense.

He "would believe" the recompense abundant, which is not at all the
same as saying he does believe it is so. His belief is clearly a willed
belief, one that he is trying to talk himself into accepting. Notice that
further along in the poem, after consoling himself with the compensations of adulthood, he addresses his sister Dorothy as follows:

For thou art with me here upon the banks
Of this fair river; thou my dearest Friend,
My dear, dear Friend; and in thy voice I catch

> The language of my former heart, and read
> My former pleasures in the shooting lights
> Of thy wild eyes. Oh! yet a little while
> May I behold in thee what I was once,
> My dear, dear Sister!

This surely is not the language and desire of someone who has made an equivalent exchange. And realizing this, we see that Wordsworth earlier in the poem has been trying to depreciate a loss which he really feels very acutely. He had spoken of the "coarser" pleasures of his boyish days, of "thoughtless" youth, as if such words could by themselves banish his very real longing to regain the raptures he once had known.

If then we cut cruelly into this beautiful poem and examine what it has to say of the childhood-adulthood dilemma, we see that Wordsworth tries hard to give credit to the different and often opposing pleasures of each condition, that superficially he seems satisfied with adulthood, that here and there he honestly includes hints of nostalgia. The dialectic of the poem is created by these alternating currents of feeling, but because the nostalgia is not given the full strength of image and statement that it deserves, the reconciliation effected in the poem, the synthesis of opposites, is not completely satisfying. Put another way, there is more tragedy in the poem, more tragic loss, than Wordsworth is prepared to acknowledge fully. The "sad perplexity" remains unresolved or is a little too easily dismissed. The optimism and "cheerful faith" in the poem are not completely earned.

Intertwined with the childhood-adulthood conflict are the ones between freedom and necessity and between the self and society. Wordsworth's youth was unbridled ("when like a roe I bounded o'er the mountains"), passionate (with "aching joys" and "dizzy raptures") and unrepressed. As an adult he has become considerably tamed through humanity's "ample power to chasten and subdue." Both youth and nature are unrestrained: "wild," a key word in the poem, is used in conjunction with his youthful sister ("wild eyes," "wild ecstacies") and with nature ("a wild secluded scene," "sportive wood run wild"). Age, in contrast, is thoughtful and "sober." Yet Wordsworth joins together the seeming opposites of freedom and constraint when he tells us that he is

> well pleased to recognise
> In nature and the language of the sense
> The anchor of my purest thoughts,

and even more daringly, that wild nature and the senses comprise the "soul of all my moral being." Thus wildness anchors thought and produces morality! Of the self and society, Wordsworth implies that along with childhood and freedom went egocentricity—his youth was "thoughtless" in the double sense of being unreflective and unconcerned with other people. For this offence he has been chastened by "the still, sad music of humanity." But this music, paradoxically, is not heard when he is in the midst of humanity. Driven in on himself "in lonely rooms and 'mid the din of towns and cities," he hears the sad music of humanity only when looking at nature. Thus nature and the self are dialectically preserved at the very moment his ego is being subdued by thoughts of human society.

On the last of our four Wordsworthian dilemmas—that between the seen and the unseen world—"Tintern Abbey" is almost schematically clear. The boy had an intense love of the mountains and woods, "their colours and their forms," in and for themselves. They "had no need of a remoter charm/ By thought supplied, nor any interest/ Unborrowed from the eye." The man, on the other hand, has felt a sense of something behind as well as within all things:

> A motion and a spirit, that impels
> All thinking things, all objects of all thought,
> And rolls through all things.

The unseen world becomes visible to the mind's eye when the physical eye is, as it were, asleep, when

> we are laid asleep
> In body, and become a living soul:
> While with an eye made quiet by the power
> Of harmony, and the deep power of joy,
> We see into the life of things.

The boy, in short, is a passionate naturalist whereas the man is able to have the quasi-mystical moments of supernatural illumination. The opposites here, as were the ones between childhood and adulthood, are neatly kept apart, and because they are not grappled with as a dilemma, they are not at all synthesized. Consequently, the formulation betrays an important weakness: the adult requires for his mystical moment "the deep power of joy," but joy has throughout the poem been associated with youth, and chastened and muted pleasure, humanity's "sad music," with age. Whence then, as an adult, does the poet receive the joy he says is needed to see into the life of things? This last set of opposites, in other words, like the first one between childhood and adulthood, remains unreconciled and unconvincing in "Tintern Abbey," and will not be fully grappled with until the "Immortality Ode."

We may be grateful that Wordsworth did not resolve the difficulties, for had he done so he quite likely would not have felt the inner pressure to continue pondering the issues and we probably would not have had the magnificent Ode, which gives richer and deeper expression, and major reformulations, to essentially the same subjects as treated in the earlier poem. But before turning to the Ode, we must say a word about "Tintern Abbey" in relation to the theories put forth in the Preface. The poem adequately fulfills the language demands of the Preface, being free of "arbitrary and capricious" expressions, relatively plain and emphatic, with a minimal amount of "poetic diction" and even of imagery. In subject matter, also, though this is less obvious, Wordsworth is not really running counter to his prescriptions. He is, after all, dealing with rustic life as experienced by an unsophisticated boy and an almost primitively responsive girl, and in effect he tells her of the complex ways in which, amidst natural beauties, "the essential passions of the heart find a better soil in which they can attain their maturity." While not the best poetic illustration of Wordsworth's theories, the poem can certainly not be said to achieve its impressive success by flaunting those theories.

In the "Ode: Intimations of Immortality from Recollections of Early Childhood," we are immediately struck by the degree to which it goes beyond "Tintern Abbey" in paying homage to childhood. Indeed the poem contains the most extravagant praise of childhood ever to appear in an English poem:

> Thou, whose exterior semblance doth belie
>   Thy Soul's immensity;
> Thou best Philosopher, who yet dost keep
> Thy heritage, thou Eye among the blind,
> That, deaf and silent, read'st the eternal deep,
> Haunted for ever by the eternal mind,—
>   Mighty Prophet! Seer blest!
>   On whom those truths do rest,
> Which we are toiling all our lives to find,
> In darkness lost, the darkness of the grave;
> Thou, over whom thy Immortality

Broods like the Day, a Master o'er a Slave,
A Presence which is not to be put by;
Thou little Child, yet glorious in the might
Of heaven-born freedom on thy being's height,
Why with such earnest pains dost thou provoke
The years to bring the inevitable yoke,
Thus blindly with thy blessedness at strife?
Full soon thy Soul shall have her earthly freight,
And custom lie upon thee with a weight,
Heavy as frost, and deep almost as life!

With such terms of praise, Wordsworth obviously gives to childhood that full measure of nostalgia and longing he had held in check in "Tintern Abbey." And consequently the compensations of adult life are not going to be as easily established in this poem as they were in "Tintern Abbey." What compensations there are will have to be affirmed against the truly wonderful *lost* joys of childhood, and the compensations cannot be complete. What adult life has to offer cannot really make up for what has been lost.

This of course means that the poem deals with a tragic experience, and the tragic hero of the poem is the child himself—who begins his career "glorious in the might/ Of heaven-born freedom on [his] being's height," and who falls into a manhood marked by an earthly freight of cares, a cold weight of custom, a loss of truths once known. After his fall into adulthood, the former child is a chastened hero, like King Oedipus, and like Oedipus he too lives in darkness, among the other blind people known as adults. What we call growing up is really, according to Wordsworth, a process of growing down, and it is a universal experience. It constitutes for Wordsworth the fundamental tragedy of human life, and he hopes we can bear it with dignity.

Now most of us know that Wordsworth has grasped and eloquently expressed a tormenting truth, a truth we dare not dwell upon unless we share Wordsworth's courage and strength of character. To feel that each year will be worse than the preceding one is guaranteed to produce melancholy and perhaps suicidal thoughts. Hence we devise means of evading the truth—we forget the past, we call those who dwell upon it morbid, we paint attractive pictures of the future and try to be optimistic. (If the Garden of Eden mythologizes our secret longing, the prospects of heaven assuage our pain.) Yet Wordsworth would say that those who harden themselves against feeling the pains of life thereby incapacitate themselves for feeling its deeper joys. Indeed Wordsworth goes so far as to assert that only by remembering the lost joys of childhood can we have the strength to surmount the trials of adulthood. As complexly expressed in the great ninth stanza:

> O joy! that in our embers
> Is something that doth live,
> That nature yet remembers
> What was so fugitive!
> The thought of our past years in me doth breed
> Perpetual benediction: not indeed
> For that which is most worthy to be blest;
> Delight and liberty, the simple creed
> Of Childhood, whether busy or at rest,
> With new-fledged hope still fluttering in his breast:—
> Not for these I raise
> The song of thanks and praise;
> But for those obstinate questionings
> Of sense and outward things,
> Fallings from us, vanishings;
> Blank misgivings of a Creature
> Moving about in worlds not realised,
> High instincts before which our mortal Nature
> Did tremble like a guilty Thing surprised:
> But for those first affections,
> Those shadowy recollections,
> Which, be they what they may,
> Are yet the fountain-light of all our day,
> Are yet a master-light of all our seeing;
> Uphold us, cherish, and have power to make
> Our noisy years seem moments in the being
> Of the eternal Silence . . . .

The apparently irreconcilable opposition between the pleasures of the child and the pleasures of the man, which had been developed in "Tintern Abbey," is here reconciled and synthesized. The sustaining strength of adulthood derives from childhood, for it is then that our powerful "first affections" are expressed and nourished, and it is then that we experience life spontaneously and have not yet submitted ourselves solely to the world of "sense and outward things." In his insistence on the importance of childhood, Wordsworth echoes the New Testament's injunction (except as you "become as little children you shall not enter the kingdom of heaven") and anticipates our contemporary knowledge of the profound influence a person's earliest years exert upon his entire life.

The particular types of experience Wordsworth feels are perpetuated take us to that other set of opposites—between the seen and the unseen world—that we found him treating in "Tintern Abbey" somewhat unsatisfactorily. There the child was the naturalist and the adult was the mystic. Here the formulation is changed. The child is not only a sense-absorbed naturalist but simultaneously a mystic, reading the eternal deep, haunted forever by the eternal mind. It is the youth who has the mystic sense of oneness with nature, and a sense-absorption so intense that it strangely transcends the senses, investing the grass with splendor and the flowers with glory. The visionary gleam is mystical, and it is lost as one advances into adulthood and the light of common day. In adulthood we can only be naturalists, regarding nature's creatures as lovely, to be sure, but no longer feeling their religious radiance. Yet in the ninth stanza, opposites are combined and a reconciliation effected, for we learn that we can recapture *through memory* the sense of the unseen world, the "thought of our past years" producing "those obstinate questionings/ Of sense and outward things"; and "those shadowy recollections" are "the fountain-light of all our day," are "a master-light of all our seeing." Through the power of memory, the past and its mode of being return to us—we are re-entered by them even as we re-enter them.

This great synthesis of opposites Wordsworth has been creatively laboring for throughout his career, but the passion with which it is expressed, the heat of thought and emotion with which the fusion takes place, should not blind us to the essential fragility of the synthesis; it rests on the elusiveness of memories and the arduousness of remembering actions and feelings correctly. Our memory is necessarily selective and is a mechanism for self-preservation. Keen as it was, Wordsworth's memory was not often able to recollect the past and his past feelings accurately. It might have caused too much present pain to have done so. But when his memory betrayed him, his poetry declined in force and tension.

Of the last two sets of the dialectic, little need be said since their synthesis had been effected in "Tintern Abbey" and are preserved in the Ode. As in the former poem, though even more explicitly, the Ode associates freedom with childhood and bondage with age; but the two states are reconciled through the power of memory and the training the moral faculty has received from cultivation of the senses. Hence the poet can still "love the Brooks which down their channels fret,/ Even more than when I tripped lightly as they." Much more extensively and dramatically developed, however, is the conflict between the one and the many, though again the reconciliation is similar to that secured in "Tintern Abbey" and indeed to that of "I Wandered Lonely as a Cloud." The lonely self, burdened with its pain of loss, is contrasted with the joyous crowd of children, animals, "Fountains, Meadows, Hills, and Groves." Then in stanza X the self joins the others ("We in thought will join your throng") and receives strength from sympathetic identification with their lives. But the poet does not thereby lose his sense of self. Nature and man are yoked together through the agency of the poet's meditations on both of them, and he preserves and heightens his sense of self through such meditations; not necessarily to others but to *him,* to one who has "kept watch o'er man's mortality/ . . . the meanest flower that blows can give/ Thoughts that do often lie too deep for tears."

So much then, in brief fashion, for the thematic dialectic in the Ode. But of course the poem would not move us if this dialectic were not conveyed with poetic power. Indeed, this poem is one of those remarkable works that stir us even if we do not closely follow its argument or agree with its contentions. It does this by the magic of its diction, imagery and rhythm. A heightening of language is felt as soon as we reach the fourth line of the first stanza:

> There was a time when meadow, grove, and stream,
> The earth, and every common sight,
> To me did seem
> Apparelled in celestial light.

Substitute for the last phrase the more plebeian "clothed in heavenly light" and one sees at once how rich a diction Wordsworth is using, richer than that used in any of his other poems. Much of it is the diction of intensity and joy, such as "festival," "bliss," "glorious," "splendid." Some of it is richly regal, such as "coronal," or "imperial palace," and a great deal is richly religious in association, such as "blessed creatures," "Nature's priest," "jubilee," "the eternal mind," "mightly prophet." The imagery, also, is highly charged, filled with suggestions of brightness and spaciousness, and accompanied by a great variety of items suggesting the freshly new and youthful—young lambs, fresh flowers, Maytime, children. Even the poet's voice is richly orchestrated against a background of pleasant noises—singing birds, drum sounds, trumpets, echoes through the mountains, shouts of shepherd boys, the laughter of heaven itself. And cooperating with this vivid diction and imagery is a great flexibility of rhythms and line lengths, giving the poem its singular animation and conveying its pulsations of emotions.

Yes, we may say, but does not all this prove how unrelated Wordsworth's great achievement is to the theories of his Preface? Is he dealing
here with peasants? Is he using their diction? The answers seem obvious,
and commentators on the Ode have not been reluctant to give them.
But if we avoid literal-mindedness and attend to the dialectic we have
explored in the Preface itself, then we can see that Wordsworth is
marvelously holding together the divergent thrusts of his theory. It is
not only his modifications of that theory that save him from a charge
of inconsistency, such as his claiming the right to employ a "selection"
of language really used by men, and the right to throw a certain coloring of imagination over scenes and incidents. The Ode also fulfills central
specifications of the Preface in profound and subtle ways. Wordsworth
had wanted poets to subordinate themselves to their material and not
use self-glorifying language, and in the Ode we hear the child praised
at the poet's expense. Beyond all else, Wordsworth had wanted the
language to be dictated by the realities of common life and to disclose
the essential passions of the heart. And surely in the Ode it is not a
special child who is being described but the universal child, the child
of common life, the child as the purest carrier of the essential passions
of the heart. In the light of the Ode we can recognize that it was the
child preserved in the peasant that always had received Wordsworth's
acclaim. The person living close to nature preserved more than others
a knowledge of truths best known by that ultimate primitive, the child.
And in celebrating its "silent" knowledge of truths which "we are toiling
all our lives to find," the poet manifestly could not employ the child's
non-language or use baby-talk.[1] Rather, in dialectical fashion, the subject matter in being pushed to an extreme, bred in the language its opposite, perhaps the only language fully suitable to the occasion. Only
a heightened language could pay just tribute to the child's holy prim-
itiveness and innocent wisdom.

Lastly, the Immortality Ode embodies Wordsworth's definition of
poetry and extends it to all human creativity. Like poetry itself, creativity in life involves "the spontaneous overflow of powerful feelings;
it takes its origin in emotion recollected in tranquillity: the emotion
is contemplated till, by a species of reaction, the tranquillity gradually
disappears," or, put poetically:

---

[1]In his *Songs of Innocence,* Blake often employs the simple language of children
to convey their ingenuous view of the world, and thereby he indirectly celebrates
their wisdom. But to talk directly about a child's wisdom in child-like language is
unnatural for an adult who uses adult language.

> in our embers,
> Is something that doth live,
> That nature yet remembers
> What was so fugitive!
> The thought of our past years in me doth breed
> Perpetual benediction . . . .
> Those shadowy recollections,
> Which, be they what they may
> Are yet the fountain-light of all our day . . . .
> Hence in a season of calm weather
> Though inland far we be,
> Our souls have sight of that immortal sea
> Which brought us hither,
> Can in a moment travel thither,
> And see the Children sport upon the shore,
> And hear the mighty waters rolling evermore.

Or, put in dry modern terminology, creativity summons up the past (embedded in the unconscious) and makes memory the necessary component for living life fully in the present. Creativity in life, in the most humble activities, is exactly like Wordsworth's definition of poetry in that it imaginatively fuses tranquillity and powerful feelings, premeditation with spontaneity, the past and the present.

Faithful to the spirit of the Preface, the Immortality Ode reflects in its sustained eloquence a mastery over the dilemmas that haunted Wordsworth's mind and art, and in that very mastery it achieves its final dialectical triumph. For the poem laments a loss of the visionary gleam of childhood and of the capacity to feel intensely, yet so honestly is the loss accepted, so reverently is the child praised, that the poem generates its own visionary gleam and pulses with deep intensity. The poetical act, at its most successful, finally becomes an equivalent substitute for the original experience of the visionary gleam—"the tranquillity gradually disappears, and an emotion, similar to that which was before the subject of contemplation, is gradually produced, and does itself actually exist in the mind." Hence the Ode harmonizes even as it creates an ultimate tension between substance and manner: the substance, reduction in the capacity to feel, points in one direction; the manner, conveying great depth of feeling, points in an opposite direction. And this ultimate union of opposites Wordsworth is able to achieve because he is living fully within his total dialectic, powerfully molding its centrifugal forces into a synthesis, and thereby giving to the poem its vivid and enduring life.

Suggestions for Further Reading

Abrams, M. H. *The Mirror and the Lamp* (1953). A superb critical exposition of Romantic theories of poetic creativity.

Bloom, Harold. *The Visionary Company* (1961). A careful reading of the major poems of the major romantics.

Davis, Jack, ed. *Discussions of William Wordsworth* (Heath Discussions of Literature Series, 1964). A collection for students which includes several illuminating essays on Wordsworth's art.

Ferry, David. *The Limits of Mortality* (1959). A brief but penetrating study.

Hartman, Geoffrey. *Wordsworth's Poetry, 1797-1814* (1964). The most important single work on Wordsworth to appear in recent years.

Lindenberger, Herbert. *On Wordsworth's Prelude* (1963). An excellent examination of Wordsworth's great long poem in relation to earlier and later poetic traditions.

Richard J. Williams

Plot as Motive:
The Structure of <u>Crime and Punishment</u>

◈

The psychological coherence of Dostoyevsky's complex Raskolnikov seems definable only if one adds his own inferences to recapitulations, however accurate, of the book's events and statements.[1] Hence perhaps the sweeping, frequently irrelevant generalities with which studies of it abound. Mr. Edward Wasiolek's essays[2] have helped to alter a tendency to ignore the correlation of Raskolnikov's psychology and the book's structure, and it is the intention of this essay further to extend the inquiry into that correlation.

If one permits the simple assumption that every character is pertinent to an exposition of the central character,[3] the unifying pattern of the novel becomes apparent: Dostoyevsky shapes it in terms, and within the limits, of three fundamental characters (or motives, because a "character" is the set of qualities which move each agent through the work) each of which has different stages of development. The book is unified by interactions among three characters; its development, or coherence, is the result of the development of these characters.

---

[1] All page references are to David Magarshack's translation in Penguin edition (Baltimore, 1951).

[2] Edward Wasiolek, "On the Structure of *Crime and Punishment*," *PMLA*, LXXIV (March, 1959), 131-136. In his later essay on the novel, a chapter in *Dostoievsky: The Major Fiction* (Cambridge, 1964), pp. 60-84, Mr. Wasiolek illustrates, using the novel, the system of thought which he feels is in Dostoyevsky's mind and governs his work. It is difficult to correlate the system of thought and the structure of this novel.

[3] This is not to suggest that subordinate characters "symbolize" the central character, but only that their qualities extend our experience of what is relevant to and therefore part of the design of that character.

The most apparent threesome, that which defines Raskolnikov's crime, consists of Raskolnikov, the pawnbroker, and her half-sister Lizaveta. The threesome which gave immediate definition to the problem leading to crime was that of Raskolnikov, his mother, and his sister. Another is that of Marmeladov, his wife, and Sonia or the children. Another is that of Luzhin, Mrs. Raskolnikov, and Dunya. Svidrigaylov, his wife, and either the maids or Dunya compose two more. In short, what is being asserted is that wherever one turns, from whatever perspective one sees the novel, a pattern of three characters is found. Svidrigaylov and Sonia are the limits of this pattern and finally cause it to be completely exposed. But they, and the pattern, are there from the beginning, notably in the episode of the Horseguards' Boulevard, wherein a man Raskolnikov calls "Svidrigaylov" wishes to exploit an innocent, victimized girl. In reacting against the impulsive act of charity by which he saves the girl, Raskolnikov imagines her mother cruelly beating her and casting her into the street; an alternative possibility is that a procuress will pick her up and use her as a bit of property. This relationship between a Svidrigaylov, a helpless victim, and a cruel or exploiting older woman is reestablished in the climactic vision of the actual Svidrigaylov's life: the five-year-old girl is associated with an image of some mother who had thrashed the unloved child. And Svidrigaylov had of course intended, with the help of a procuress and an exploiting mother, to marry a child. Raskolnikov kills Lizaveta as a consequence of his relationship to the exploiting pawnbroker. Marmeladov causes the sacrifice of Sonia, and in a sense of the other children, through the instrumentation of his wife; Luzhin almost brings about, with the help of Mrs. Svidrigaylov but especially of Mrs. Raskolnikov, the sacrifice of Dunya, whose position is so far made parallel to Sonia's. Even quite minor instances reveal the habit of Dostoyevsky's imagination: Nastasya, for example, is in a slight way a victim of Raskolnikov because of the "exploitation" of him by his landlady. A most curious instance: among the anonymous members of humanity to be driven "home" by the surrogate Raskolnikov, Mikolka, Dostoyevsky singles out "a fat, red-cheeked peasant woman" who through all the brutality goes on "cracking nuts and just smiling to herself" (pp. 75 and 76). In so far as this first dream is considered in itself, the threesome could be seen as Mikolka, the fat woman who is one focus of the crowd he's pleasing, and the victim, the mare; or as Mikolka, the mare, and the boy. In so far however as the dream exposes what is coming to the surface of Raskolnikov's experience, the dream embodies the murder; this means that the mare killed by Mikolka includes the qualities of both of Raskolnikov's victims, being in apparent value the pawnbroker, but in spirit the willing self-sacrifice which slaves for the old hag, Lizaveta. Alter perspective as one will, the design of the novel is encompassed by three general types.

So many diversities are included in the patterns of three that it may seem pointless to assert them. But when they are explored for motivations, they expose the design of the novel, Raskolnikov.

First, then, the qualities possessed by the victims—Sonia, Dunya, the girl on the boulevard, Lizaveta, and others. Diverse though they be, they are united in a helplessness which comes with material poverty, in an experience of their being sacrificed, and in a willing or unwilling acquiescence in the sacrifice of personal "rights" to the will of the other. Raskolnikov is, first of all, one who feels himself such a victim.

He wishes not to be, and not to experience the victimization of others. When in Part I he finishes reading of the virtual prostitution, to Luzhin, with which his sister is threatened, his pain at his inability to have a "right" (pp. 62 and 68) to prevent it is intense, as intense as the need to prevent it. And this is the way he sees it—as a problem of morality, of having a right, based on power, to prevent it. Unable to endure victimization, his sister's or his own, he is led instinctively toward a solution, toward Razumikhin, and rushes off to him. But his longing to have the right to forbid victimization is too strong to enable him to be patient—it causes him to define the problem in extremes: either "to do something at once and quickly, too" or "renounce life altogether" and humbly "give up every right to act, to live, and to love" (p. 63). This pride—the desire to sense within himself the immediate power and therefore the right to support the good—which makes him pose the problem in these extremes precludes any but extreme resolutions.

And because he is proud, Raskolnikov's decision is to make an effort to reject, by virtue of possessing a right, vindicated by power, all victimization. This effort is presented in the novel as a destructive antithesis to the giving up of "every right to act, to live, and to love." It creates in Raskolnikov qualities antagonistic to the victims and embodied in greater or lesser development in the victimizers—Marmeladov, Luzhin, Svidrigaylov, and others.

But Raskolnikov, in spite of his having killed, never succeeds in fully joining the Svidrigaylovs: the possibility of doing so hinges on his *genuinely* gaining a right: as Porfiry and Razumikhin agree, what is the original (and hence only truly relevant) part of Raskolnikov's superman theory is that it makes the shedding of blood a matter of conscience. To dare then to transform his conscience and thus gain the right to gain the power to have the right—this is the attempt and this is the circularity of thought which leads to the murder and is the "lie" (p. 553) in Raskolnikov's convictions: the contradiction between his belief that such a conscience is given by an impersonal law of nature and his personal need to create such a conscience by a fear- and disgust-ridden personal trial. A yearning to transform his conscience, ultimately and imaginatively for the sake of all victims but immediately and for the sake of making himself a master of good (as a master of conscience one *is* master of good)—this leads to crime. But the effort fails.

The best he can do is vacillate between being an impulsive victim (giving away his money), and a theoretical victimizer seeking the right lines and the right inspiration to play the part genuinely. To confront Raskolnikov and the reader with the conflict between these antagonistic positions, Dostoyevsky invents the third group of characters, the intermediary group: Mrs. Raskolnikov, Mrs. Marmeladov, Mrs. Svidrigaylov, and others. Being intermediary, they are both victims and victimizers, and give way under the pressure of circumstances to either side of their natures. They are self-sacrificing, yet aggressive; humble, but proud; helpless, but make demands; they victimize others, and themselves as well. They are like Raskolnikov subject, against their natural inclinations but in an effort to prevent victimizations, to the spirit of Svidrigaylov. Mrs. Raskolnikov for her son's sake is virtually duped into encouraging the victimization of Dunya by Luzhin; Mrs. Marmeladov for the sake of her children turns on Sonia; Mrs. Svidrigaylov throws the maids to Svidrigaylov to protect herself; Raskolnikov's landlady is only trying to protect herself when she gives the promissory note to the rapacious Chebarov.

What the Svidrigaylov principle does is magnify a relatively weak demand until it becomes intolerable. For example, Raskolnikov's landlady has a right to make a demand for rent. But she will not; as she promised she will be patient so long as she is not victimized. But Raskolnikov's pride, seeking as it does to transcend *all* demands as irrelevant to him, creates a "criminal destitution," as Marmeladov calls it, and makes the landlady's demands magnify by means of Chebarov. Thus too Raskolnikov's pride turns the pawnbroker's demands and his mother's demands into unbearable exploitations. Marmeladov, enduring the partially justified and only modest demands of his wife, gives away to destitution through drink (rather than through dreaming and theorizing), with the result that her inclination to assert her rights and make demands is turned into a destructive victimization first of Sonia, then of her children, always and finally of herself. In these intermediary characters, then, the

Sonia and Svidrigaylov principles, Raskolnikov the victim and Raskolnikov the victimizer, meet and contend.

And Raskolnikov's progress, unified in terms of the three possibilities available to him—Sonia, Mrs. Marmeladov, or Marmeladov, say—is traced as well by watching the intermediary characters as by watching his relationships to the extreme characters. Some signposts of his progress can now be fixed.

When the story opens, Raskolnikov, who we later learn had at one time been living, perhaps experimentally, with Sonia's principles—had supported a consumptive fellow student and his father, had heroically saved two children from a fire, had promised to marry a cripple—has more recently crossed, so to speak, the empty place between where Sonia lives and where Svidrigaylov lives, and permitted the egotism of his nature to develop. Another way of saying this is that when the novel opens he is more tormented by the unmet demands of his landlady than by the way his chosen destitution is victimizing her. His pride has developed to such an extent that he is, not actually, but virtually, a Svidrigaylov—that is, he has come to experience crime as a practical thing: "he had unconsciously got accustomed to looking on his 'hideous' dream as a practical proposition . . ." (p. 22). He is not, then, making a clear moral choice to kill; in fact, he does not fully experience the morality of the situation until the end of the novel, which is designed as his moral education. Still, he is responsible for allowing himself, as a matter of irrational habit, to be shaped by chance, or the devil, into a Svidrigaylov.

Thus the novel opens with a "rehearsal," and the theater metaphor perfectly indicates the extent to which Raskolnikov is committed to the performance of the crime, and at the same time the theatrical, partial, or actor's way in which he is involved in it. He has suspended his own real identity. The theatricality of Raskolnikov's opening condition is sustained by the posturing Marmeladov who, like Raskolnikov, has created that degree of destitution which is, he says, criminal. Marmeladov's motives, especially his pride, nowhere more evident than when he delivers judgment on himself and saves himself because he is humble, his culpability —all expose the character of Raskolnikov; both are at this point only incipient Svidrigaylovs. When Raskolnikov brings Marmeladov home to his wife we experience, so to speak, Raskolnikov moving from his "role" as Svidrigaylov back to a confrontation of the victims, the children. But fully to experience the victimized children, the ineffectuality of their goodness yearning to be cared for, is to confront as well the pride—embodied in Mrs. Marmeladov—which makes the victim's yearning an unbearable demand.

In the Marmeladov encounter, Raskolnikov experiences directly only the minimal developments of what is latent in the situation: though Sonia is referred to, though Lebezyatnikov (another violent man—he has beaten Mrs. Marmeladov and tried through the landlady to exploit Sonia, and is so far one of the Svidrigaylovs) is referred to, Raskolnikov confronts only the Marmeladovs. Marmeladov himself, who is not yet violent (he will be, a virtual suicide), is only potentially a Svidrigaylov and the children are only potentially Sonias. Throughout Part I this quality of potentiality persists—all of the major characters are still "distant," only implicit in the situation; Sonia, Luzhin, Dunya, Svidrigaylov are all referred to but are not to Raskolnikov actual. When they become so, after the crime, it is because Raskolnikov is discovering the actual nature of crime. Razumikhin, incidentally, who can correctly imagine the events of the crime, is thought by Zossimov to be in error because everything in Razumikhin's account fits "just as if it were on the stage" (p. 161).

In fact, Raskolnikov commits the crime without yet fully realizing what he's doing. And, like Marmeladov, he is much to be pitied; both suffer intensely for the victimization of those they love. But both suffer even more from their inability to satisfy the demands of those who look to them to save the victims. What is wrong is that pride can make them turn both the victims and those who make demands into objects of hatred rather than objects of love. To the extent to which one visualizes himself as great, that is, as the possessor of the good, to that extent will he feel all demands as challenges. If one's greatness is illusory, any demand which cannot be met destroys the illusion, which can be sustained only in isolation from all demands, hence from all people. But the immediate source of pain is the inability to prevent victimization, and in Raskolnikov's experience of the Marmeladov children, of his sister's impending sacrifice, of the mare's impotent, self-sacrificing striving and his boyish inability to prevent that sacrifice, Raskolnikov feels original pain.

It is the basic pain, feeling ineffectual, that supports the other, feeling exploited by unfair demands. Dostoyevsky constructs this relationship by having the mare's impotence enrage Mikolka, by having Lizaveta support the ugliness which is the pawnbroker, Dunya's willingness to sacrifice support the ugliness which thereupon threatens to develop in Mrs. Raskolnikov, the suffering of the children support the ugliness which develops in Mrs. Marmeladov.

Pride, then, not fully understood but allowed to live in oneself as an actor playing a role, gives to Raskolnikov's consciousness of impotent sacrifice and insatiable demand the shape of obstacles to be destroyed; there occurs the performance of the removal of that intolerably ugly demand, and of course a murder as well of what lies behind it and really supports it, the ineffectual yearning which characterizes the victim.

Sketched, then, are the situation and conflict of the novel as they exist in Part I, the first stage of development. Part II begins a process of punishment which ends only when Raskolnikov surrenders to "life," to Sonia. "Begins," but there is no beginning here: from Part II on there is simply an ever more developed exposure, to the anguished consciousness of Raskolnikov, of the real nature of those forces which, only partly developed, had impelled him into becoming criminal. In short, the novel progresses by making actual the theatrical motives of the opening movement. Indeed, Raskolnikov commits crime as "drunkenly" as Marmeladov kills himself; sober, he moves toward it only, when finally he understands its nature, to choose Sonia. The movement of the novel is not so much the revelation of a character caught up in the consequences of its actions as it is the revelation to a character and to the reader by means of the actions of others of the way potentialities of that character could further develop.

To go on is to trace the developments occurring in the rest of the novel. To do this completely would be to follow Dostoyevsky's plotting in great detail, which is here impossible. Still, one can define and trace Raskolnikov's meeting with the characters in whom he after Part I confronts ever more directly the nature of crime.

Only one completely new principle enters the novel after Part I, and this because the crime has to be committed before the principle comes into play. It is that embodied in Porfiry and partly in Zossimov. Both examine Raskolnikov, one because he is seeking the identity of the guilty, the other because he seeks the identity of sickness. Zossimov enters the novel first, possibly because Raskolnikov is experiencing an effort to believe his failure was mental, not moral, but Dostoyevsky plots the vanity of the superficial Zossimov; Raskolnikov's sickness is a matter of guilt, not mental or physical health.

Porfiry is the important figure, and brings into the novel the question of the "examining magistrate," of conscience: Who *is* the criminal? Is it you? He is a person who epitomizes the question as Raskolnikov experiences it—he is shrewd, probingly curious, unofficial, deceptive, never definitely understood, ultimately humane but unpleasant as well as tenaciously oppressive, and ugly to look at. He is the question which shapes the novel after Part I because Raskolnikov, having acted the part of a criminal, which is to say having tried to submerge and tranform conscience, must go on to recover his real identity, his real conscience.

Raskolnikov is not ready for the question of the examining magistrate until Sonia, the power to endure victimization, enters his immediate experience, his room. When she enters his room to be united, at his insistence, with those—his mother and sister—who had originally given crucial intensity to the problem of suffering, the problem of suffering is associated with its solution, and this because of the pity Raskolnikov feels for Sonia. And even though Svidrigaylov now "shadows" Sonia home, to live almost side by side with her, the threat he ultimately poses for Raskolnikov is blunted by the fact that Sonia has become real to Raskolnikov before Svidrigaylov does. (That Svidrigaylov will be seen and judged by Raskolnikov only from the perspective given him by the presence of a Sonia character is plotted out by having Raskolnikov protected from Svidigaylov through his effort to prevent the victimization of Dunya. Which is not to say that the effort to live with a criminal conscience is precluded; it overhears and mocks every effort to surrender.)

Sonia has now been experienced in person (she comes to Raskolnikov's room in her own dress, not in the costume worn on the night of Marmeladov's death); on the other hand Svidrigaylov, now that Sonia is attached to Raskolnikov, lives near her, but is not yet consciously present to Raskolnikov. Enter Porfiry, the question of conscience. Porfiry understands that the basic principle of Raskolnikov's essay is the assertion that the shedding of blood is a matter of conscience. And he forces Raskolnikov to reexamine his theory. After this interview, and to indicate how Raskolnikov has failed to answer to his own conviction the questions Porfiry raised, he hears the accusation "Murderer" from a stranger. He is beginning vaguely to awaken to a sense that he *is* a murderer, accused by a humanity unknown to him. (Dostoyevsky is as usual evocative with his details: in this case he makes both Porfiry and the old man who accuses Raskolnikov look like old peasant women.. Surely an image of shrewd accusation? pp. 267, 288.) What follows is Raskolnikov's third dream, a dramatization of his approaching recognition that *he* was the figure played by Mikolka and the second Lieutenant but that he has not killed and cannot kill his conscience, the principle he tried to kill; but he comes to this only in a dream, not yet in reality. There is still one last possibility, apart from madness, the possibility of keeping his conscience in a practical way defeated: Svidrigaylov "dawns," so to speak, on Raskolnikov; he slowly comes into consciousness, and is in the room.

The Svidrigaylov group of characters includes notably the destitute drunk, Marmeladov, the drunken Mikolka, Luzhin, who would surely drink only with caution, and Svidrigaylov himself, who can't drink. The unity of this group, which defines the murderous potentialities of Raskolnikov's solution to injustice, lies in their being (1) ultimately nihilistic; (2) suicidal, because for Dostoyevsky murder is suicide; (3) victimizers of the innocent helpless. The coherence of Raskolnikov's experience of them lies in the way Dostoyevsky develops their nature from Marmeladov through Luzhin to Svidrigaylov. (In one sense Luzhin is less evil than Marmeladov, being the first stage of Raskolnikov's discovery of what leads to crime whereas Marmeladov is already a befuddled victimizer. Still, Luzhin's conscious and deliberate pride and rapacity, though they are made ineffectual, are potentially of greater evil.) Marmeladov can find utter destitution, that infinite of nothing which is the ultimate goal of the Svidrigaylovs, only with the help of an emptied glass. Mikolka too destroys his "property" in drunkenness, but also rage. Luzhin is, one can say, drunk with "blind self-conceit" (p. 322) and so loses his human property, Dunya, an event which fills him with "vindictive hatred" for Raskolnikov. Marmeladov's suicide is inadvertent; Svidrigaylov performs his consciously and systematically. Marmeladov is not completely responsible—his wife helps—for the victimization of the innocent; Svidrigaylov simply amuses himself in manipulating the greed of the mother of his bride-to-be. Marmeladov, though in his pride-inspired vision of the Last Judgment he forgives himself, implicitly acknowledges the need for forgiveness; Svidrigaylov can experience no such need. And so on.

Of this group it is Luzhin who is the most immediately hateful because in him the evil of this potentiality in Raskolnikov is most accessible, most evident. Marmeladov exists at one extreme, the point where Raskolnikov, the novel, began, where a willingness to help the victimized becomes united to a demand which victimizes, where in short one marries Mrs. Marmeladov. Svidrigaylov exists at the opposite extreme where, the intermediary figure, his wife, being dead, there is only the victim to be exploited. Into these extreme areas one imagines his way with difficulty because the moral perversions and paradoxes multiply. But Luzhin is a more stable, middle-class type, easier to measure because his identity is public property.

When, as a Crystal Palace exhibit of the latest fashion, he comes into Raskolnikov's presence, it is to reveal that self-interest is his motive for echoing the shibboleths of "science and economic justice" (p. 167). And when Raskolnikov, a murderer trying to justify murder, tells Luzhin,

"Well, if the principles you've just been advocating are pushed to their logical conclusion, you'll soon be justifying murder," we experience how little help Raskolnikov's transvaluation of murder is being given by his and Luzhin's rationalizations about progress and justice. For in both these characters the real motive is self-interest, pride, and Luzhin makes the nature and working of pride clear: his intention is to have the object of his "love" so destitute that he will be able to "lord it over her and— and taunt her with owing everything" to him (p. 171). Pride, the principle of self-interest, the principle of having a "right," based on property, to judge oneself, requires utter destitution, suicide finally. The very proud man insists he is above others; the measure and test of this is to experience the dependence of others upon himself. In the last analysis, one must make certain he gains control over the emergence, strength, distribution, ultimately the nature of the good. This ultimate responsibility is evidently conceived by Dostoyevsky as being not that for the existence, the being, the truth of things (as for Goethe's Faust, say) but for the good, and so he makes Raskolnikov's ultimate and criminal ambition that of being responsible for determining what is good. As a direct corruption of the good is more evil than an attempt to construct a personal good by making others one's property, so Svidrigaylov exceeds Luzhin in the practice of evil. Of course Luzhin does finally attack Sonia herself, but only her public property, her reputation, not her real innocence.

Luzhin thus contributes much to making the middle stage of Raskolnikov's recognitions clear. One instance is the scene, already referred to, where Luzhin loses his intended victim, Dunya (IV, ii.). He loses because Raskolnikov rejects him, a Raskolnikov braced now not only by his experience of Sonia, but also by his first actual experience of Svidrigaylov. What Raskolnikov is rejecting in himself is what Luzhin is. Luzhin enters Mrs. Raskolnikov's rooms feeling "a sense of his own importance," behaving with the "air of a man of sterling virtue whose dignity had been hurt and who was quite determined to demand an explanation." Hating "uncertainty," and feeling that "everything depended on him," he is excessively self-confident. When that self-confidence is shattered, there develops a confused rage and he bursts out: "But do you realize, Madame, that I have a right to protest?" (p. 320). Luzhin is a business man and lawyer; that is, he defines "rights" or property materially and legally. The only way he can kill himself is by losing property, and the only way he can attack Sonia is through property. Raskolnikov however does not, like Luzhin, confuse having rights with controlling property according to the law. In his first dream, we learned that for him the identification of something as one's property—this is Mikolka's cry, "My property"—is both proof that a man hasn't the "fear of God" in him and is the proper justification for murder (p. 77). For Raskolnikov, unlike the bourgeois Luzhin, the only adequate basis for rights is absolute power. Raskolnikov's cynical outbursts about rights (pp. 57, 59, 62) and the requirements of the social "system" are caused by his sense of being ineffectual. Not absolutely owning the good, he has no right to do anything good.

His motive is to evaluate all things himself. Luzhin, again, is deluded into imagining this good as property in a material and legal sense; Raskolnikov, not so short-sighted, defines it as property rights in conscience. He wishes "to dare," to dare to try to gain mastery over good. If what he wills to be good is for that reason good, the good is indeed in his possession and he can meet all demands.

Now these demands on Raskolnikov are plotted out in terms of practical and material necessities (from the landlady's rent to the care of Dunya), but Dostoyevsky makes us aware of their full range. For example, Raskolnikov's crime includes his making absolute the "demand" imposed by life on his intellect, the "demand" that it be understood. (See p. 133.) His intellect exhibits *its* drive for mastery over all such demands by eliminating mystery and generating a theory which would organize his whole life and establish mathematically certain laws for the entire race.

And with regard to his will, what Porfiry says of Raskolnikov best defines the set of a will opposed not to this or that but to everything: "a man who is dispirited but proud, domineering, and impatient, especially impatient" (p. 462). In the matter of theory, Raskolnikov wanted mathematical clarity; in the matter of will, he is impatient—he wants to abridge what Razumikhin calls the "living process" of history. This means fundamentally the effort to master time—to get rich, for example, at once, and as a prerequisite to master what time measures, change, or process. Everything human being temporal, Raskolnikov is set in opposition to everything. Unwilling to let the circumstances of history bring about a better condition, Raskolnikov's impatience of restraint and pride-rooted sense of being a victim lead to a form of rebellion which is finally suicidal. Ways and means are humiliations. As Luzhin, who is of course only aping the progressive, puts it: "The ways and means I hardly need mention" (p. 167).

But what, after all, is ultimately desired? Not total organization; not a victory over the problem of ways and means. No, nor anything actual either. Raskolnikov wants no particular thing, like money. He wants no particular good; he wants the good itself, the adjective, not the noun. He wants, again, an ultimate power—actually to bring into goodness what he wills to be good, and by that act itself of willing.[4] Such an ambition finds its final challenge and temptation in those creatures who, like children, awaken one's sense of goodness yearning to be cared for. Because the good is not within the self as such, the attempt to place it there requires gaining it from without, as a self-made business man, as a seducer, or as a "rapist" of the good experienced in the innocents themselves.

To see that crime is finally the devouring of innocence is to see Svidrigaylov. But Raskolnikov has in the meantime been moving toward Sonia. En route there are experienced the intermediary positions. Especially important and poignant is that of Mrs. Marmeladov, seen in Part I as more victim than victimizer. But when she dies, after Raskolnikov has first confessed to Sonia, she has come full circle, from the helpless victim left in poverty by her relatives, to the victimizers of her own helpless children, driven into the streets as was Sonia. (When, in dying, she speaks of herself as a mare driven to death, we have warrant for saying the mare of the first dream was both victim and unwitting victimizer.) But it is the condition in which she dies—demanding forgiveness as a right, demanding justice, forgiving herself as it were—that tells us what is still gripping Raskolnikov and alive even in the death of the furious energy which had supported it and brought Mrs. Marmeladov into consumption. If there be something excessive, something therefore unjust in Dostoyevsky's vision of how life or Sonia is reached, it is revealed in the way he has Mrs. Marmeladov die. Pity her though he does, he indicts her, and what after all is the case against her? Sonia says: "She's just like a child really. . . . She looks for justice. She's pure. She believes there

---

[4]Does Raskolnikov commit crime for the sake of punishment? (See for the discussion of this thesis W. D. Snodgrass, "Crime for Punishment: The Tenor of Part One," *Hudson Review*, XIII [1961], 202-253.) Well, punishing oneself for being too weak to satisfy the demands of justice is certainly one way to achieve that satisfaction. And the rejection of self by punishment (which is, considered in itself, destructive) is also a way to experience that self-sacrifice for the other which Dostoyevsky believes is basic to human nature. But the more important probability is that if there is deliberate self-punishment it is because the individual seeks to make himself responsible for judgment and punishment. That is, the root motive is not to punish oneself but to do so because one wants to get into his own control the power to evaluate and judge. In *Crime and Punishment* suffering is exalted because if God does everything, to suffer is to seek a direct experience of divine agency. And this whether the divine is the process of history, life working itself out in the heart, or a divine humanity (Christ) restoring a man to life.

ought to be justice in everything, and she demands justice. And even if you tortured her, she wouldn't do anything that wasn't just. She doesn't realize that it's impossible for people to be just" (p. 333). Mrs. Marmeladov dies (1) demanding that justice come into existence, and (2) doing so by forcing her children into the street. Dostoyevsky's significant, if slight, censure of her is that, in spite of her goodness, her vanity-supported demands, her sense of having a right to demand justice, consume her and victimize those around her.

So painful is this truth, so unable yet is he to surrender his sense of having had a right, that Raskolnikov's experience of the death of this attitude, Mrs. Marmeladov, leads him further into an experience of what, were he not coming to see its ugliness, would trap him—despair, that is, Svidrigaylov. The love for Sonia which protects him is, nonetheless, still dominated or resisted by pride; Raskolnikov is at this point able to commit himself to no more of Sonia than what is embodied in Dunya and Razumikhin. He instructs Dunya that she should find her support in Razumikhin (p. 439).

And Razumikhin, the antithesis of Luzhin as Sonia is of Svidrigaylov, is what supports an extraordinary person until he can fully unite with Sonia. Razumikhin provides a more ordinarily human, Sonia an heroic, definition of life. Razumikhin does more: he provides a set of terms for a "living process"—and therefore too a process of living—into which one can translate the particular experience of Raskolnikov. His opponents, "Socialists," wish like Raskolnikov to abridge a living process. The conflict, as Razumikhin defines it (p. 273), is *not* that between reason and "life," but that between full rationality and mathematical calculation or logic; between human nature and that to which it would be reduced, a thing of environment; between history and mechanics, freedom and servility, the mysteries of human aspiration and simplistically conceived comforts. He also exposes the motive basic to those he calls socialists: the desire to create at once and by one's own power a "sinless and righteous society." As he sees this effort, it demands the avoidance of genuine thought and the surrender of freedom. Profound certainly is his observation that it is man's hunger for a morally perfect order which leads him to seek a systematized mastery of his own nature, a mastery which requires servility to the processes of mathematical organization and comfort engineering.

Not in his comments on the "socialists," then, but in his own character lies the sentimentality. For this character, which helps Raskolnikov endure long enough to reach Sonia, *is* sentimentally conceived. He is an enthusiast, one whose living energies overflow in antithetical ways (evidently a guarantee of extreme vitality). He is a little simple, but has depths and is far from stupid; can run wild but work very hard; play tricks but be serious; can drink like a fish or abstain. What is more revealing than the stoical achievements of his fortitude is the fact that his life is devoted to an improvement of his circumstances, his great skill being that he knew "all sorts of ways of making money." In principle he accepts the given history, and because history includes evils, he is tolerant of bribes, talking rot, lies, on the condition of course that, they originate "honestly" (pp. 70, 17, 209, 219, 221). Sentimentality being attractive to one whose powers to respond are rudimentary, our seeing him always from the perspective of Raskolnikov's terrible ennui keeps him, perhaps, more attractive than his simplistic character would otherwise be. The many ways in which he very humanly adumbrates Sonia, especially in his capacity for self-sacrifice, need no comment. What now needs scrutiny is the self-sacrifice itself, the goal of Raskolnikov's enduring, Sonia.

Her fundamental beliefs are revealed when Raskolnikov is prepared to seek them (IV, iv). What she finally says is quite simple: God does "everything" (p. 339). God being good, man's effort to shape life in terms of his individuality will be neither good nor, indeed, possible. Man can only be an instrument of the divine agency, and is so when he negates his personal will. Otherwise there is only denial. The will can avoid opposing God and can successfully act only when, denying itself, it serves the nonself, the other. Dostoyevsky presents this valid exercise of will, this self-annihilation for the sake of the other, as Christian love. It is, rather, prostitution, and is so plotted in the novel.

In moving through crime and punishment to Sonia, Raskolnikov experiences a negation of those things—understanding, free will, individual desires—which constitute a human person. This loss of his personal share in humanity is plotted in terms of Raskolnikov's alienation from others. But by the same loss he comes to know a selfishness which, were it voluntarily chosen, would be the greatest achievement of freedom, because freedom is voluntary self-negation in the service of humanity defined as the other.

He becomes aware after the crime that he had had and has no desire: he can't find a tangible thing sought for or found. He experiences like Sonia an ignorance, confusion, mystery, doubt. He learns that his mind, far from providing a plan for living, was able to organize nothing, not even the crime itself; on the contrary, the unforeseen or accidental guides him. Above all, his thinking wasn't even original; as Razumikhin and Porfiry point out, superman theories were old hat. As for will power:

what characterizes Sonia's will is that it shapes itself voluntarily to conform to that of someone else. And Raskolnikov is forced to experience
the being directed by others.

But the most significant demand for self-sacrifice is not that pertaining to desire, to mind, or to will; it is that pertaining to morality.
Dostoyevsky seems to feel that to permit God to do everything requires,
as a climax to the foregoing negations, the represssion of conscience.
Sonia cannot in her mind excuse her prostitution. What, using only the
material of the novel, is surely in her case guiltless and even saintly behavior, must by her be experienced as a sacrifice of her conscience.
And so too Raskolnikov: the last thing to give way is his control over
his conscience; even in the epilogue his evaluation of the killing remains
what it was.

There is this possible qualification: Raskolnikov may not have been
convinced even "consciously" of the approbation of his conscience. In
the epilogue Dostoyevsky speaks of his having been "perhaps dimly
aware of the great lie in himself and his convictions" (p. 553). Still, the
emphasis is on the priority of a will to live over a reason, or moral judgment, for living; the latter is simply overwhelmed by the former. What
must happen is revealed by the book's double ending. The novel proper
ends with Raskolnikov's acceptance of union with humanity in its legal,
demanding guise. In his confession to the assistant superintendent he,
like a prostitute, exposes himself to the eager eyes of the people, awaits
and tolerates their manipulation. He is without desire or understanding;
he has committed his will to another, Sonia, and implicitly to her faith in
Lazarus' resurrection. The rest is a matter of time, and is quite properly
narrated in an epilogue. For Dostoyevsky "life" will overwhelm the
last vestige of personal assertion, the assertion which began Raskolnikov's
crime, the assertion that he can control his own conscience.

Another way of saying that the epilogue *is* an epilogue and that
self-negation has been achieved is to say that Svidrigaylov is dead. He
has tried to live in the absence of any sense of guilt. He has acknow-
ledged the fact of crime, but not the guilt of crime. So in Part VI has
Raskolnikov, for whom Svidrigaylov is an alternative to Sonia, a way
out, a focus of hope as hope becomes specious. To sketch Svidrigaylov
again is to emphasize why the novel properly ends with his death and
Raskolnikov's virtual prostitution.

Svidrigaylov's motive is Luzhin's, is Marmeladov's: to be master of
the good itself. Marmeladov wishes by alcohol to reach a fictitious destitution and pity, the guarantee of his humility. He needs this humility
because it is the condition of salvation. He has tried by force and in an

ecstasy of criminal destitution to achieve his own favorable final judgment. Because he is seeking property rights in morality he is, like
Svidrigaylov, a suicide. Luzhin's motive is essentially the same, to possess
good, or rather goods, within himself. Svidrigaylov systematically lives
the principle that all good is subject to his judgment. He lives so long
as he can ingest, so to speak, moral good in a pure form and feel
his control over it. He gets this experience from innocence and from
helplessness.

On his way toward Sonia Raskolnikov, on the other hand, has been
moving toward her type of prostitution; he has had to experience all
surrenders except one, the final one, the surrender of the belief that he
is or at least should be, though a criminal, without guilt and able to live.
But this belief, embodied in Svidrigaylov, is what dies at the end of
Part VI. Hearing of Svidrigaylov's death, Raskolnikov is driven from
confession by the heavy weight of a vicarious despair. But in leaving
he confronts Sonia, and is moved once more to accept the kind of voluntary surrender—itself almost a despair—she demands. The novel is
virtually over. It requires only that what has implicitly died with Svidrigaylov die explicitly in Raskolnikov's consciousness. Thus the epilogue
is concerned with the problem of making value judgments explicit. First,
Dostoyevsky presents the legal evaluation of guilt, which is essentially
irrelevant. Second, there is the effort to support illusion—this is plotted
in the account of Mrs. Raskolnikov's insistence upon keeping her image
of Rodya innocent. But she as a consequence begins to go mad, and
finally dies. Finally, there is Raskolnikov's dream of how terribly destructive self-righteousness is; the very principle of destruction is irrational, stubborn, moral assertiveness. And as with the other dreams in
the novel, this one indicates what is emerging in Raskolnikov's awareness.

Dostoyevsky then manages with great skill to make the feeling of life
sweep everything before it. This god that brings about Raskolnikov's
resurrection, which forces into his mind the "great lie in himself and his
convictions," is not manifested in reasoning, nor in a willed habit of
loving, nor even in the discovery of a definable desire; it is rather a
sudden and dramatic quasi-religious renewal, one full of tears and yearning, of a sense of being once more a child of earth, a sense too of being
now in the grips of a force which will work *itself* out in time. Dostoyevsky evokes the new "will to live" by stressing the prisoners' love of life,
by stressing their tenderness for Sonia, by having Raskolnikov dream his
dream in a context of Christian death and resurrection symbols, of
spring, and of recovery from sickness. There is too the fear of losing

Sonia through sickness. The climactic vision follows—it is a vision of vast distances, and a sense of timelessness; it is a vision too of continual movements, the movement of nomads. What is engendered is a sense of boundless freedom, of infinite, that is, romantically indefinite, possibility. "There there was freedom . . ." (p. 557). Love, life, the will to live seizes him and throws him at the feet of Sonia.

Morris Golden

On
Crime and Punishment

Like any other major work of art, *Crime and Punishment* is *one* thing, a unity; but, again like other artistic achievements, it is many things as well. *Crime and Punishment* is a sensitive psychological study, an experiment in the art of fiction, a reflection of and commentary on the intellectual movements of its day, and an examination of human nature, of morality, and of man's place in the world around him, both human and divine. If it is a success, then its many aspects are integrally related to its central unifying substance: "a psychological account of a crime," as Dostoyevsky described it.[1] That is, whatever is said of human nature, or of current issues, or of anything else considered at any length, must be directly related to this core.

The constitution of human nature, as exemplified by the characters in Russia at the time of the action, is central to the question of why a decent, educated young man would commit a brutal double murder. Man, to judge by these people, is a creature acting by a combination of impulse and reasoning. Some, like Porfiry the police investigator and others, are only partially alive, because they are too much addicted to and dependent on reason; others, like Razumikhin, the Marmeladovs, and the Raskolnikovs, are saved because they notably possess the qualities of irrational faith, of intuition, of energy, of romantic refusal to be bounded by the limitations of common-sense reason. Though the moral terms are the same as in other periods, their psychological basis is exactly opposite to what it was for Swift and Molière—now it is reason which signifies selfishness, while emotion or passion is the spur to

---

[1]In a letter translated in Edward Wasiolek, ed., *Crime and Punishment and the Critics* (San Francisco, 1961), p. 4.

172

brotherhood. Neither side of character can be found isolated in whatever is human: Raskolnikov is forced to murder the saintly fool Lizaveta though he intends only to murder her viciously anti-human sister Alyona; the ideal is as much of the Lizaveta and as little of the Alyona as possible. For women, the ideal is the meek and suffering saint of limited intelligence, like Lizaveta or the book's heroine, Sonia, since such a person can, like a particle of divine grace, bring the suffering sinner to God. The male ideal, perhaps more adaptable to action in this world, is someone like Razumikhin, who through energetic acceptance of man and the world is able to sweep his way even into a decent practical life.

People are also defined by the nature of their fantasies. The whole novel traces Raskolnikov's change from holding a totally destructive dream of himself in relation to the rest of the world to his adjusting this dream, after a good bit of psychological suffering. Others have different fantasies (which can, however, be seen as facets of Raskolnikov, or of every man). Marmeladov, whom we meet first of the major characters after the hero, is consumed by a dream of his own worthlessness; but unlike the intellectualized version of this kind of concern, Svidrigaylov, he is saved by his humility and faith in a forgiving God. Marmeladov, seeing himself as worthless and yet representative, is led by his charity to perform the godlike act of pitying all other sufferers—he had married his current wife because "I could not bear to see such suffering," and he knew that she had married him because "she had nowhere to go."[2]

Luzhin, who represents a major facet of modern man's nature, is at various times described specifically in terms of the fantasy he loves to spin. In the first reference to him, in Mrs. Raskolnikov's letter to her son, he is mentioned as having said that he wanted to marry an impoverished girl who would owe all to him (as a significant indication of changing views of the dignity of women, Molière's misanthrope had, without odium, indulged the same wish). As the symbol of the new businessman with a laissez-faire ethic, Luzhin is eager to get rid of the past, which had presumably put the rights of the acquisitive self in perspective with more important rights, primarily the right of people to dignity as souls, not economic units. He is all for progress, envisioning new ideas as useful, scientific justifications for his predatory selfishness. As he understands utilitarian economics, by selfishly growing rich

---

[2]Fyodor Dostoyevsky, *Crime and Punishment,* trans. David Magarshack (Baltimore, 1951), p. 33. All references to *Crime and Punishment* are to this Penguin translation.

he is helping his country to progress, providing jobs, raising living standards. This remarkable anticipation of the view of a recent American official that what is good for General Motors is good for the country is immediately characterized by Razumikhin, the most admired man in the book and within his limits Dostoyevsky's spokesman, as "empty chatter and self-deception" (p. 168). Even Raskolnikov comes sufficiently out of a temporary apathy to say that Luzhin's theories would justify murder, thereby indicating an aspect of his own mind which had led to his crime: pure selfishness, which means placing oneself above and judging humanity, considering all people but oneself as mere machines to serve one's pleasures.

Like Svidrigaylov, the other great symbol of psychological temptation, Luzhin is unable to imagine other people as real, as having desires and even souls of their own; but unlike the greater tempter, he takes his own reality very seriously: "Having risen from insignificance, Mr. Luzhin was morbidly fond of admiring himself . . . . He loved the money he had amassed . . . it put him on the same level with everything that was higher than himself" (pp. 322-3). He had been dreaming—as Dostoyevsky examines his fantasy of buying sexual esteem—of a girl like Dunya, young, pretty, and so grateful for his saving her from hardships that she is his adoring slave. Living as he does in this self-enclosed dream, Luzhin plots his otherwise senseless calumniation of Sonia, since he is convinced that everyone else must act on the basis of material self-interest, and therefore that Dunya and her mother will seize on anything, even what would discredit Raskolnikov, to restore their respect for him. When he is exposed by Lebezyatnikov, who is acting against his own principles as a lackey of the new, he disappears from the story, much as wicked witches in fairy tales habitually disintegrate once the sources of their strength have been revealed. If we see Luzhin also as a hugely exaggerated version, in the world outside Raskolnikov's mind, of a tendency within that mind, it is significant that only after this disintegration is Raskolnikov able to take the step of visiting Sonia, who is to lift his purified nature to salvation.

Most of the other characters also have their fantasies with which they replace the grimy world of common sense. Dunya and Mrs. Raskolnikov, particularly the latter, want a world in which Raskolnikov is brilliantly successful; when this dream is completely shattered by his crime, Mrs. Raskolnikov prefers not to abandon it, and goes over into the nearby world of madness, a world which for similar reasons Mrs. Marmeladov often inhabits. Mrs. Marmeladov is mad, in the manner of a Tennessee Williams belle, though her illusion (or, as it might more grandly be called, her myth) is more noble: not only does she like to dream of herself as having been a lady in the past, increasingly with time a greater lady, but she also has the unattainable dream of realizing justice in her life. Nikolay, the painter who gives himself up for the murder, though he manifestly has not committed it, is presumably subject to delusions; and since his madness is really a specialized form of his religious extremism, since he feels the need to suffer, to expiate a sin which he and everyone else has committed, he too is among the saved. For Dostoyevsky madness is not the horror which it had been for Swift or the joke of Molière. In general, romanticism tends to be sympathetic to madness, for at least two reasons: the romantic agony, to borrow Mario Praz's term, derives from the sensitive response to the discovery that man's yearnings must be frustrated by society and the conditions of his life, and this response may be madness; also, the madman may be the one who has a truer vision of reality than the man whose vision is bounded by matter.

Razumikhin, whose name as Svidrigaylov points out is derived from the word meaning "reason," is something of an exception to the patterns of fantasy. He is too much oriented to human decency and worthwhile action—things of this world, things involving morality more than religion —to be deluded. In his case, therefore, it is not reverie but a possibly attainable goal which becomes a guide: the dream that mankind, organically developing through history (itself a romantic idea) "will at last be transformed into a normal society" (p. 273). He is the one who can put western ideas into proper perspective—when we first see him he is busy translating what he considers German nonsense, though aware that it has some value—and he is the one who gives the Raskolnikov women a future through his venture into publishing.

Finally, we meet Svidrigaylov, who has no delusions or utopian dreams and therefore no hopes. Nor is he fooled by others' delusions. His view of human dignity had been reflected in his treatment of women, who he says like being humiliated: "I'd even go so far as to say that that's the only thing that matters to them" (p. 298). He is "not particularly interested in anything" (p. 299); the only absolute in which he believes, as we learn from his seeing ghosts and from his early references to his journey, is death. So fearful was he of discovering that anything was worthwhile that he had never wanted to leave his torpid existence in the country to travel, since he would be depressed by the beauty of, say, Naples: "The horrible thing is that it really makes you yearn for something" (p. 301). He hates drinking, but now "there's nothing left for me to do except get drunk" (p. 301). He is afraid of any sort of life, since its independent existence would make his own self-enclosure meaningless. It would remind him that he must die, and that he had never lived.

When Svidrigaylov lies in his dirty hotel bed preparing to commit suicide, he realizes that he has never hated anyone, never wanted revenge, never argued, never been really excited about anything for any length of time, and he knows that all of these are bad signs (p. 517); and if one feels, like Dostoyevsky, that emotional energy is the *sine qua non* of virtue, the signs surely are bad. He disposes of his money most decently —unable to corrupt Dunya with it, he gives a good part to his fiancée, who is innocent and good (though he is aware that her corrupt mother will control it) and the rest to the Marmeladov children, thereby saving Sonia from the destructive life of the streets and the others from the same or the equivalent. For someone like Svidrigaylov, Dostoyevsky implies, this charity is purely arbitrary: if all ideas are the same, and all actions, in the light of inevitable death, are also the same, then the money might just as well have been spent on depraved as on virtuous people. Perhaps, however, his awe of Dunya shows one kind of influence that female virtue can have (to parallel Sonia's effect on Raskolnikov); and he is, after all, actually a person, not a devil. If reason makes no difference in his disposal of the money, the human ties of impulse may well determine the election of virtue.

The other reasoners, Dr. Zossimov and Porfiry, tend to have some delusions, being more alive than Svidrigaylov. The doctor, while a decent enough fellow, is described by Razumikhin as too addicted to sensual pleasures, and deluded by modern pseudo-scientific social theories. Porfiry, who combines sympathetic understanding with keen reasoning ability, and who refuses to think of people as units though he is not intensely emotional, does indulge in some fantasies, notably those involving detection of crimes. He is something of a specialist in military tactics (which however he is not fool enough to confuse with reality), and he dreams of solutions based on his new psychology. On the whole, however, he is aware that the rational life is too limited, and in his most sympathetic conversation with Raskolnikov he advises him to confess, suffer, and be redeemed, implying his own envy of anyone who is capable of such strong emotions. Raskolnikov is one of those who will live, he says, while he himself, as a reasoner, lacks the essential spark.

Emotion, then, is a central quality of virtue; even when it seems to constitute all that we know of the person described, it leads to approval: even the assistant superintendent of police, "Lieutenant Gunpowder," while gauche and vain and pompous and sometimes bullying, is nonetheless a sensitive and kindly person. But there are other criteria of virtue, or perhaps one should say constituents of virtue. The most important of these grow from the idea of brotherhood, or fellow-feeling with humanity and its corollary of denying the self for the sake of charitable deeds for others; and an essential element in brotherhood is a sense of humility.

Marmeladov, for example, worthless as he is, still has the virtue of humility and charity. He has the capacity to suffer, and tears are as much a sign of virtue in Dostoyevsky as in "This Is Your Life." Of his daughter's humility and charity there is no point in speaking—she is almost divine in this respect. But her childishness, or childlikeness, is another quality notable as an aspect of virtue in the novel. For Dostoyevsky, Svidrigaylov's doubting everything is the essence of the adult's attitude, in that it is the opposite of innocence; gullibility, lack of education, in more attractive form a bluff refusal to disguise oneself, these are the childlike qualities connected with innocence, without which virtue cannot really exist. Most of the attractive figures, particularly the sufferers like Sonia, Lizaveta, and Mrs. Marmeladov are at some point compared to children, and Razumikhin has a child's openness.

The introduction of Razumikhin as a thought occurring to Raskolnikov (and they are all, in a sense, thoughts occurring to him) is also the introduction of the decent and healing virtues. He is evidently the energetic, excessive, natural man, who in a situation objectively much like that of the hero does not despair but instead throws himself into his work and has the natural goodness to think of others. When we meet him, he is working hard; and we meet him only because Raskolnikov, finding himself completely cast out of human society by his own guilty feelings, has unconsciously wandered to the only person whom he can think of as both responsible and compassionate. Nursing Raskolnikov back to consciousness after his illness, Razumikhin has endeared himself to everyone in the house, especially to the insanely reticent landlady, to whom his warmth had communicated itself so that she is able to respond charitably, whereas her lodger's self-isolation had evoked in her the same withdrawal of compassion.

Generally, Dostoyevsky's favorite virtues, as they appear in Razumikhin, Mrs. Raskolnikov, and Dunya, are warmth of heart, simplicity, sincerity, kindness, vigor, strong convictions, and a sense of right. Engagement, a passionate feeling for a cause, and the willingness to carry it into action, are essential components of virtue—one reason why Dostoyevsky is admired by our contemporaries the Existentialists. Some causes, for example nihilism, are shown as worthless precisely because people like

Lebezyatnikov, drawn to them out of simple-minded desire to be advanced, do not act on their ideas when these conflict with basic decency. When the causes are wholly right, the humblest are strong. Even Sonia, the meek and acquiescent, becomes passionately assertive where her feelings are committed: in reading the Bible to Raskolnikov, as she approaches the account of Lazarus she speaks powerfully and passionately, in the joyous hope that he will hear and believe (pp. 342-3).

These, then, are the various predispositions of human nature. They manifest themselves in a number of major interrelated themes, some constituting conscious approaches by the characters, some unconscious rationalizations, some implied, and all relating to the conflict and contrast of selfishness and brotherhood. From one group of viewpoints, only one's own self is alive, with other people to be used as instrumental to its satisfaction, essentially with other people being denied life and merely perceived as machines. From the other side, men are seen as tied to each other by their humanity and by Christ's sacrifice, which they are to imitate. The awareness of this tie is emotional, not rational, and it acts to persuade us that others as well as we are alive. Raskolnikov's theory of the great men and the lice, which as the rationalization for his murders is a central plot device, becomes symbolic of a whole inhuman cast of thinking as well as of his psychological alienation from humanity and from God.

Among the issues connected with this central one are reason (cold and inhuman) as against intuition and feeling, both warm and human; rational clarity, as in Luzhin's speech accusing Sonia, as against complexity and confusion in human relations, epitomized in the close but fuzzy ties between Razumikhin and the landlady. Science and innovation, particularly as applied to social relations (what we would now call social science) are inventions of the devil, who is marketing them as laissez-faire capitalism, utilitarian socialism, and the Napoleonic superman; against these are balanced the human warmth of religion and tradition. Westernism is the selfish modern development of impersonal, intellectual science; Russianism, by contrast, attempts to express the traditional, chaotic, expansive, vague, childlike, unselfish, suffering, pious heart of humanity. Centrally, the statement about man's nature that makes explicit Dostoyevsky's position is Razumikhin's rejection of socialism in the midst of the long scene in which Raskolnikov and Porifiry argue about greatness. The socialists, he says, are wrong in considering crime "a protest against bad and abnormal social conditions," since such a view exalts environment as the single cause of morality and denies the living complexity of human nature, free will, and God (pp. 272-3). Mankind, he argues, is organically developing through history, and "will at last be transformed into a normal society" (p. 273). The socialists, he says, want a mechanical system, not a *"living soul"*; but "Human nature wants life. It has not completed the living process. It is too soon for it to be relegated to the graveyard" (p. 273). Though Dostoyevsky is well aware of the rot in contemporary Russian society (which he vividly illustrates through the effects of widespread drunkenness and through the examples of sexual exploitation based on the unfair economic system), he does not advocate a change in the form of society. The proposals for change, being systematic, intellectual, "scientific," would lead to even greater inhumanity. The cure, he implies, is simply for man to develop, through humility, innocence, and religion, into a better being. Dostoyevsky thus is stamped by his century's ideal of progress, though he wishes to envision it purely as a moral quality.

Even more central in the novel than the moral principles to be chosen is the theme of the relations of the individual with mankind, as that theme illuminates Raskolnikov's condition and psychological development. Fundamentally, the principles and the theme are aspects of each other. For Dostoyevsky, the natural human feeling, which leads also to a natural piety, is brotherhood, which wells instinctively from the hearts of children and child-like adults. Concentration on the self, a sense of alienation, is the conduct of a sick mind (Svidrigaylov, for example, admits there is something wrong with him mentally, though he doesn't know what it is). The person capable of salvation will suffer agonies while he is alienated, but if he survives the suffering, it will have been redemptive, leading him to reunion with mankind.

Raskolnikov's Napoleonic heresies are the outward manifestations of his inward alienation from humanity. When we first meet him, he is wrapped in self-absorption, vacillating between nervous excitement and apathy, immensely alone in a great city (p. 20). He tends to be disgusted with human squalor, considering himself superior to the grimy lives of the many. But while contemplating the murder, which is the ultimate assertion that another person is not human, he has an irrational impulse to seek company, and wanders into a dirty tavern, where he approaches Marmeladov. Marmeladov's own character, and the circumstances of his family as he describes them, are vastly worse than even Raskolnikov's, and yet the message that Marmeladov extracts is not of despair but of hope for himself and for humanity—a message in direct contrast with Raskolnikov's tortured abondonment of humanity.

The murders, which are in some ways a bitter response to the call of his mother's letter and of Marmeladov's confused hope as these are mixed in Raskolnikov's mind with the pains of poverty, constitute the act by which he separates himself from humanity. But the form of separation is lower, not higher than the thing itself, being bestial; and he loathes the process and himself all along, which suggests that he can be redeemed. After the deeds, he finds his first safety when he is lost in the crowd (p. 105).

From this point largely, Raskolnikov's sense of his relation to others vacillates with his psychological condition. For example, in the police station (a place full of humanity and the untidy problems which life entails), he is at first extremely cordial and animated, but then feels completely indifferent to the police officers' opinions, completely empty of feelings toward others, overcome by his own solitude (pp. 121-2). He feels a sudden horrible "sensation rather than a conscious idea" that he will never be able to speak to these people humanly or directly again. Outside once more, he intends to throw the loot into the canal, but there are people around, and he has a strong sensation that they are all watching him (a recurrent image in his dreams, deriving from a sense of guilt).[3] After realizing again how he has taken on a new life now that he is a murderer, Raskolnikov has a sense of animal hatred for everyone (p. 129). He has set himself off and, like Cain, finds every man's hand against him.

An instinct toward picking up a human tie leads him to Razumikhin, but he is no sooner with him than he tries to run off, since he wants to meet no one face to face, wants no contacts at all. After Razumikhin's spontaneous charity and kindness, he does escape, and in the street is whipped by a coach driver, the sort of action that can confirm for him his hatred of mankind. But Dostoyevsky does not allow him this satisfaction long: a woman who has observed the whipping, again spontaneously charitable, gives him a coin. Raskolnikov looks across the Neva and sees the Palace and the cathedral shining in the sun, and he recalls now he has always had a "vague and mysterious emotion" at this view (p. 132). He sees all his past, including these past feelings, as completely separated from his current life as a murderer, and throws the coin in the water, symbolically rejecting the charitable ties of brotherhood. Returning home, "He felt as though he had cut himself off from everyone and everything at that moment" (p. 133).

Passing over a good many more examples of Raskolnikov's vacillation, we can see the central theme made explicit in the big scene with Porfiry

---

[3]For a perceptive examination of Dostoyevsky's sense of his characters' unconscious in another novel, see Simon O. Lesser, "The Role of Unconscious Understanding in Flaubert and Dostoyevsky," *Daedalus*. XCII (1963), 363-82.

in which Raskolnikov's article is discussed. Soon after, however, is the first major scene with Svidrigaylov, as much an outcast from human concerns as Goethe's Mephistopheles (and for the same reasons), and it is immediately evident that Raskolnikov can never be as objective or as lost as he. Though they have both murdered, Svidrigaylov has sinned through polluting the souls of others, while Raskolnikov's crimes have been largely animalistic; and animalism is more tolerable, because more humanly passionate, than cold negation. The next grouping is at the Raskolnikovs', where Luzhin is properly cast out as anti-human; but just as the scene becomes a picture of human solidarity, Raskolnikov says that he must leave, and that he wants his mother and sister to leave him to himself or he will hate them (p. 328). Razumikhin remains with the women: "In short, from that night, Razumikhin became a son and brother to them" (p. 329). With the healthy, Razumikhin has replaced the sick son; in his new life as a murderer, Raskolnikov cannot inhabit the family of his past innocence.

He therefore goes to Sonia, whose own condition as a sinner and pariah makes her a suitable companion. It is immediately clear that she is an example of the need for the closest possible human connections: the Marmeladovs, though not her blood relatives (as his mother and sister are for him), are absolutely essential to her. She defends Mrs. Marmeladov, who had sent her to the streets (and who was therefore part of her *whole* life, her sin as well as her innocence), and gladly works for them all. Raskolnikov, pointing out that her self-pollution has not saved the Marmeladovs from anything, asks whether she would not have been better off with suicide. Having often considered this solution, she responds, "But what will happen to them?" For the first time, Raskolnikov realizes what other people must mean for an integrated person (p. 338). At the end of the scene, when Raskolnikov sees that true reconciliation with God (and humanity) requires commitment and pain, he frantically proposes that they two, both damned, go together, though he doesn't know where. Though he seems in an irresponsible agony, this first open willingness to associate himself with another person is a major step toward his redemption.

A period of confused mental states follows for Raskolnikov, a time misty in retrospect, in which intense panics are followed by apathy (p. 450). At times, he has yearnings to be completely alone; but in the country, away from people, he feels strongly a sense "of some close and alarming presence" and has to get back among the crowds. Evidently the pressure of his conscience, which manifests itself as a painful awareness of alienation from humanity, will either combine with the influence

of Sonia (an agent for divine forgiveness) and of Porfiry (of human
law) to cause him to confess and secure a regular position in human
society, or it will drive him to suicide.

In Svidrigaylov's suicide, so hauntingly developed toward the end
of the novel, we have a symbolic version of one of Raskolnikov's possible
choices (we are even told that he was contemplating the same act at
the same time); that is, Svidrigaylov goes in the direction to which
Raskolnikov's intellectual nature would lead him, if not for his saving
emotions and impulses. Svidrigaylov wanders pathetically from contact
to contact, attempting to communicate with his fiancée and the Marmeladov children through the medium of money, and drifts through cheap
places of entertainment in search of the bonhomie of drinks and songs.
His dreams are full of evidences of his guilt—one of a girl corrupted by
him and driven to suicide (pp. 518-9), another of a small child, whom
he puts to bed innocent and who then leers at him with the face of a
French prostitute (pp. 519-21). Finally, he kills himself before a
witness, symbolically again defying and blaming humanity for his lack
of commerce with it.

After further uncertainty, Raskolnikov warmly takes his leave of
his mother and sister, telling the latter that he is about to confess,
and goes to Sonia for his crosses. He is not yet ready for redemption,
for the soul must suffer long before it can move from alienation: at the
same time that he is troubled by Sonia's tears for him, he thinks of
her with self-contempt as "My future nurse" (p. 534). But he is becoming more and more convinced that he needs her, and that he has been
very wrong to think of a grand isolation for himself. For his symbolic
confession of humility, he seeks the Hay Market: "He had an aversion,
a strong aversion, for being among the common people; but now he
deliberately went where the crowd was thickest" (p. 536). But even
this action merely shows a dominant tendency in his mind at the time,
not a steady conviction. Not until he had suffered through the trial and
a year in prison was his reunion with mankind completed. At Easter, the
time symbolic of resurrection, he realizes that his theories have been
dangerously foolish. He dreams of a modern madness, in which people
are infected with microbes which have reason and will: "Each of them
believed that the truth only resided in him" (p. 555). And after he has
been united with Sonia through her love—"the heart of one held inexhaustible sources of life for the other" (pp. 557-8)—he begins to talk
to his fellows and can face a human future.

The structure of *Crime and Punishment* and the techniques which
Dostoyevsky uses beautifully fuse the plot, the central themes, and
the underlying movement. The novel is divided into six parts, each

developing a clearly separated and yet dependent part of the whole. Part I gives the preparations for the murder and its accomplishment (along with the unforeseen and totally unjustifiable second murder). All the themes connected with the crime are begun, particularly the issue of Raskolnikov's alienation from humanity; the letter from his mother provides us with a picture of his old ties, and the Marmeladovs, whose new ties are to be decisive, are introduced. Symbolically, the young and innocent man commits the sin after which there is no going back to complete innocence.

Part II presents the immediate consequences of the murder. Also, it includes the death of Marmeladov, which is intimately connected with what is to become of Raskolnikov, in one way through his temporary rejection of thoughts of suicide and in another through his necessarily closer contact with Sonia. This section develops Razumikhin as Raskolnikov's Good Samaritan and introduces Raskolnikov's mother and sister, his natural human ties, with whom (since they are essentially pure) he finds little directly to hold him. It also becomes clearer that he has much more in common with Sonia and (though we don't yet know this) perhaps with Svidrigaylov, who insists on their bond, than with his family.

Part III includes the scene in which the central issues are discussed by Raskolnikov and Porfiry, the formal presentation and refutation of the theories which Raskolnikov has developed to rationalize his alienation from humanity (pp. 272ff). The examining magistrate's suspicions are strong, and from the point of view of the detective-story plot their discussion is crucial. Raskolnikov is made aware that he is not likely to be one of the privileged murderers. As the part ends with one of Raskolnikov's guilty dreams, Svidrigaylov (as yet unidentified) faces him from the foot of the bed, and we may suspect that the novel may be undergoing a major turn. Edward Wasiolek has very plausibly argued that this is the case: "Parts I-III present the predominantly rational and proud Raskolnikov; Parts IV-VI, the emerging 'irrational' and humble Raskolnikov. The first half of the novel shows the progressive death of the first ruling principle of his character; the last half, the progressive birth of the new ruling principle. The point of change comes in the very middle of the novel."[4] Seen this way, the novel is perfectly symmetrical around its center.

Part IV is the most closely packed with emotionally and intellectually powerful confrontations, beginning with the eerie dialogue with Svidrigaylov. Immediately following is the family scene of the Raskolni-

[4]"Structure and Detail," in *Crime and Punishment and the Critics*. p. 110.

kovs, Razumikhin, and Luzhin, in which the women show their integrity
in repudiating Luzhin (an action initiated by Raskolnikov and illustrative
of his superiority to corruption by money). This scene, realistic and
even satiric in places, is followed by the emotional intensity of the
first Raskolnikov-Sonia dialogue, with its high point in her reading of
the Bible and his frantic response.

While the hero is still quivering from this fusion of hope and despair,
he faces the psychologically and intellectually important meeting in
Porfiry's suite at the police station. The pressure from the outside is,
however, lessened with the inundation of people surrounding the con-
fessing Nikolay. Where in Part III everything had led to the likelihood
that Raskolnikov was going to be caught or at least exposed by others,
Part IV indicates that the moral choice and the psychological problems
will be his alone: Porfiry cannot find the evidence, Svidrigaylov is more
interested in what he can make of his knowledge than in revealing it to
the police, and Sonia is desperately struggling for his soul's salvation. It
is purely up to Raskolnikov to decide whether to rejoin humanity and
God.

Part V further develops the themes already set forth, beginning with
the funeral dinner at Mrs. Marmeladov's and its focus on her desperate
attempt to live within her delusion of an aristocratic past. The exposure of
Luzhin, which has been awaiting development since he was mentioned
in the letter of Part I, is essential to central themes in the novel:
under the surface of attractive clichés, laissez-faire business ethics sub-
stitutes selfish success for morality, brotherhood, and faith. Significantly,
even after Sonia is cleared of the charge of theft she is in a state of shock,
since she has learned how helpless she actually is, how her meekness cannot protect her against a world of Luzhins. There is no real compromise
possible between laissez-faire and God; one cannot exist where the
other is. In the next scene, however, the emotional meeting with Raskolnikov in which he confesses his crime, she is in her element, a source
of strength and hope. In a way, these two scenes objectify the great
movements of the earlier parts: first we are shown the consequences of
the individualistic, rational ethic, and then the exaltation of the emotional,
brotherly, divine.

Part VI is of course the section which must resolve the themes,
being the last. In its first major scene, Dostoyevsky uses the examining
magistrate to mediate between God's way and the law's. Porfiry gives
up his trickery to show the hero that he cannot arrest him without a confession, but argues that psychologically he expects a confession. At the
same time, he points out kindly that a confession would be good for

Raskolnikov, uniting him with humanity and easing his conscience, mainly because of the healing influence of suffering. The next person whom the hero consults is Svidrigaylov, who dominates this last section, constituting the current psychological alternative to Raskolnikov, that state of the soul to which Raskolnikov will tend unless he follows the path of Sonia. The whole lyrical stage occupied by his suicide is a projection of one aspect of Raskolnikov's mind, the acting out of various hopeless desires and their death. Once this extreme of the dead reason is gone, Raskolnikov can speak with emotional directness to his mother and he can take the crosses—symbols of intuitive faith—from Sonia. He is ready now for the Epilogue, there to yield to Easter, a dream, and Sonia, to become reunited with man and God, and to live happily at some time in the future.

Here, then, is the frame of the work, which so clearly delineates the chief movement; the clash between godly brotherhood and that selfish mechanicalism which is exemplified in different ways by Luzhin and Svidrigaylov and to which Raskolnikov's theories of aloof superiority inevitably lead unless they are countered and destroyed by a saving reassertion of solidarity with mankind.

Another large-scale movement is intertwined with this major one: the working out of the change from innocence to experience which is inevitable for all. The contact with evil from which feelings of guilt are produced is in this work a double-murder, as in "The Rime of the Ancient Mariner" it is shooting an albatross. But the specific form which the symbol takes is secondary to its effects, and the effects in both works are the same: a sense of clear division in one's life, psychological suffering, and in time and if one is lucky, penitence and redemption. Connected with this theme is the great emphasis on sexual corruption, which has often elsewhere (notably in "Genesis") been symbolic of first sin.

An allied element which helps to lend unity to the novel is the formal influence of the contemporary *Bildungsroman*, the story of the growth and development of a young man. Although the ostensible frame is that of the novel of detection, for Dostoyevsky as for the other giants of his time fascinated by crimes (Dickens, Browning, Stendhal, Balzac, etc.) the mind of the criminal and the human significance of what has happened far outweigh the question of detection and capture. In the process of growing, Raskolnikov confronts talkative representatives of various approaches to life. Luzhin, Razumikhin, Zossimov, Porfiry, even the silly Lebezyatnikov, Marmeladov, Sonia—all these have much to say about what direction of life can most satisfy a young man. Of all those opposing virtue, the most dangerous is Svidrigaylov, the counsellor of despair, who kills himself when he cannot effect yet another corruption. But against despair Raskolnikov has his own living impulses, the example of the Marmeladovs, and particularly the encouragement of Sonia, which comes from God. From her he learns love, which is both childlike and, in a deliberate paradox, the central quality in emotional growth.

Above all other techniques and structural devices, that which gives special effectiveness and unity to *Crime and Punishment,* and which stamps it as uniquely the work of Dostoyevsky and of no one else, is the steady and marvellously perceptive rendering of the mental states of the hero. At the beginning, for example, we focus not on the past of Raskolnikov, the various economic or moral factors which have led him to his present condition—these are skillfully woven into the narrative as they come to his consciousness—but on his mental condition as he is contemplating his projected crime.

From there, we are taken through all the stages of this sensitive and suffering mind as it copes with the idea of murder, repelled and attracted at the same time, one part often objectively watching while the other part is involved; one part responding to the sound of the apartment bell, while the other considers the oddity of responding to the bell; one part horrified by fear of detection, the other part frequently eager to confess, to trick the self into giving up; one part passionately acting in the affairs of the moment, the other apathetic, disgusted by the involvement. Only in the marvellous symbolic dreams does the unified self perceive. There the underlying, sensitive self can make of the revolting old pawnbroker a suffering horse and of all the exploiters (the Luzhins, the Napoleons, and the murderous side of Raskolnikov) a drunken peasant who is himself, after all, a man and a sufferer. Or again, it can make of the sufferer his landlady and of the mindless attacker the assistant superintendent; or finally, it can show that he himself, the murderer, is also the victim, and that the old woman—his guilt—is laughing with everyone else at his folly in thinking that he can resolve his human longings through an inhuman act. *Crime and Punishment* stands or falls by whether the picture of this vacillating sensitive self, horrified by the world and its own actions, and seeking some way to escape from division and brutality, is persuasive. The past century has testified that it is.

Suggestions for Further Reading

Lesser, Simon O. "The Role of Unconscious Understanding in Flaubert and Dostoyevsky," *Daedalus*, XCII (1963), 363-82.

Trilling, Lionel. "Manners, Morals, and the Novel," in his *The Liberal Imagination*. Garden City, 1950.

Wasiolek, Edward, ed. *Crime and Punishment and the Critics*. San Francisco, 1961.

Yarmolinsky, Avrahm. *Dostoyevsky, His Life and Art*. New York, 1960.

Joseph R. Hilyard

Eliot's <u>Ash Wednesday</u>: The Structural Function of Christian Paradox

✦

A poem is an ikon of life and must be, like life, a multiple yet unified thing. If we unify and master the manyness of life through the emotions of irony and wonder, perhaps those poems which most fully evoke these emotions most fully embody the mystery of existence. And so, perhaps paradox, the verbal mode that sets one wondering, is the most successful way to enmesh in words the contradictions of being. For only in its most contradictory and paradoxical patterns is language a flexible enough medium for the shaping of an ikon of life.

Eliot has Sweeney say plaintively at one point, "But I've gotta use words when I talk to you" (*Fragments of an Agon*). Here Eliot has voiced the crux of the problem of language and has voiced it very appropriately through the inarticulate Sweeney. Words, which we depend upon to convey meaning, are inadequate conveyers of some kinds of meaning. In many ways all of us are as verbally inept as Apeneck Sweeney. Words do quite well at the objective, rational, scientific level of discourse, but when we come to try to put into words other equally *real* entities—feelings, values, and the conflicts thereof—the words often fail. And they fail most dismally when we attempt to hold them to their literal, denotative meanings and to their usual logical syntax.

If words are inadequate, both thought within our skulls and communication with other skulls will be inadequate. Eliot, acutely aware of the problem, says that

> words strain,
> Crack and sometimes break, under the burden,
> Under the tension, slip, slide, perish,

188

> Decay with imprecision, will not stay in place,
> Will not stay still.
>
> *(Burnt Norton, V)*

And so poets are trapped between their vision of an often illogical reality and their verbal medium, which is constructed largely upon a tacit acceptance of the categories and relationships of logic. Poets, therefore, are constantly searching for ways in which language can be used so that its neat logic does not strangle the vital but unneat emotions and notions that the poets wish to embody in poetry. Paradox is one powerful way to embody in words these unneat things that a poet needs to say.

By using paradox poets have been able to capture in words some of the seeming contradictions that logical discursive language cannot capture. In purely logical language love and hate cannot be shown to be related, God cannot be described as both just and merciful, matter and energy cannot be seen to be other than distinct, paired categories like chance and choice or reason and emotion can never be shown to merge and mingle. And yet the poet's experience of life demonstrates that within each of these pairs the members are frequently interacting and interdependent, so much so that the two must often be considered, not as separate entities, but as the components of a larger entity that encompasses them both. And so, if consciousness and all other levels of being are double and paradoxical, then poetry, which results from the impact of consciousness upon being, must be permeated with the verbal doubleness of paradox.

Paradox, then, does loom large in life, and therefore, looms large in poetry, an attempt to say some almost unsayable things about life. Religion is one area of life wherein there are many ideas that are almost unsayable. To conclude our syllogism we would, therefore, expect that religious poetry be full of paradox. (Here is an example of the ultimate irony of language—we must use logical language even in our discussion of the illogical uses of language.) Since Eliot writes within the Christian religious tradition, we would expect his poetry to contain many instances of Christian paradox. In *Ash Wednesday* we find a particular Christian paradox, not merely present, but present in such a manner as to be the main shaping force or principle of organization in the poem.

What are some of the salient Christian paradoxes? Most of us have encountered some of them, such concepts as the *felix culpa*—the idea that the fall in Eden was good because it made Christ's blessed coming necessary, the simultaneous immanence and transcendence of God, the

Incarnation in which spirit and matter interfuse, the Beatitudes with all of their illogical blessedness, and the Crucifixion in which defeat conquered, in which passion became action. The Christian paradox that informs *Ash Wednesday* is the healthful suffering and enlightening darkness of penitence and purgation.

Religion, then, grapples with some of the abiding ironies of the human condition. The religious poet, to express these complex and apparently contradictory relationships, needs complex and apparently contradictory patterns of language. Paradox is the term which we use to denote all of the ways in which diction can be patterned so as to express these seeming contradictions of man's state.

But even if we accept this last—the need for paradoxical language to express the contrarieties of existence—we are still a long way from accepting paradox as a principle of structure in a poem. How can paradox, which seems to be disorderly, irrational bunching of unlike ideas, help to shape and order a poem? If structure is the means by which a poem is put together and held together, how can an apparently destructive device like paradox pull a poem together? How can an expression whose existence breaks logical forms, patterns, and categories help to make the form and pattern of an organically whole poem? These are questions that bite deep, and to pull their teeth we must look closely at *Ash Wednesday*.

Ash Wednesday derives much of its power and most of its structural patterns from the mind-wresting religious paradox mentioned above— the illogical process of penitence, penance, and purgation. The poem depicts the crisis in the growth of the soul when it renounces its earlier commitment to the self and to the world of sense and painfully redirects its will toward God through what mystics have called the "negative way." The "negative way" is simultaneously a good and an evil experience—the dark painful route to the bright joyful reality. The day, *Ash Wednesday*, is, of course, the beginning of the Lenten Season, a season of suffering, but of a constructive, soul-making kind of suffering. The soul, according to many religious thinkers, must become spiritually dark and dry and dead before it can become the spiritual opposites of dark, dry, and dead.

This strange, but strangely true, notion of a healthful and helpful pain is the central paradox around which *Ash Wednesday* shapes itself. If most of the parts of the poem are related in some way to this central notion, then the notion imparts to the poem a structure, a shaping relationship through which the parts conjoin to form a whole thing.

Up to this point I have shied away from words like "single" and "unity." I do this to avoid suggesting that the unity of a poem in which both idea and structure are paradoxical is a *single* sort of unity. The one-ness that constitutes any poem, and particularly the poem of paradox, is not a static, monolithic oneness but a dynamic equilibrium of polar op-posites. The poem of paradox, even more than other kinds of poetry, de-rives its intensity, its vibrancy, from what Coleridge calls "the balance or reconcilement of opposite or discordant qualities" (*Biographia Lit-eraria*, XVI). The logically "opposite or discordant qualities" of pain and pleasure, of a denunciation of the world of sense and a celebration of that world, strain against each other in *Ash Wednesday*. But though these opposites strain apart, they do not break apart. The reader (or, to an even greater extent, the *hearer* since so much depends on sound in Eliot's poetry) perceives relationships between the opposed elements that he had not been aware of before. It is this dynamic balance and interdependence of polar opposites that knits the poem together, that endows the poem with the exciting "many-in-one" quality that aesthe-ticians in discussions of non-verbal art have called *significant form*.

The structure or significant form of *Ash Wednesday* results to a large degree from the tensions or interacting forces generated by the two re-lated paradoxes suggested above. The first is the idea that to lose the self is to gain the self. The corollary paradox is that the losing of one's worldly self is valid only when one feels the loss, only when one values the beauty of the sensory world enough to make the renunciation of this beauty meaningful. This pair of paradoxes give the poem its central principles of structure, its significant form.

How do the various parts and the relationships between these parts sustain these focal paradoxes? A poet has available to him several kinds of literary devices with which he can bring together and hold together the antithetical ideas of a paradox. These devices help to free the logic-bound mind of the reader so that he can grasp the essential rightness of this apparently wrong joining of things logically distinct.

Eliot often uses parallel sentence structure to achieve this joining, this mixing and mingling of opposites. In the line "in ignorance and in knowledge of eternal dolour," the parallelism helps us to grasp an elus-ive spiritual concept. This concept is so elusive that any attempt to state it in logical prose would have to sound something like this: that ignor-ance and knowledge may not be distinctly distinguishable states after all, and that, for certain kinds of knowledge, knowing and not knowing are so implicated in each other that we do not know whether not know-

ing might not ultimately be more knowing than knowing. The awkward-
ness of this paraphrase proves how very skillful Eliot's parallelism is.
In the repeated lines,

> Teach us to care and not to care,
> Teach us to sit still,

the sentence structure forces the mind to confront the paradoxical kin-
ship that must exist between "caring" and "not caring" if the rejection of
the world is to have meaning in the purgative process.

The paradoxical parallelism is often strengthened by Eliot's use of
the various sound patterns—rhyme, alliteration, and assonance. Helen
Gardner[1] and others have spoken of this poet's auditory imagination.
Because of his awareness of the powers of sound in poetry, he is very
adept at pulling together allegedly opposite ideas by choosing words of
similar sound to convey them. The passage, "those who walk in darkness,
who chose thee and oppose thee," makes vivid the dilemma of the souls
that deny and affirm their love of God and affirm and deny their love
of the world. The rhyming of *chose* and *oppose* makes the paradox more
easily assimilated by the reader.

Another way in which Eliot manipulates sound so that it strengthens
paradoxical meaning is the device of alliteration. In the words, "stops
and steps of the mind over the third stair," the alliteration makes us
more attuned to the tension between the passive or *stopping* forces and
the active or *stepping* forces in spiritual growth.

Like the other figures that depend upon a similarity of sound, a
pun can be useful in making us see relationships between two senses
of a word that logic says are unrelated. The two meanings of an ambiguous word can be interdependent polar opposites of each other. Freud
believed that the two opposed meanings of a word like "cleave" are both
to some extent present in any one use of the word.[2] *Cleave, to separate,*
can be more fully comprehended because the counter meaning, *to join,*
is also buzzing about in the brain whenever we hear the word. The word
burden in

> "And the bones sang chirping
> With the burden of the grasshopper"

---

[1]Helen Gardner, *The Art of T. S. Eliot* (London: Cresset Press, 1949), ch. I.
[2]Sigmund Freud, "The Antithetical Senses of Primal Words," *On Creativity and the Unconscious* (New York: Harper, 1958), p. 60.

displays this type of "pun-able" ambiguity. The word reconciles within itself the paradox of purgation, an experience that is both an oppressive *burden* or *load* and an expressive *burden* or *chorus* of a joyful song. Discordant pain and harmonious joy join in the pun as they do in Dante's Arnaut Daniel, "who weeps and goes singing" in "the fire that refines" (*Purgatorio*, XXVI).

What is true for ambiguous words is also true for homophones and near-homophones. In the second section the speaker, now purged down to the bare and scattered bones of the spirit, says,

> "And I who am here dissembled
> Proffer my deeds to oblivion."

Here *dissembled* suggests *disassembled* because the disjoined bones *are* disassembled. But it is quite probable that the word also means what it says, for the bones are merely *dissembling* or pretending weakness. In their bare and disassembled condition they are probably stronger and more spiritually unified than they were in their earlier articulated state. This paradox, the apparently *disassembled* discord of the bones being in reality a *dissembled* or disguised harmony, is reinforced by the idea of music when the bones begin to sing. And so by punning upon two nearly homophonic words the poet is able to communicate an almost incommunicable paradox.

In addition to these sonic figures Eliot uses that capsule paradox, the oxymoron, with good effect. In these noun-verb or adjective-noun phrases the meanings of the two strange verbal bedfellows strain away from each other. "The silent Word" exhibits this tendency to fly apart but on second glance seems to be a successful way to embody in words the "deep but dazzling darkness"[3] of God, the bright Logos who is dark incomprehensible silence to a deaf, blind world. In the phrase,

> "The veritable transitory power,"

veritable has a connotation of eternal and permanent truth, a connotation which shocks somewhat in conjunction with the term *transitory*. The shock jars the mind out of its smug preconceptions about permanence and stirs it to reconsider the relationship between things that pass and things that stay. Another oxymoron, "the blessings of sand," condenses

---

[3]Henry Vaughan, "The Night."

the central paradox, the illogic of a beneficial bane, down to a morsel which the mind can ingest all at a gulp. The compactness of the paradox in an oxymoron causes the two unlike terms to enter the mind almost simultaneously. Their likeness makes its impact before the cleaving reason can split them by reason of their unlikeness.

Another weapon in Eliot's armory of paradoxical devices may not be named as yet by rhetoricians. It is the use of a key clause in two places in the poem with a change in the subordinating conjunction in the second instance. Williamson points out that the passage from the beginning,

> *Because* I do not hope to turn again,

becomes at the end,

> *Although* I do not hope to turn again.[4]

Eliot in his essay on Pascal speaks of "the demon of doubt which is inseparable from the spirit of belief." *Ash Wednesday* is given form by this close interaction of a believing hope and a doubting despair. A gradual evolution in tone from a dominant despair tinged by hope to a dominant hope tinged by despair gives shape to the poem. Such shaping results to a large degree from these clauses, this changing of an earlier causal *because* to a later concessive *although* with the basic clause remaining unchanged. If form in art is an inexplicable mingling of difference in sameness, of the Many in the One, this evolving clause, that binds together the beginning and the end of the poem, that merges the contrary concepts of cause and concession (anti-cause), that conjoins hope and despair, imparts form to the poem.

Another pair of contraries, implicit in these lines and related to the hope-despair paradox, helps to shape the poem. This related paradox is a doubleness in the speaker's attitude, a doubleness that grows as the poem progresses. The speaker has increasingly complicated feelings toward his own repudiation of the world and the senses. In the first section this paradoxical tone is less pronounced, for the speaker seems to be shoving away something valueless. He does sound somewhat nostalgic for the time when "the usual reign" of the senses was valuable, but that time is no more. But in the last section, "although" he "does not hope to turn," he is powerfully drawn by "the white sails," by "the bent golden-

---

4George Williamson, *A Reader's Guide to T. S. Eliot* (New York: Noonday, 1953), p. 182.

rod," by "the lost lilac and the lost sea smell." The attractive power of the "lost" world seems to surge in the final section where that world is rejected, not as something worthless, but as a thing of worth that has been eclipsed by something of even greater worth. The sterile rejection of the earlier *because* clause intensifies by contrast the more fruitful rejection of the *although* clause with its paradoxical concession that the rejected values, despite their rejection, are still valuable. The poem, to a great extent, is constructed around the evolving meaning of the words "I do not hope to turn again."

This tonal paradox, this doubleness of attitude toward the "lost" world, is implicit in the persuasive turning metaphor. In addition to the lines just discussed we have other "turnings":

> At the first turning of the second stair . . .
> At the second turning of the second stair . . .
> At the first turning of the third stair,

and the turning of the whirling "unstilled world." In *The Book of Common Prayer* the epistle for *Ash Wednesday* reads

> "Turn ye even to me, saith the Lord" (*Joel*, ii, 12),

and our usual term for the turning of the will toward God in the progress of the soul is *con-version*, a *turning with*. Thus the image is peculiarly appropriate in a poem of purgation entitled *Ash Wednesday*. This appropriateness is underscored by Williamson when he notes that the passage from *Genesis* used in the Ash Wednesday ceremony, "Unto dust thou shalt return," reminds us of the exile from Eden and of the need of the soul to return to God since the body will re-turn to dust.[5]

But this turning, as I have suggested in discussing the "although" clause, is not an uncomplicated redirecting of the self toward God. There is in the turning of conversation a turn within a turn. The growing soul turns through the healthy pain of purgation toward God, but at the same instant turns away from God and back nostalgically toward the world of flesh and sensation and natural beauty. The very act of renouncing the beauty of the world becomes a subtle celebration of that beauty. The delightful scene viewed from "the first turning of the third stair," from "the slotted window bellied like the fig's fruit," is a "distraction" and must be turned away from. But the loveliness of the

---

[5]Williamson, p. 168.

world is so intense "beyond the hawthorne blossom and a pasture scene"
that the soul can turn its back upon this loveliness only with regret and
nostalgia (the Greek *nostos, return* and *algia, pain*). Miss Gardner describes this double turning or double wishing of the soul with a deft
play upon an already deft phrase from the poem (VI, 7). She feels that
"the distinction between what the poet wishes to wish, and what he
does not wish to wish, but still wishes, gives to *Ash Wednesday* its
peculiar intensity."[6]

This binding thread of double attitude that knits *Ash Wednesday*
together is nowhere more evident than in the lines mentioned above in
connection with parallelism:

> Teach us to care and not to care
> Teach us to sit still.

The speaker here and throughout the poem is simultaneously committed
to and uncommitted to the mystery of gain-through-loss, of growth-
through-suffering. The soul oscillates between acceptance and rejection
of the non-world, between retaining and relinquishing the world, between caring and not caring. Eliot says elsewhere that

> The moment of the rose and the moment of the yew tree
> Are of equal duration. (*Little Gidding,* V.)

Sometimes in *Ash Wednesday* these contradictory moments with their
countering tones alternate in cyclic, sequential patterns. Section I, III,
and V seem to express more rejection, pain, and doubt. Sections II, IV,
and VI seem to express more acceptance, joy, and certainty. But none of
these sections is unmixed in tone, and often both the acceptance of and
the rejection of the needful agony are enmeshed in a single vibrant
passage:

> Will the veiled sister between the slender
> Yew trees pray for those who offend her
> And are terrified and cannot surrender
> And affirm before the world and deny between the rocks.

The affirmation and the denial, the surrender and the offending, are not
separate attitudes but are the inseparable components of the total
double tone that suffuses the poem. The ambiguous prayer at the end,

---

[6]Gardner, p. 104.

"Suffer me not to be separated," may be the soul's ultimate realization of a logic-wrenching paradox—that denial and affirmation are inseparable and that every repudiation reaffirms the value of that which is being repudiated. The self-purging soul must thrust away the flesh, the senses, and the world, but in the act of depreciating them the soul appreciates their value.

The recurrent wet-dry, garden-desert images in *Ash Wednesday* strengthen further this central ambivalent tone. In the lines:

> The desert in the garden the garden in the desert
> Of drouth, spitting from the mouth the withered
>   apple-seed,

the double "objective correlative,"[7] the garden-desert, makes the reader "feel" the paradoxical concept of merged attraction and repulsion "as immediately as the odour of a rose."[8] But Eliot does not force the imagery to carry the burden of the paradox alone. Because in purgation the desert drought of the spirit can be refreshing, and, conversely, because a certain kind of garden lushness can desiccate the soul, the poet wishes to dissolve the logical distinctions that separate *garden* and *desert*. He wishes to do this more completely than he can do by merely placing them together in the line. And so he uses syntax and punctuation to help the imagery achieve this synthesis, this mutual intermingling of barrenness and fruitfulness in the purged soul that is both empty and full. By the interchanging of *garden* and *desert* in the parallel but inverted syntax (A in B B in A), by using both words in both syntactic positions, he stresses the likeness of these words which logic insists are unlike. This paradoxical blending of *desert* and *garden* he emphasizes further by omitting the logically expected punctuation in the middle of the line.

But paradoxical imagery is not restricted to pairs of antithetical images like this garden-desert combination. Often the doubleness of thought and feeling is embodied in a single ambivalent image, an image with clashing associations. "The withered apple-seed" that is spit from the mouth compacts within itself the essential paradox of the poem, the paradox of acceptance in rejection, of fruitfulness in barrenness. The act

---

[7] T. S. Eliot, "Hamlet and His Problems," *Selected Essays*, new ed. (New York: Harcourt, Brace and Co., 1950), pp. 124-125: "The only way of expressing emotion in the form of art is by finding an 'objective correlative'; in other words, a set of objects, a situation, a chain of events which shall be the formula of that *particular* emotion."

[8] T. S. Eliot, "The Metaphysical Poets," *Selected Essays*, p. 247.

of spitting suggests the dryness of a parched mouth but also the wetness of saliva. The dry seed is spit but only after one has been refreshed by the moisture of the fruit. The seed is withered and dry and yet contains within itself a promise of nourishing juice, for in the rejecting of a seed lurks the chance of accepting a fruit from the possible tree. This dry-wet image goes both ways in order to flesh forth a doubleness of tone and concept that is structurally central to the poem.

This carefully constructed couplet with its garden-desert and apple-seed images demonstrates how syntax and imagery can give life to paradox. The keystone position of the couplet, near but not at the end of the poem, and the way in which opposed forces resolve at this keystone demonstrate how paradox can give form to a poem. The counterpoise of unlike notions and emotions that exists in these two lines is the total architecture of the poem in miniature.

Another image that merges contraries and thus gives shape to the poem is, of course, the Lady. As she walks brightly veiled and eloquently silent, she incarnates the mystery of purgation. Her double singleness is first hammered into our consciousness by the "Lady of silences" litany in Section II. From that point on she serves to organize the poem more than any other single element. Her varied yet similar reappearances give to the poem a coherence that it would otherwise lack. But most important for structural purposes is her function as an imaginative link between the central garden-desert paradox and the related paradoxes of bright darkness, of constructive destruction, of articulate silence, and of motionless movement. She is "veiled," a word that connotes darkness, but veiled "in white light folded." She is "torn" but "most whole." She is silent, but her contemplative silence seems to be an intercessory prayer, a silent communion with "the silent Word." She moves but in her movement there is stationary permanence—the curious moving immobility of a walk in a rose garden or of "the still point of the turning world" (*Burnt Norton*, IV). Thematically, then, the Lady is the summation of all of the separate paradoxes, a Mary, Mary, Quite Contrary in whose garden hope and despair, affirmation and denial, are reconciled. Structurally, since she fuses the forces generated by these several pairs of antithetical images, she stands like a central caryatid supporting the shaped thing that is the poem.

And so in *Ash Wednesday*, because paradox is both what is said and the way of saying it, we have a poem in which matter and manner are inextricably melded. The tensions that give shape to the poem are engendered by the counter-pull of finely balanced values and commitments. The Christian paradox, that to lose is to gain, and its corollary, that the lost gains value in the losing, appear to determine every element of style in the poem. Perhaps both the texture of individual passages— imagery, puns and other sound patterns, sentence structure—and the gross structure of this poem have to be paradoxical. Perhaps there is no other mode capable of depicting the necessarily illogical relationship of man and God. Perhaps words in their usual logical patterns "too much discuss, too much explain," too much destroy the unneat complexity of a soul growing through pain. Since paradox is the principle of structure in all existence, perhaps paradox is the fittest principle of structure in a poem, an attempt to capture existence in weak words. For despite their weakness, "I've gotta use words when I talk to you."

Suggestions for Further Reading

Drew, Elizabeth. *T. S. Eliot, The Design of His Poetry*. New York, 1949.

Eliot, T. S. *Selected Essays*, new ed. New York, 1950.

Gardner, Helen. *The Art of T. S. Eliot*. London, 1949.

Kenner, Hugh, ed. *T. S. Eliot, A Collection of Critical Essays*. Englewood Cliffs, N. J., 1962.

Matthiessen, F. O. and C. L. Barber. *The Achievement of T. S. Eliot*. Oxford, 1958.

Maxwell, D. E. S. *The Poetry of T. S. Eliot*. London, 1952.

Rajan, B., ed. *T. S. Eliot, A Study of His Writings by Several Hands*. New York, 1948.

Unger, Leonard, ed. *T. S. Eliot, A Selected Critique*. New York, 1948.

Williamson, George. *A Reader's Guide to T. S. Eliot*. New York, 1953.